The Compl

The Complete Father

Essential Concepts and Archetypes

Michael O. Weiner *and*
Les Paul Gallo-Silver

McFarland & Company, Inc., Publishers
Jefferson, North Carolina

All photographs, illustrations and tables were created by the authors for this book unless otherwise noted.

LIBRARY OF CONGRESS CATALOGUING-IN-PUBLICATION DATA

Names: Weiner, Michael O., author. | Gallo-Silver, Les Paul, author.
Title: The complete father : essential concepts and archetypes / Michael O. Weiner and Les Paul Gallo-Silver.
Description: Jefferson, North Carolina : McFarland & Company, Inc., 2019 | Includes bibliographical references and index.
Identifiers: LCCN 2018050943 | ISBN 9781476668307 (softcover : acid free paper) ∞
Subjects: LCSH: Fatherhood—Psychological aspects. | Father and child.
Classification: LCC BF723.F35 W45 2019 | DDC 306.874/2—dc23
LC record available at https://lccn.loc.gov/2018050943

BRITISH LIBRARY CATALOGUING DATA ARE AVAILABLE

ISBN (print) 978-1-4766-6830-7
ISBN (ebook) 978-1-4766-3434-0

Front cover images © 2019 iStock

Printed in the United States of America

McFarland & Company, Inc., Publishers
Box 611, Jefferson, North Carolina 28640
www.mcfarlandpub.com

To my children, Benjamin,
Eleanor and Nathaniel, who give me
every reason to try and be the best father I can be.
Michael O. Weiner

To Richard B. Gartner, PhD, with deepest gratitude,
and in loving memory of Moe Davis,
Salvatore T. Gallo and Dick Miller.
Les Paul Gallo-Silver

Acknowledgments

Being a father is an imperfect act at best and more often resembles that moment when we are fumbling with our keys at the front door, hoping that we will not drop them. With this in mind, I want to name some of the fathers in my life and to acknowledge that each in his own way has greatly influenced me, my life, my parenting, my fatherhood. They have shared their successes, their missteps, their genuine attempts to do the right thing for their children and their bravery in the face of having no way of knowing how it will all turn out. Thank you, each of you—John, Jerry, Dani, JT, Ferdy, Dan, Kevin, Stephen, and, of course, Rooster. You are all amazing and your children are luckier for it.

Michael O. Weiner

Special thanks to Allison Rupprecht and Joan Gallo-Silver for their invaluable assistance in moving this book along and, more importantly, for their ability to find the good within imperfection.

Les Paul Gallo-Silver

Table of Contents

Preface

The Complete Father takes a positive view on fatherhood by emphasizing the myriad manifestations and benefits of fathering within a child's life, rather than focusing on the difficulties and struggles. The book's chapters highlight, from many different angles and perspectives, the potential in every father. In essence, we underscore the idea that to become a father is to enter a club that has existed since time began.

The father's role in the family is critical. It is also somewhat misunderstood, overly gendered, and often stereotyped. There has been a significant amount of theoretical literature and research in the area of fatherhood, and we attempt to capture this information and synthesize it. We provide the reader with a means to increase an understanding of fatherhood and the current re-shaping of fathering skills.

Our contemporary exploration into fatherhood replaces the stereotypical view of fathers as strict, absent, rejecting, emotionally or physically unavailable, lacking in self-awareness or too busy to father as emotionally complex, multi-faceted individuals. In a world of dynamic family structures, evolving gender roles, awareness of the effects of childhood maltreatment, the vicissitudes of intergenerational trauma and oppression, the demands on fathers and on fatherhood are changing quickly. This book is inclusive of adoptive, divorced, and non-custodial fathers as well as men that reflect the ethnic, racial, cultural, sexual and religious diversity of the United States.

Our work is grounded in brief summaries of psychological, sociological, anthropological, and philosophical concepts. Our intention is to engage two groups in gaining a more hands-on understanding of the nature of fathering and fatherhood: (1) students in the fields of men's studies, sociology, psychiatry, psychology, social work, mental health counseling, family therapy, and family dynamics interested in deepening their understanding of this population and (2) parents seeking to ground their skills in theory. Coming at the topic from a variety of directions offers a comprehensive parenting exami-

1

nation of many facets of fatherhood. The text visualizes essential concepts of fathering through the use of numerous figures, scenarios, and tables, providing the reader with easy to digest snapshots of detailed material. Clinicians, physicians, and educators will find easy to understand explanations and descriptions of types of fathers and fathering to share with parents. Beyond the practitioners, our book is written to engage the community of fathers—first time, biological, adoptive, foster or stepfathers—in an in-depth discussion of what it means to be a father, the psychosocial and humanistic context of their place as fathers, and what they can do to be proactive in the process of fathering.

Beginning with an historical context, *The Complete Father* examines how fatherhood has undergone various transformations driven by the influence of societal changes, culture, faith, gender identity, and gender roles. Through all this, there have been some immutable constants often obscured by the individual and group histories of communities buffeted by the technological advances, economic changes, and traumatic experiences of war, mass displacements, environmental changes, genocides and slavery. The book uniquely highlights these unchanging, and powerful, constants that are part of what Carl Jung called the "collective unconscious."

Focusing on the collective unconscious, *The Complete Father* uses this repository of humankind's shared thoughts, connections, behaviors and feelings that all human beings hold inside them, as the fundamental framework motivating all fathers' actions in connection to their children. We pursue Jung's theories, further, by including the collective unconscious' companion idea of "archetype" or patterns of interpersonal beliefs and activities based on these central motivations. While these theories are equally applicable to mothers, *The Complete Father* focuses on men as a population needing more education, support and reinforcement of the importance of their role in raising children within a context of diverse families. We choose this path not to diminish the importance of the mothering role, but to enhance the current trend in fatherhood of fathers as active co-parents.

Fathers of today confront a rapidly changing world where children with their more flexible developing brains are learning and acquiring knowledge quickly due to technological advances, globalism, and information overload. We stress the idea that fathers need to be able to take in, contain, evaluate, and participate in this same rapidly changing world as their children. This takes a level of flexibility that recent generations of fathers were not required to develop, but that were required of generations from further back in history. Increasing self-awareness, creating options, choices, and alternatives, identifying and engaging different role models, and establishing a support structure are all ways that fathers can keep up with our fluid fatherhood landscape.

The path that *The Complete Father* takes will lead the reader through a process that deconstructs and rebuilds the concept of fathering and provides a highly practical understanding and road map of what can be accomplished as a thoughtful father in today's society.

Introduction

The concept of the father and fatherhood is one of the foundational cornerstones of the family. We write this with full respect for the importance of the mother's role. It is our contention that there are noticeable changes that are happening in the area of fatherhood, such as the increasing numbers of fathers as primary caretakers, stay-at-home fathers, mothers in the workforce, different configurations of families and fathers carrying with them intergenerational oppression and maltreatment. It is crucial to understand the evolution of fatherhood, from the parent who once was peripherally involved in the child's day-to-day development to a parent that exhibits equal participation with mothers in all parenting roles from practical ones to emotional ones. As a fundamental component of family, the perception of father has gone through various alterations through the influence of culture, faith, economics, gender identity, gender roles and technological advances. In addition, notions of fatherhood have morphed to meet the demands of sociological conflicts, anthropological transformations and traumatic experiences including, but not limited to war, mass displacements, genocide and slavery.

A contemporary exploration into fatherhood alters the focus from the problematic absent father, rejecting father, and/or emotionally or physically uninvolved father to one that focuses on the father as a co-nurturing parent of his children. As a way to reinforce this new focus, we believe and want to emphasize that fatherhood is a life-long process. For each man, his development as a father is filled with uniqueness and individuality defined by his childhood family, his culture, his experiences and his society's expectations. In a world of dynamic family structures, evolving gender roles, awareness of the effects of childhood maltreatment and oppression, the demands on fathers and on fatherhood are changing quickly.

That said, we believe that, through it all, there are some unchanging, and powerful, constants in fatherhood that are often obscured by the variation in parenting styles, changing ideas of masculinity, fluidity of the male role, and a growing acknowledgment and acceptance of diversity in our society.

4

This book centers on these enduring constants of fatherhood. From these, we construct a framework for the "Complete Father"—one who has the innate knowledge to provide for the emotional, physical, developmental, and knowledge needs of his children. To understand this framework, we redefine the notion of "fathering" by re-envisioning a man's inherent responsibilities in the raising of his child.

To begin, we turn to Carl Jung, a Swiss psychotherapist and theorist, and a contemporary of Sigmund Freud, who developed a concept called the collective unconscious (Jung & De Laszlo, 1958). It centers on the notion that within the human race there exist thoughts, connections, behaviors and feelings that all human beings hold inside them—belonging, love, death, fear, etc. These ideas stem from humans' shared experiences through all of human history, from common day-to-day experiences to significant societal and cultural altering events.

We apply Jung's collective unconscious to our ideas about fathering. The resulting "shared fatherhood unconscious" consists of the aspects and traits of being a father that exist in all men and, in turn, affect our definition of masculinity in relation to fathering. Because these traits reside in all men, the work for all men is to become increasingly aware of these traits, to take control of them, and to use them effectively. This process will look different for each and every man. The term "Complete" indicates that we believe that every man has the potential, inside him, to grow and develop confidence in his abilities to parent his children in any situation and under any circumstance. Complete, in this way, means whole.

The underpinnings of Jung's collective unconscious are his concept of archetypes. An archetype is a pattern of interpersonal beliefs and activities that serve as a model for others to follow. The "father" (authority, rules, power), the "mother" (food, nourishment), the "wise old man" (experience, wisdom), the "hero/wounded healer" (safety, empathy), the "trickster" (rule challenge, play), and other historical roles are Jung's archetypes (Jung & De Laszlo, 1958). Our shared fatherhood unconscious modernizes the Jungian archetypes, altering them in name, but not purpose. Our modernized archetypes describe five fathering functions that exist together in an interconnected system and can, if cultivated, reinforce each other within today's father. All, are essential fathering skills for him to have in light of the myriad circumstances and events of his child's life (see Figure A.1).

The Captain archetype (Jung's "father" archetype) contains a father's participation in creating, establishing and reinforcing clear, fair and understandable rules and structure, through which his child may make productive life choices. The Captain part of a father tries to pass on to his child the important concepts of control, decision-making, analysis and prioritization. In addition, the father as Captain attempts to have an understanding of a

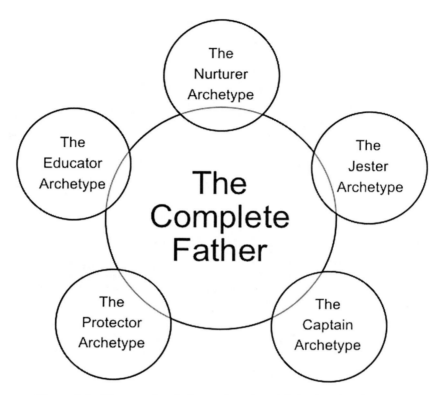

Figure A.1—The complete father and its shared fatherhood archetypes.

child's developmental trajectory and tries to address his child's requirements, both proactively and reactively, as needed and to provide navigation for his child.

The Educator archetype (Jung's "wise old man" archetype) holds a father's participation in passing on knowledge to his child for the purpose of improving his child's abilities to think critically, synthesize data, and learn. The Educator part of a father focuses on his child's intelligence, learning style, and acquisition of new information, and endeavors to teach his child "how to" do, "how to" understand and "how to" think.

The Protector archetype (Jung's "hero/wounded healer" archetypes) retains a father's involvement in helping to establish safety for his child within a containing, responsive, and empathic environment. This allows his child to experience life and manage any difficulties that inevitably occur while growing up including the hostility towards children of color in racist societies and those in which there is the tyranny of misogyny. The father as wounded healer is aware of how intergenerational trauma affects him, his fathering role as well as his children. The father as Protector tries to understand at a basic level the nature of his child's experiences and serves as an empathic companion on the journey.

The Nurturer archetype (Jung's "mother" archetype) contains a father's involvement in providing actual nourishment and food for his child to grow and thrive that comes in a variety of forms from the physical realm (hugs, food, resources, shelter) to the emotional realm (love, emotional support, affection). The Nurturer facet of a father attempts to have a working knowledge of the realms of a child's experience including emotional expression, self-love, and physicality.

The Jester archetype (Jung's "trickster" archetype) contains a father's active contribution to his child's enjoyment of life by, from time to time, shifting the focus, from society's requirements of rules and regulations to play, in all its forms, and even to mischief, in its effort to test limits and boundaries. The Jester aspect of a father relishes in spontaneity and creativity and attempts to convey to his child not to take life too seriously, to challenge the status quo, and to focus on the self.

By looking at the father through the lenses of these different archetypes, we see individual fathering as a system of thoughts and responses defined and shaped by varying combinations and interactions of these archetypal roles. In this way, the balanced application of the elements and underlying influences of these five archetypes is the work of every father. Coordinating these dynamics within distinctive parenting structures, diverse cultural norms, and unique familial histories, is the work of every family.

We examine changing social norms and evolving expectations of fathers and incorporate these elements into our new definition of fathering. We believe integrating the concepts of archetypes, cultural histories, and personal histories of fathers creates the optimal way to understand the development of the fatherhood of the future.

To this end, this book traces the development and transformation of the father role throughout socio-economic history, from primitive subsistence provider for his pastoral family, to farmer and/or animal herder following the development of agriculture and settled communities, to the post-industrial worker and economic provider of the increasingly technological world, and finally, to the modern era father, in societies that are redefining the makeup of families, altering who works and who cares for the child, and changing traditional views of masculinity. As an important sociological perspective, we also examine how societies have perceived a father's relational connection to his partner and his children throughout history. This angle of exploration tracks a father's accessibility to his family and sheds light on different ways that fathers of today may relate to their families.

In assembling the book in this way, we do not focus on providing parenting "strategies"—the guidance, skills and advice that we receive so often from other fatherhood books, websites and workshops. The decision to steer clear of "strategies" centers on our belief that if one understands the underpinnings of fatherhood—the structural components that drive all father's instincts, choices, and decision-making—then the specific details of what he may achieve as a father, should he choose to search for them, will follow.

We examine, in detail, the nature of fathers—ranging from their personalities, to their experiences, to their outlook on life and their world-view—and believe that it is the awareness of these that will help men be Complete Fathers. We consider ideas about a father's personality, his developmental journey, his seminal experiences from traumatic to jubilant, and other personal factors as influences of and inspirations for his unique implementation of the fatherhood archetypes. These ideas fall into five categories (see Figure A.2): Temperament (innate qualities of a person), Relational Dynamics (ways of relating to others), Time Orientation (past, present or future-focused), Emotional Intelligence (ability to access and interpret emotions), and World-View (perception of the world as it relates to optimism and pessimism with a context of trust and safety).

The path that we take in this book leads us through a process that deconstructs and rebuilds the concept of fathering. This book focuses on the idea that fathers, based on a variety of factors, tend to emphasize certain archetypes over others sometimes to the complete exclusion of some archetypes. We look to identify ways to rebalance fathering by adding new ways of thinking about fatherly instincts, choices and decision-making. The destination we intend to reach is a bold one, *The Complete Father*. It is a destination that we believe can be reached by all fathers.

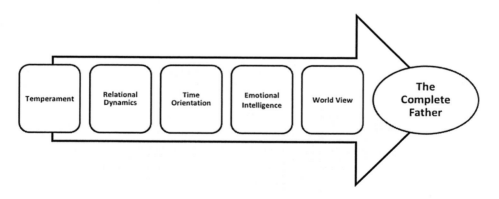

Figure A.2—The driving forces behind archetypes: A father's individual interaction with the world.

List of Figures and Tables

List of Scenarios

The authors would like to thank the many fathers who appear in this book. Although names and identifying characteristics have been changed to protect their privacy, their stories are an essential and valued part of this book. Some scenarios are revisited throughout the book.

Chapter 3—Balancing Fatherhood

Name	Relation to Father	Age(s)	Scenario
Javier	Son	5	Grieving from loss of a parent

Chapter 4—The Captain Archetype

Name	Relation to Father	Age(s)	Scenario
Juan	Daughter	10	Protesting bedtime
Eran	Daughter	13	Cleaning up after oneself
Mark	Son	7	Breaking rules at school
Louis	Son	6	Throwing temper tantrum
Errol	Daughter	14	Breaking rules at home (curfew)
Dan	Son	12	Under-age drinking
Xavier	Daughter	7	Not listening to parent (with parental frustration)
Alexander	Son	5	Protesting wearing weather appropriate clothing

Chapter 5—The Educator Archetype

Name	Relation to Father	Age(s)	Scenario
Steven	Son	8	Viewing inappropriate material on Internet
Pedro	Son	6	Learning the rules of a game
Jeffrey	Daughter	11	Teaching/learning to use technology
Kamal	Son	12	Sharing school material with parents
Hubert	Daughter	14	Managing homework assignments
Damon	Daughter	11	Needing assistance with homework

Chapter 6—The Protector Archetype

Name	Relation to Father	Age(s)	Scenario
Leonard	Daughter	10	Considering sleep-away camp
Pablo	Son	7	Crossing the street safely
Steven (revisited)	Son	8	Viewing inappropriate material on Internet
Errol (revisited)	Daughter	14	Breaking rules at home (curfew)
Dan (revisited)	Son	12	Under-age drinking
Jamal	Son	17	Dangers of driving as an African American youth
Arthur	Daughter	3	Adjusting to preschool (overprotection)
Rick	Daughter	15	Choosing when to share difficulties with parent
Kwame	Son	7	Walking to school on one's own

Chapter 7—The Nurturer Archetype

Name	Relation to Father	Age(s)	Scenario
Sergey	Granddaughter	4	Preparing for preschool
Louis (revisited)	Son	6	Throwing temper tantrum
Jacob	Daughter	5	Struggling with transitions (bedtime)
Toby	Son	11	Needing comfort (when parent is already struggling)
Steven (revisited)	Son	8	Viewing inappropriate material on Internet
Mark (revisited)	Son	7	Breaking rules at school
Antoine	Son	18	Adjusting to/preparing for college
Jamal	Daughter	16	Driving a car and seeking independence
Jude	Son	11	Feeling anger about being punished (with parental uncertainty)

Chapter 8—The Jester Archetype

Name	Relation to Father	Age(s)	Scenario
Katsuo	Son	10	Making decisions during play
Billy	Daughter	5	Playing to distract from sadness and fear (illness)
Hassan	Son	6	Choosing play instead of work
Ted	Son	13	Showing interest in child's interests (Internet videos)
Brandon	Son	4	Playing in "girl" clothes
Victor	Daughter	5	Imaginary play with dolls (increasing comfort)

Name	*Relation to Father*	*Age(s)*	*Scenario*
Rodney	Son	15	Fighting
Antoine (revisited)	Son	4	Communicating through play (autism)
Carmine	Sons	11/7	Rough housing in the house
Kenneth	Daughter	13	Setting limits on telephone use
Cliff	Son	8	Competing with child (video games)

Chapter 10—Fathers' Temperament and Impact on Archetype Access

Name	*Relation to Father*	*Age(s)*	*Scenario*
Katsuo (revisited)	Son	10	Making decisions during play
Leonard (revisited)	Daughter	10	Considering sleep-away camp
Steven (revisited)	Son	8	Viewing inappropriate material on Internet
Errol (revisited)	Daughter		Breaking rules at home (curfew)
Alexander (revisited)	Son	5	Protesting wearing weather appropriate clothing
Kenneth (revisited)	Daughter		Setting limits on telephone use

Chapter 11—Fathers' Relational Dynamics and Impact on Archetype Access

Name	*Relation to Father*	*Age(s)*	*Scenario*
Manush	Son and daughter	17/14	Adjusting to divorce and different homes
Dieter	Son	16	Fearing learning how to drive
Amir	Daughters	3/5/7	Wanting to play with an exhausted parent
Gabe	Son	6 months	Crying (infant)
Matthew	Son	3	Adjusting to death of a parent
Jacob (revisited)	Daughter	5	Struggling with transitions (bedtime)
Miguel	Daughter	5	Identifying discrimination in Kindergarten

Chapter 12—Fathers' Time Orientation and Impact on Archetype Access

Name	*Relation to Father*	*Age(s)*	*Scenario*
Gary	Son	15	Walking in on son masturbating
Nicholai	Daughter	27	Getting married
Solomon	Twin daughters and son	4/7	Adjusting to trauma, death of a parent

Name	Relation to Father	Age(s)	Scenario
Sebastian	Son	3	Preparing for preschool (with nervous parent)
Stuart	Sons	13/15	Managing homework and after school activities

Chapter 13—Fathers' Emotional Intelligence and Impact on Archetype Access

Name	Relation to Father	Age(s)	Scenario
Manuel	Daughter	15	Struggling with friendships
Donald	Son	8	Dealing with hyperactivity

Chapter 14—Fathers' World-View and Impact on Archetype Access

Name	Relation to Father	Age(s)	Scenario
Errol (revisited)	Daughter	13	Breaking rules at home (curfew)
Miguel (revisited)	Daughter	5	Identifying discrimination in Kindergarten
Devlin	Twin daughters	2	Struggling with complication related to premature birth
Saito	Son	12	Becoming interested in girls

Chapter 15—The Future of Fatherhood Archetypes

Name	Relation to Father	Age(s)	Scenario
Freddy	Daughter	14	Discussing a mass school shooting
Benjamin	Daughter	11	Helping parent get used to new technology

1

Fathering Beyond Conception

The Concept of Fatherhood and Historical Trends in Fathering

The heart of a father is a masterpiece of nature.—Prevost Abbé

There is a humility of being a father to someone so powerful, as if he were only a narrow conduit for another, greater thing. That's how it feels right now, he thinks, kneeling beside her, rinsing her hair: as though his love for his daughter will outstrip the limits of his body.
                                                            —Anthony Doerr

The father who would taste the essence of his fatherhood must turn back from the plane of his experience, take with him the fruits of his journey and begin again beside his child, marching step by step over the same old road.
                                                            —Angelo Patri

"Why do men like me want sons?" he wondered. "It must be because they hope in their poor beaten souls that these new men, who are their blood, will do the things they were not strong enough nor wise enough nor brave enough to do."
                                                            —John Steinbeck

I think that my strong determination for justice came from the very strong, dynamic personality of my father.... He is a man of real integrity, deeply committed to moral and ethical principles.... If I had a problem I could always call Daddy.
                                                            —Martin Luther King, Jr.

A book like this one—about fathers, fathering and fatherhood—requires a definition of the word "father." This provides a point of reference from which to identify how these concepts are being used today, have changed over time, or still may need to be expanded. In everyday language, the verb "to father" refers to the act of a man's participation in conceiving a child. At its core, the statement "I fathered a child" does not denote any type of relationship or role with the child other than a biological one asserting man's fertility. The Merriam-Webster Dictionary defines a father similarly, as "a man who has begotten a child" and "one who originates or institutes" (Merriam-Webster, 2018). In this use of the word, "fathering" is a wholly narcissistic action—and a momentary one at that—that is self-referential to the individual man. Its emphasis on fathering as only a procreative act that ends when the act is completed creates a disconnectedness from the family system. Using this narrow definition demands a clarification of role—if a father creates a child, what then, if any, are his ongoing responsibilities?

The Oxford Dictionary defines a father in several more expansive ways including (1) "a man in relation to his natural child or children," (2) "an important figure in the origin or early history of something," (3) "a man who gives protection to someone or something," and (4) "the oldest or most respected member of a society or other body" (Oxford Dictionary, 2018). Within this source, we can see a variety of themes developing—biology, connection, respect, age, authority, creation, protection, and experience—that society has noted are important in relation to the concept of "father." This definition of a man as "father" comes with strings attached in the form of continuing relational and experiential responsibilities to the child that he "begot."

As we define fatherhood and fathering in this book, the details concerning (1) the diversity within the role itself and (2) the specifics of the men who fill the role are essential. The word "father" conjures up countless ideas, thoughts, memories and details. Each person's experiences shape his or her own meaning of what a father is and the important qualities that define the word.

Relationship
- My father adopted me
- My father was a hard man
- My father left us before I knew him
- My father traveled for work and was not really around
- My father died when I was young
- My father was divorced from my mother and I lived with him

Description
- My father was gay
- My father was a proud man
- My father smoked a pipe
- My father was an immigrant

- My father was a different race than my mother
- My father was tall

Activities
- My father taught me chess
- My father showed me how to clean a gun
- My father coached my baseball team
- My father played board games with me
- My father came to my basketball games
- My father and I cooked together

Quality of the Interaction
- My father loved to give me hugs
- My father was really strict
- My father yelled a lot
- My father never smiled
- My father abandoned me
- My father was always there for me

One's own connection to fatherhood is only one aspect of understanding this complex role. Looking further back into history elucidates even more. What follows next is by no means a comprehensive historical account of how men's roles in society have changed over the centuries as that type of analysis is well beyond the scope of this book. Our purpose, here, is narrower, but crucial to this discussion of how the role of "father" changed over time and contributed to creation of different themes within the fathering arena. These themes are the work of this book and this chapter gives this work some historical roots. To accomplish this, we use a linear historical format, while acknowledging that societal growth and change is not a linear process and that a whole culture does not move in unison as innovations and new attitudes create changes in family structure. In addition, not all societies develop on the same time frames or in the same ways.

Maslow and Fathering as a History of Providing Needs

A father in today's developed world is the latest incarnation of an evolution of the role over centuries. Many varying elements—some of which can be found embedded in our current definitions of fathering—developed for specific reasons throughout history. Depending on the structure and framework of the society during that period, different aspects of fathering seem to have been emphasized where other were de-emphasized (Bernard, 1981; Kimmel, 2012; Kimmel & Stout, 2006; van den Berghe, 1979).

Abraham Maslow, a human development theorist, established a hierarchy of needs that individuals require in order to develop (Maslow, 1968; 1971; 2013). Maslow's ideas have a methodology that lends itself nicely to the purpose of understanding the bio-psychosocial structures that individuals need to thrive. By bio-psychosocial we mean, a structure derived from the biological, psychological and social requirements of human beings. Since we are endeavoring to grasp the building blocks of fathering, we felt this theory is highly applicable.

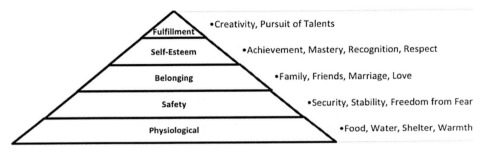

Figure 1.1—Maslow's hierarchy of needs (Maslow, 1968).

Maslow's concept centers on the idea that healthy, well-functioning systems—whether they be individuals, families, or societies—are built from the ground up. At the most basic level are the individual's "physiological" requirements such as air, water and food. Without these, we do not survive. All biological systems need these basics to flourish. Maslow believed that each subsequent level was built on the previous and without sufficiently meeting the needs of one level, a system or individual was not able to meet the next.

The Hunters and Foragers—Physiological (Food)

The hunter/gatherer or "forager" societies were comprised of tribes/clans founded on group nourishment, with men and women having very different roles (although still exhibiting a great deal of egalitarianism between genders) (Winterhalder, 2001). Males hunted, and women gathered (fruits, edible plants, seeds, nuts and fungi), ultimately helping children survive to procreate and continue the human race. Some believe Darwinian natural selection rewarded a family unit with infant survival if the man could provide adequate protein to the woman and child by successful hunting (which also included fishing) (Hewlett, 2004; Hewlett & Lamb, 2005; Inhorn, Chavkin & Navarro,

2014; Kraemer, 1991). This centers on the Male Provisioning model of understanding fatherhood (Lee & DeVore, 1968; Gray & Crittenden, 2014).

Hunting in hunter/gatherer societies, though imbuing the men with the idea of strength and virility, put the men at risk and created a level of insecurity due to the life-threatening nature of the occupation. In addition to managing uncertain and inconsistent food sources, hunting required trips away from the families' living area to track and kill game, and so these hunters could not often protect their families adequately. The nomadic nature of these societies left families with inadequate shelter from the environment, competing tribes and animals. In fact, in these communities, some research indicates that up to 40 percent of children died before the age of 15 due to illness, violence and/or inadequate sustenance (Gurven & Kaplan, 2007).

Seemingly paradoxical to the sustaining of their families, the need to provide food via hunting may be the origin for fathering's outward focus as opposed to inward and family-connected focus that we will see exhibited in fathers later. By outward focus, we are referring to the linked concepts of externality and internality. These concepts address the issue of "locus of control" or point of control—the way a father feels that he can provide the most significant influence over the course of his family (Riddick, 1975). Outward focus is a reference to externality. External needs of a family can include, among others, the size of the home, where the family lives, and the type of employment a father has in order to support his family's financial needs.

If physiological needs are met, individuals continue to develop up through the Maslow's hierarchy. Next comes the family's need for "safety." Maslow saw safety as the individual's need for security and stability within the world (Maslow, 1968). Dangerous environments, homes, or communities—actual or perceived—undermine this in two fundamental ways. One, for some there is little growing an individual can do when required to shelter in fear and, two, danger often encourages isolation in individuals (as in the flight reaction of fight or flight) (Cannon, 1915; Bracha, 2004). It is fairly clear that this sense of safety was not often sufficiently established by fathers (or mothers) within the hunter-gatherer/forager communities and so a change was required. One version of this change came in the form of Sedentism, the practice of living in one place for an extended period of time (Railey, 2010).

The Herders and Farmers—Physiological (Food, Shelter), Safety (Security, Stability) and Belonging (Family)

While we realize that the development of hunter-gatherer communities into farming/herding communities occurred over thousands of years and involved a very slow progression that included hunter-gatherer communities "becoming" sedentary, we accelerate the process in order to maintain the fathering narrative (The Oriental Institute, 2010). To that end, Sedentism includes the domestication of both animals (via farm raising and herding) and food (via the growing of crops). This shifts the motivation behind fathering and fatherhood from a Male Provisioning Model to a Direct Care and Protection Model (Owen, 2006; Gray & Crittenden, 2014).

These new communities provided fathers with a variety of new opportunities. First, they were able to build stronger and more stable shelters for protection from the environment and dangerous animals. Second, they were able to fortify their communities against outside intruders now that they were not required to move their communities on a regular basis. Third, the consistency created by the regular food sources enhanced a sense of stability within the communities and for the father within his family (Owen, 2006).

With this sense of safety and security, Maslow believed that it was possible to achieve the next set of elements in the hierarchy—namely a clear sense of connection with others that allows for the development of healthy, mature relationships with intimates, friends, and offspring. This connecting or "belonging" has its roots in the relational dyad that newborns have at birth with mothers and primary caregivers. Maslow's third stage is the circling back to this construct as adults when, hopefully, we have the agency and knowledge to create and shape these relationships (Maslow, 1971).

Another way of referring to this connection is the inward focus of a father or his internality. This idea centers on the belief that what happens within the home is the determining factor of the success of a family. In these cases, an inwardly focused father's notion of control centers on his family's relational needs such as trust, sense of safety, empathy, attention, emotions, feelings and love. This type of fathering typified the "patriarchal," protective father that harkened back centuries to a time when the father was in charge of all (LaRossa, 1997).

Called one of the "important developments in the 13,000 years of human history," the domestication of certain animals and plants provided opportunities for men and boys (often "in charge" of the herds and the fields) to develop caregiving and nurturing behaviors—what had been the purview of females in the family (Diamond, 2002). This represented a shift and highlighted men's ability to exhibit both internality as well as externality and re-oriented the fathers away from risky and isolating activities that undermined the family cohesion to ones that enhanced closeness and the belonging that Maslow highlighted.

The advent of farming created an environment for even more family closeness and cohesion. Farming required a massive group effort, and there was increasingly less difference between what men and women did to nourish the family. Children that were once gender-selected as hunters or gathers did similar farming functions when physically able. The nurturing (introduced to fathers through animal husbandry) was also required for successful farming.

This family farming activity further developed men into sources of cultivation (as educator, supporter, and sustainer) of their children and their animals as well as their crops and put them on the road toward Maslow's next stage—that of mastering the family's internal dynamics, relationships and structures and working to achieve a level of confidence and self-esteem about parenting. The adult men and women were in charge of caring for a larger brood due to increased fertility and economic incentives for having more children as potential laborers. This led to opportunities for more interactions with their families (Owen, 2006).

However, in the United States, or what would be the United States, this process was interrupted. Whether through the systemic dynamics of slavery, the specific logistical requirements of the Industrial Revolution, or the personnel needs of other novel economic models of production, family were once again split apart.

The Factory Workers, Wage Laborers, Share Croppers and Office Workers— Physiological (Food, Shelter) and Safety (Security, Stability)

Slavery and the Industrial Revolution, though we do not equate them, greatly disrupted the close-knit family life for many people. Family members were separated from one another in different ways and for different reasons (servitude is far more brutal, violent and traumatizing), but each with similar effect—the internal focus of these families was diminished. Fathers (and mothers), shifted their focus, because of income-based logistics or lack of choice over their familial structure and autonomy, away from closeness, personal growth and relational dynamics and toward more basic concerns of security, shelter, and food.

In the South, among slaves, we want to emphasize that the effort to maintain some semblance of internality continued, but with great forces stacked against it. Kin networks were developed by African American families and communities affected by the slave trade with secondary kin and non-blood kin taking on the role of parent to children who lost their fathers or mothers to another owner (Tolman, 2011). Fathers sold and separated from their nuclear families made attempts at staying in contact—at times successfully, if on a plantation nearby in what was called an "abroad marriage"—and were able to provide some "emotional support, moral instruction, discipline, affection and physical protection when possible" (Stevenson, 1996).

After the Civil War and emancipation, freed slaves (both fathers and mothers) attempted to reunite and re-orient or re-establish their familial bonds, with some success. Yet, due to the United States government's inadequate assistance in transitioning freed slaves into even a subsistence wage-based economy, the attempt to stave off the poverty for their families required many fathers (and mothers) to enter a highly time-consuming and rigorous labor force as cleaning staff or other low-wage laborers (Berlin & Rowland, 1998). While share cropping provided an opportunity for Southern fathers (and their families) to live together, harkening back to the "internal" era of Herders and Farmers, the onerous "rental" arrangements created a level of risk that undermined family's sense of security (Davis, 1982). While slavery attacked the very foundation of the African American family system, and fatherhood itself, as part of the subjugation of black adults and children, there is a great deal of evidence that these men did not lose their sense of commitment to their children but adjusted their interactions in response to circumstance (Stevenson, 1996).

In areas not dominated by the slave-based economy, factory work removed men and women (and even children) from the home for many hours a day throughout a 7-day work week (Laslett, 2000). Rather than working together for the same hours and days to manage a herd or crops, urbanization made work an activity outside of the home environment for everyone. Urbanization in the developing world destabilized families as the fathers and mothers sought work leaving children with other family members. For some, men and women left families to travel to urban centers far from their homes for factory work. The older extended family members remained at home to raise the children who were not working on farms and in factories (Taylor, 2004). In addition, children (boys mainly) were swept up with rebellious thoughts connected to revolution and change and pushed back on their father's authority further disconnecting the family (LaRossa, 1997).

In a return to norms of the hunter/gatherer societies, this was a shift back to externality and an outward focus with regard to family life. Family size decreased, fathers in western societies were decreasingly engaged in domestic undertakings, and the father's role returned to an economic one, providing tangibles for his family (Knox, 2016). Fathers who were more successful in providing these basics were better able to keep their families and home environment intact. However, their internal family life often suffered. Still, the historical experience of prior family development—that of the herding and farming families—persisted in the fathers as an inherent ability (an unfulfilled wish for this type of connection). The shift to a focus on the nuclear family over the extended family in western societies, maintained fathers' abilities to support, protect, teach and nurture a smaller number of children (Goloboy, 2008). To reinforce and acknowledge their innate abilities, there was even some societal push back on fathers' increasing externality, with popular media focusing on a concept of masculine domesticity (LaRossa, 1997). "It was ... a model of behavior in which fathers agreed to take on increased responsibility for some of the day-to-day tasks of bringing up children and spent their time away from work in playing with their sons and daughters, teaching them, taking them on trips" (Marsh, 1990).

Post-industrial family life changed the nature of jobs and employment, once again, but did little to alter the specific responsibilities of fathers. Two major responsibilities—providing for family and productivity at work—remained inexorably interrelated for fathers. This construct of externality was taxed again and again, with the multiple World Wars, the Great Depression, and the systemic oppression of populations of color. In addition, this seemingly inescapable externality tended to lead to a tainted version of quasi-internality that focused on consumeristic love, financial support and material things as replacements for affection and attention. This created a new dilemma—the father who could not find employment or was stuck in low wage jobs due to racism or the shifting needs of local economies (i.e., the mechanizing of industry) became disheartened in his ability to provide for his family often further challenging these fathers' ability to provide for their children both emotionally and physically. These events altered fathers' sense of masculinity and strength in connection to their patriarchal family role (LaRossa, 1997).

The Preoccupied Co-Opted Father—Physiological (Food, Shelter) and Safety (Security, Stability)

The closer we get to the present, the more difficult it is to fully characterize society's impact on fatherhood. That said, we have selected two areas of focus that we deem important to acknowledge. Both contend with a level of preoccupation which directly affects fathering by somewhat co-opting the role and its ongoing purpose and focus. They are selected as representative of sub-groups of fathers. We feel it has become more and more important, as this environment has become more polarized (economically, politically, culturally, and socially), to acknowledge the individualized experiences of these populations.

To this end, within the group of fathers in lower income socio-economic strata, there has been an increasing sense of futility, in connection to income inequality and the dramatic rise of growing poverty-challenged communities.

We have seen an intensification of what we call individual preoccupation and co-option—a general distractedness and apprehension that perpetuates a deepening focus on the external over the internal. The insecurities, fears, and general anger that fuel this preoccupation drive fathers in these communities to focus on Maslow's more basic developmental needs for their children. As with the previous era, we are not suggesting that fathers have not wanted to participate in the various roles of parenting that venture beyond the basics—and do not succeed in many ways—yet, environmental pressures have made this increasingly difficult.

There are many systemic reasons for this, but those reasons that have nothing to do with any shortcomings of these men. The overstated claims, which have been reinforced by fear mongering in the media and superficial talking points by politicians, position fathers who are unemployed or who are not married to the mothers of their children as less-than-willing participants in providing support ("dead beats") (U.S. Department of Justice, 2017; Cordell, 2014). This characterization has derailed a true national discourse on any number of concerns regarding fathering and parenting, in men who are oppressed by poverty, racism, and traditional gender norms. The superficiality of the discourse has created a feedback loop that compromises men's roles in all areas of parenting.

A compromised welfare system, a minimum wage that challenges low-income single parents to provide basic necessities, racially and economically biased judicial, law enforcement, and incarceration institutions, and even, the changing notions of marriage (that it is an option and not a requirement) have all, individually and together, fostered an environment in which many more children are being raised in single parent homes. While many fathers try to provide support (emotional, physical and financial), they are confronted by Federal and state laws that include being jailed for failing to pay child support, yet not for failing to provide emotional and/or physical support. This conveys the notion that these un-wed fathers, in the eyes of the State, are viewed not as co-parents in complete sense, but in the limited role of financial providers. Fathering that is persistently defined by the externality of financial support cannot be in balance and becomes increasingly co-opted and less effective over time (Cordell, 2014).

In 2013, more than 1.6 million individuals were incarcerated in federal or state prisons in the United States, with many more in local jails. There were 2.7 million children who had at least one parent in prison. Almost all (close to 99 percent) of incarcerated parents are fathers. At some point in their lives, 7 percent of all children in the United States will have a parent who has been imprisoned. According to the Bureau of Justice Statistics, about half of the parents that go to prison are the primary financial providers for their family. These statistics disproportionately negatively impact people of color, the poor, and the less educated. As an example, and an acknowledgment of the unbalanced environment in which we are inviting fathers to engage in a process of re-balancing, approximately 1 in 9 children of African American decent in the United States will have an incarcerated parent, versus one in 57 Caucasian children (Coates, 2016; Hinton, 2016; Wakefield & Uggen, Mallet, 2016; Smith & Harper, 2015; Pew, 2010; Murphey & Cooper, 2015).

The reasons for these dramatic numbers are well beyond the scope of this book. That said, with most research indicating that the imprisonment of fathers affects their children in a variety of ways including increased aggression, increased difficulties with attention and concentration, and increased behavioral problems, the importance of fathers to balance internality and externality is ever more critical. We are asking a great deal from fathers by asking them to contend with these and other environmental disparities.

The Technocrat—Physiological (Food/Shelter)

Within a different population of fathers, social media, smart phones, 24-hour connectivity, and superficial talking-head news coverage, have all created a frenetic pace that often lacks attention to detail. Consumerism, materialism, discussion of the 1 percent, 401(k)s, and cable TV dominate discussions. This externality has been further perpetuated as the definition of workplace has changed. The line between home and work has blurred and work hours have been informally extended throughout the day and night, and on all days of the week (Shapiro, 2014).

Smart phones and computer technology have perpetuated the idea that boundaries no longer exist between the personal and the professional lives of individuals. The technology-based worker has inevitably had the effect on fathers of perpetuating a disconnectedness from the family. The technology-based father must contend with information external to his family being "pushed" to him at all times of the day. The structure of today's society and the ubiquitous implements of communication seem to focus fathers' attention away from internality when it comes to family. What we see is these new technologies perpetuating and reinforcing previously established trends of externality that have been happening for some time. This is not the fault of the new tech and it is not really an issue of full attention or partial attention (for these have been banes within the parent-child relationship forever). This is about the society's bias toward work and money (the concrete) versus family and relationships (the abstract). It is the choice of financial well-being over emotional well-being.

The Future—Uncertain

With all these pressures, it seems clear that based on the most recent research, expectations regarding fathering and fatherhood are demanding that men dig deeper and access all their historical skills to meet today's parenting requirements (Barker & Weingarten, 2016). According to Kilmarten and Smiler (2015), it seems that the trend is to ask fathers to be able to provide financial, emotional and physical support to their offspring and to understand that all these are critical to healthy child development. This seems to be the prevailing bench mark for being a "successful" father and a vibrant part of the family (Cabrera, Tamis-LeMonda, Bradley, Hofferth & Lamb, 2000; Genesoni & Tallandini, 2009; Stewart & Newton, 2010; Levant & Wimer, 2009).

The counterpoint to the data that reports increasing demands on fathers, is the unfortunate reality that in many parts of the society some of the most basic underpinnings that could allow for this well-rounded fathering are changing (U.S. Census, 2013). A variety of factors (economic, social, legal) are altering decade and century old norms and are causing men—who once may have conceived of fatherhood in the same way as having an education, a home, or a job—to re-consider or delay becoming a father as their opportunities to father in the ways they believe are strong and masculine are becoming more difficult to attain (Gray & Anderson, 2010). This is by no means happening en masse, and it may be driven by a more self-oriented societal change in priorities, but it is something to be cognizant of for the future, as the age average age of first-time fathers has increased by 3.5 years over the past 50 years or so, to 30.9 years old. This trend of later entry into fatherhood is being seen across educational, geographic, racial and ethnic lines (Aubrey, 2017; Zamon, 2017). With change comes opportunities, but also some concerns. Recent studies indicate that the increased age of the fathers parallels some risk of some medical, psychological and developmental issues (Zamon, 2017; Zickl, 2017). That said, older fathers, possibly more established, may be more financially, socially, and/or personally secure, allowing for a return to fathering that is more balanced between internality and externality.

Maslow and the Accomplishment of the Complete Father

This modest, linear and all too simplistic historical summary of a father's connection to his family begins to establish the fluctuating foundational roles of the father. Throughout history, fathers have worked within the structures of their societies and cultures to be responsible for and to their families, while facing and confronting an infinite variety of unique experiences and challenges. If we use Maslow's ideas as a measuring stick, fathers and their families, have for the most part navigated up through his first three stages of need—Physiological, Safety and Belonging. Unfortunately, we believe that this is akin to subsistence living—providing just what the family needs to survive—and, even these levels are at risk. We blame this uncertainty on broad societal and historical pressures and constraints enumerated in this chapter.

Maslow's final two stages are the central to the purpose of this book—Self-Esteem and Fulfillment. These levels within the hierarchy are about truly exploring and enjoying fatherhood. This process centers on pushing oneself beyond the practical elements of fathering and beginning to tinker with making these elements the best they can be. In any work, examining and understanding can lead to a sense of mastery that leads to increased confidence and self-esteem. Having a family is one thing; having it be the family you want and have consciously participated in shaping it is another. Being a father is wonderful; being a father that feels in control and truly confident is another. The evolution can lead to self-assurance, inner peace and accomplishment that Maslow deemed to be the final two pieces of the puzzle, Self-Esteem and Fulfillment (Maslow, 2013).

The process of becoming this "complete" father begins with the thoughts and ideas that a man may have about himself becoming father. It continues within the act of reproduction and the birth of his child. From there, we see fathering as fluid progression of interactions grounded in mutuality and togetherness. Whether the man is a hunter, a gatherer, a farmer, a herder, a factory worker, an athlete, a welfare recipient, a soldier stationed overseas, an office worker, an inmate, a stay-at-home parent, or a non-cohabiting parent, fathering is the act of meeting the changing demands of family within a given societal/economic structure and offering flexible responsibilities that are established and/or adapted to meet these demands. *The Complete Father* is a compendium pulled from human history, with all of the richness of the achievements and failings of fathering available to a man willing to search for the capabilities inside of himself.

This semi-historical construct becomes the foundation for the mythology of the father. This perspective can be augmented by enhancing it with Carl Jung's cosmology of archetypes which we cover in depth in Chapter 2 (Jung, 1981). Jung's formulation of archetypes describes the psychological internalization of human history in each person. In this way, the purposeful strength of the hunter, the commitment and dedication of the food gatherer, the protection and nurturance of the herder and farmer, all remain embedded in the disparate fathers of today and create connections between fathers that transcend culture, race, ethnicity, socio-economic strata, trauma, and geography. Holistic fathering includes both the internality of emotional and conscious connection and the externality of providing for the basic needs, life lessons and wisdom that children need to exist and thrive. The goal of the successive chapters of this book is to explore our Jungian influenced ideas of archetypes and how fathers can access them to uncover their hidden talents of holistic fathering.

2

Carl Jung, the Collective Unconscious and the Archetypes

Your vision will become clear only when you can look into your own heart. Who looks outside, dreams; who looks inside, awakens.—Carl Jung

Children are educated by what the grown-up is and not by his talk.—Carl Jung

Mistakes are, after all, the foundations of truth, and if a man does not know what a thing is, it is at least an increase in knowledge if he knows what it is not.—Carl Jung

If there is anything that we wish to change in the child, we should first examine it and see whether it is not something that could better be changed in ourselves.—Carl Jung

Consciousness rises out of the depths of unconscious psychic life, at first like separate islands, which gradually unite to form a "continent," a continuous landmass of consciousness.—Carl Jung

We cannot change anything until we accept it. Condemnation does not liberate, it oppresses.—Carl Jung

Before we begin this chapter in earnest, we want to acknowledge to our readers that there is no proof, scientific or otherwise that the unconscious exists (Ellenberger, 1970). We say this because, while we believe in the unconscious, we also welcome skepticism and challenge. We believe that Carl Jung was on to something significant and we find that as a way of understanding and examining fatherhood, his theories have real resonance and serve as a powerful organizing principle. One chapter on a theorist as complex and creative as Carl Jung cannot possibly do justice to his large body of work. Nonetheless, this chapter of the book reads more like an introductory psychology lesson than the other chapters.

We acknowledge that Carl Jung as a man was shaped by his gender, race, sexuality and Eurocentrism. The personal limitations of theorists naturally shape and color their theories. It is also important to recognize that Carl Jung was well traveled and attempted to incorporate the ethno-cultural traditions of diverse populations. Can a white European create a theory that speaks to multiculturalism and diversity? Can we use the theories of such a man to develop ideas that resonate with fathers of every race, ethnicity, socio-economic strata, or sexual orientation? Ultimately, you, the reader, can decide how well he and we have rendered his concepts sensitive and applicable to diverse populations.

We have included multiple interpreters and interpretations of Jung's work. This provides an indication that by no means is there only one agreed upon reading of Jungian concepts. It is the very fact that Jung's work can be interpreted in a variety of ways that led us to choose his theories as the access point to an understanding of fatherhood. This use of Jung's theories does not confine fathers to be one specific brand of fathering. Rather, Jung affords each man the ability to acquire and absorb what he may from his ideas, such as an individual's unconscious, the collective unconscious and the archetypes. In this way, his concepts can be liberating as well as instructive.

Carl Jung was a Swiss psychiatrist. He enjoyed a prestigious career at the premiere psychiatric hospital at the University of Zurich, Switzerland. Dr. Jung wrote prolifically and influenced the fields of psychology, anthropology, religion, and philosophy. His work as a psychiatrist focused on psychosis as presented by his patients in the hospital. He became a major contributor to the development of psychoanalysis as a primary treatment for mental illness and had considerable influence in its adoption as a treatment methodology throughout Europe (Hall & Nordby, 1999).

Jung's work was consumed by the individual, the individual's experience of themselves, and ultimately, his attempts to create a complete psychological framework of the human psyche. He wanted people to accumulate "self-knowledge," and believed that this could only be accomplished by actively engaging in self-exploration. He did not believe that this "self-knowledge" could be gained as an intellectual pursuit, but had to be acquired through each person's experience—joy, pain, loss, accomplishment, etc. He also held that a life journey's details, nuances and specifics with regard to awareness and understanding were unique to each person. Jung expanded on this demonstrating a decided preference for in vivo observation rather than rigorous scientific inquiry (Jung, 1957).

Some of Jung's work focused on the unconscious and the related phantasmagoria of dreams that he saw as images created by the unconscious mind. The unconscious as described by psychoanalytic theory is the repository of all thoughts and/or experiences that are not currently available to an individual's active (or conscious) thought and that motivate a person's behavior and cognitive process. Psychoanalytic theory called these unconscious motivations, instincts. Sigmund Freud believed that these instincts were sexual and aggressive in nature and taboo, in some ways, and that this was the reason for having them remain hidden. Jung did not feel that these two instincts were the only aspects of a person's unconscious (Strachey, 1966). As he studied religion, philosophy, and folklore from diverse cultures and other disciplines, the patterns he identified led him to believe that there were many more motivations to human existence and that some of these unconscious thoughts, ideas, experiences congregated with one another and formed groupings (Jung, 1957; Stein, 1999).

His work included the varied mythologies of the human condition and experience. All cultures create an origin story for the advent of humankind, that includes the specific development of the cultures' founders. For many cultures, the origin story is considered divinely revealed and is included in sacred texts filled with metaphor and parables describing the development of the world, humans, and their cultural principles. Jung was fascinated by the commonalities of these origin stories—from Egyptian mythology to Australian aborigines to the indigenous peoples of North and South America—and found that the recurring themes crossed over time, continents, races, ethnicities, cultures and languages. For instance, almost every society across the globe has a story of a devastating flood. The time, place and circumstances change but the essentials of death, destruction, survival and renewal remain the same. In this way, it seems all of humankind has a Noah. That human beings often live (and still do) in flood zones is not in dispute. That floods destroy much of what is in their path is also not unusual. Some people survive floods and others sadly do not. What demonstrates to us a shared unconscious is the belief that a flood is an act of destruction (and possibly vengeance), that some deity or other worldly power warned some and not others of the impending flood, and that the flood was some sort of purification process (Leeming, 2005).

While it is true that cultures borrow from each other, the difficulty of contact between peoples from different parts of the world with no known way of interacting with one another does make one wonder. For instance, the appearance of pyramids in Egypt and pre–Columbian Mexico. It certainly made Jung wonder about the commonality among human mythology, folklore and religion. These ideas were mixed with an on-going examination of his own dreams and those of his patients and resulted in his development of a cosmology that was grounded in spirituality and metaphysics, rather than in science. He named this creation the *collective unconscious* and its backbone *archetypes* (Jung & Segal, 1998).

The idea of the collective unconscious is straightforward. Jung noted that human beings throughout history shared similar experiences and that these experiences must, in some way, be handed down generation after generation. To this end, when a person is born, Jung believed that this individual was already endowed with this "objective" knowledge; it is part of his or her essence (Jung, 1959). He further theorized that through life experiences all this embedded memory—this knowledge from our ancestors (and even before human history back to our evolutionary roots)—begins to make sense to the individual and is put to use in the here and now. He essentially believed that human beings have access to the compendium of the whole of human history.

Jung considered this compendium to be a legacy from multiple ancestors both direct and indirect. The collective unconscious was the richness of the human experience that increased in value to human kind as human history continued to evolve. For Jung, the elemental nature, albeit the instinctual aspects of human behavior, were not learned so much as inbred, in much the same way as the migratory patterns of birds and butterflies, hibernation of certain mammals, and the suckling of all mammalian babies. He believed that while each person experienced her/his own development as an individual occurrence, its repetition in all people was an aspect of collective memories held by the community of humans (Jung, 1981).

Examples such as visceral and instinctual fears of the dark, or of death, may be used to illustrate that some historical memory exists in all people. It is possible for one to believe that certain aspects of Jung's idea of the collective unconscious were actually evolutionary adaptations at work (that fearing the dark is an aspect of Darwinian survival), but the usefulness of the theory is its focus on the elements of human social interaction and psychic content (Jung, 1951; Hall & Nordby, 1973). The collective unconscious does not flow from individual experiences and, as such, is not acquired by people in the form of education or imitation. Rather the collective unconscious exists within the collective or community, shared among all, though subtly cloaked by fables, mythology, oral histories and sacred texts of diverse populations, from culture to culture, and region to region (Jung & De Laszlo, 1959)

Similar to the concept of the "unconscious" in psychological circles, the collective unconscious is not a fact or hypothesis, but a supposition—a belief without proof. That said, we believe that there are ideas, feelings, symbols, and practices that all people share. Looking closely, there is more that connects us as human beings than separates us. Typical brains are the same size as are all of our internal organs, breast milk can feed any child of any race or ethnicity from any mother on the face of the Earth, and, as Jung pointed out, the stories, folklore, oral histories, and sacred texts of many disparate populations of the world all share some common elements.

We, as humans, are part of a connected community (more so now than ever) and if one chooses to believe in the existence of an unconscious, then the belief of a collective or of common elements in all humans' unconscious is a possibility. Along these lines, Jung argued that if psychotherapists and psychoanalysts, starting with Freud, could espouse ideas and base their work with patients on uncovering and making conscious "impersonal, universally distributed, hereditary factors of a dynamic or motivating character," then his idea of a collective unconscious that contained similar elements was not that "daring" (Jung, 1956, p. 487).

In addition to his belief in a collective unconscious (a theoretical stretch that Freud was unwilling to make), Jung described a set of common elements of this shared collective unconscious that gave it meaning and life. He compared these elements, that he called archetypes, to psychoanalysis' "instinctual behaviors" or patterns of behavior related to unconscious instincts (Jung, 1956). Archetype is not a word invented by Jung, its pre–Jungian meaning is "an original sample from which all copies are made" (Jung, 1959). A more modern version of this concept might be the word template. Jung called the archetypes "the contents of the collective unconscious" (Jung, 1959; Merchant, 2009).

Jung believed that within all humans were these original patterns or samples of human roles and he called these the archetypes (Robertson, 1995). He theorized that all people, from infancy, inherit these archetypes and act on them and use them throughout their lives. He also believed that these archetypes were essential and necessary parts of our experience, noting that if humans did not need them, they would not exist (Ulanov, 1999).

Think of an archetype as a star that stands in the center of a solar system. The star's immense size and density give it a gravitational pull that attracts celestial bodies to it—planets, moons, asteroids, comets, etc. The archetype, situated at the center of a person's unconscious self, functions in the same fashion, pulling (or in this case, giving importance to) thoughts, feelings, and experiences. Just as the planets of Mars, Venus, Earth, and Jupiter define the solar system, these thoughts, feelings and experiences fill the archetype and once a critical mass is reached, give it a voice in the form of a conscious expression, be it emotional, verbal, or behavioral.

Murray Stein (1998) writes that Jung saw these archetypes as "psychic universals" (Stein, 1998, p. 89). Stein indicates that Jung believed that on the level of the collective unconscious, people are not distinctive or exceptional; that each person is ostensibly the same from this perspective, having access to all the archetypes. He called these "nature's gifts" and noted that they are "given to one and all" (Stein, 1998, p. 88). He goes on to describe the process of a man expressing distinctiveness, what Jung called individuation, as "a person's conscious engagement with the paradox of the psyche over an extended period of time" (Stein, 1998, p. 88). In other words, with the backdrop of the collective unconscious and its archetypes, the process of becoming a distinct human being is a life-long journey. During this journey the unconscious, embedded in each of us, is slowly, through thoughtful experience, brought into awareness and coalesces into a self.

Four of Jung's original archetypes were decidedly abstract compared to the ones that developed later, as his theories became more widely used. These original archetypes were the Persona, the Shadow, and the Anima/Animus. We think it is important to include these archetypes in our discussion in order to understand the evolution of Jung's concept of the archetype and to strengthen our contention that all archetypes are aspects of every human being and are therefore accessible to each of us. That said, each of these archetypes deserve far more time and words that we are able to offer in this text. Let us begin by defining each and then go on to describe their application by an individual.

The Persona archetype centers on the idea that each individual wears a mask and that this mask enables us to have relationships and interact with others (even ones with whom we might otherwise have difficulty). He called this the "outward face" of a person (Merchant, 2009; Robertson, 1995; Ulanov, 1999). Calvin Hall and Vernon Nordby called this the Conformity archetype and it is the part of a person that aids in the ability to present to others the "face" that we feel they want to see (Hall & Nordby, 1973). Based on its purpose, this archetype contains self-awareness, empathy, rule adherence, decision-making, and self-control among many other attributes. In a more problematic sense, this archetype may also contain the forces and antecedents of such historically destructive concepts as assimilation, acculturation, enslavement, disempowerment, and oppression.

The Shadow archetype centers on Jung's belief that each human being has a power, a driving force, an inspiration, that is beyond reason and practical thought (Robertson, 1995). He also compared it to "animal instinct" (Ulanov, 1999). It resembles Freud's Id in its instinctual rawness (Freud & Strachey, 1990). This is an archetype of attributes including confidence, strength, aggression and power. It is the Ying to the Persona's Yang. Jung indicated that these two archetypes needed to be in balance in order for an individual to (1) function in society in a healthy, productive way (the Persona) and (2) exhibit a vibrancy and an energy that allows for enjoyment and productivity (the Shadow) in life (Jung, 1956). Using this construct, the trend for the majority of men generally seems to favor Persona over Shadow (highlighting the lack of balance between these two archetypes). This seems especially relevant when considering some of difficulties that men from historically oppressed populations have exhibited within the realm of self-expression.

The Persona and the Shadow make up the system of a person that is connected to the outside world, to the objects or people of the world. In the language of psychology, we might characterize these two archetypes as being the conduit to one's object relations or relationships with others. In theory, the Persona expresses the part of a person that the person wants others to see, the part that the individual identifies with and wants to be identified. The Shadow is the person's hidden side, the part that exists, but that the individual feels is less acceptable for the world to see. These two archetypes do a dance together and the expression of each changes over time as the individual becomes more self-aware—as the unconscious is made conscious (Jung, 1951; Hall & Nordby, 1973; Stein, 1998).

The Anima/Animus archetypes represent more complex concepts and are Jung's attempt at acknowledging the dual nature of each person—the conscious and the unconscious. If the Persona/Shadow dyad determines the individual's connection to the world, the Anima/Animus archetypes access the inward path, the link one has with the inner self. The use of the term "the self" refers to an individual's sense of personhood, a mélange of personality, self-esteem, body image, awareness, mind and spirit as well as a person's wishes, dreams and underlying feelings (Kohut, 1971).

For an understanding of how the Anima and Animus are related in their purpose, we have to go back to the idea that the self includes two interconnected parts of consciousness. One part is the conscious part of the self, that which is known to the individual. The other is the unconscious, the part of the self of which a person has no awareness. Jung believed that this unconscious part was given its expressive subject matter by an archetype which he split into a masculine form and a feminine form—called the Animus (if the person is a woman) and Anima (for a man). The archetype's "contents" exist, based on our acceptance of a collective unconscious, but the individual has no knowledge of it, similar to uncatalogued books in a library (they are there but cannot easily be found). As we are writing about fathers, we only focus on the Anima—the archetype of the male unconscious (Jung, 1981; Hall & Nordby, 1973; Stein, 1998).

An important aspect of the discussion about the Anima is Jung's choice to emphasize his belief that all humans have masculine side and a feminine side. He further held that for a man, his feminine side was unconscious and for a woman, her masculine side was unconscious. Cleverly, he stated that these two parts were inversely related and that the underlying and humanistic striving in each person was to make the unconscious conscious. As Carl Rogers stated, "the organism has one basic tendency and striving—to actualize, maintain and enhance the experiencing organism" (Rogers, 1951, p. 487). In other words, Jung believed that all people strive to bring their masculine and feminine aspects together. This would result in a man's effort to make his unconscious feminine side (the Anima archetype) more conscious, melding with his conscious masculine side to form a cohesive whole.

According to Jung, a man who stereotypically expresses masculine qualities such as aggression, emotional distance, or a need for control, is "over-expressing" the masculine as a communication that within his unconscious, his feminine qualities are pushing to be expressed. The more a man expresses masculinity, the more Jung would characterize his archetypal expression of the Anima (his unconscious strivings) as feminine. Conversely, a man who expresses more traditionally feminine traits—compassion, tenderness, or emotion—holds in his unconscious, masculine characteristics stemming from a more masculine Anima. The Anima archetype itself is gender neutral (Jung, 1981; Stein, 1998).

As we described in the Chapter 1, these aspects of human nature, the masculine and feminine, have expressed themselves in different ways throughout history. Jung contends that this duality exists as a form of self-protection and self-preservation—that men expressing inherently feminine qualities, and women incorporating inherently masculine qualities creates stronger, more well-rounded individuals (Jung, 1970a). He goes further to indicate that for a person (and that person's personality) to be at peace, one must be able to express these two "harmoniously" (Jung, 1970b; Hall & Nordby, 1973).

For this book, we believe that the existence of the Anima archetype within the collective unconscious is the grounds that allows us to acknowledge that change is possible, that building a complete father is within reach. This is not an attempt to de-masculine fathers. Rather, it identifies a route to conceptualize fatherhood as parenting that includes disciplining, rule-making, playing, and teaching, in addition to tenderness, compassion, affection, and practical caretaking that traditionally have been seen as the purview of women more than men. This is not to criticize or attempt to dismiss what some cultures, and certain populations, have developed as traditional male roles in families, but more as a way of augmenting these ways of thinking. We see these initial Jungian archetypes as a way to remember that men are multi-layered beings. As we will examine in Chapter 3, these archetypes (and others) and their structural capability to foster change and growth, are the foundational components to rebalancing and enhancing one's expression of fatherhood.

The number of Jungian archetypes is many and varied and fall into four typical categories: Family, Story, Nature or Animal (Jung, 1970a, 1970b). Many were identified by his colleagues and adherents as his theories became more widely used. The idea of the archetype was so accessible and spoke to people on such a basic and spiritual level, that from these initial abstractions came numerous versions. Jung believed that archetypes affected the conscious parts of the personality by modulation, alteration and affirmation (Jung, 1970a, 1970b). He saw archetypes as a goal, a destination, an empty vessel to be filled. He wrote: "There are as many archetypes as there are typical situations in life. Endless repetition has engraved these experiences into our psychic constitution, not in the forces of images filled with content, but at first only as forms without content, representing merely the possibility of a certain type of perception and action" (Jung, 1936/37, p. 48).

Here are some of the Jungian archetypes that have been identified and named. We leave off a definitive meaning as a way of showing how each archetype represents an initial idea and how from this template grows each person's use of the archetype.

Table 2.1—Alphabetized List of Jungian Archetypes

Anima/Animus	God	Ruler
Birth	Hero	Sage
Caregiver	Innocent	Seeker
Child	Lone Wolf	Shadow
Death	Lover	Sun
Demon	Magician	Trickster
Destroyer	Moon	Warrior
Devious Cat	Mother	Wind
Faithful Dog	Orphan	Wise Man
Father	Persona	Wounded Healer
Fire	Power	
Giant	River	

Adapted from the work of Carl Jung.

As we prepared for this book, we selected some of Jung's archetypes to address what we believe contain the innate abilities of men to parent their children. Our selections use a full complement of skills and talents gleaned from the totality of the human experience. Like Jung, we believe that the role of father, based on the archetypes that are available to him, is outlined by and within the collective unconscious. Each man has the framework embedded within him, passed down through history, to be a whole, integrated and complete father. The archetypes that he accesses and expresses during his journey of fatherhood are filled throughout his life by each man's life experiences, his specific characteristics and the diverse cultures, societies, and historical forces that shape him. From our perspective, the Jungian archetypes that most influence and express the role of father are as follows:

- The Father—consciousness, creation, form, energy, power, intellect, rationality [Jung, 1948, 1954]
- The Wise Man—wisdom, enlightenment, holiness, insight, guidance, synthesis of information [Jung, 1970a, 1970b; Crisp, 2010]
- The Hero—adventure, exploration, danger, loyalty, protection, safety [Jung, 1970a, 1970b; Stein, 1998]
- The Wounded Healer—suffering, pain, understanding, healing, mutuality, companionship, interconnectedness [Jung, 1951; Benzimen, Kannai & Ahmad, 2012; Larisey, 2012]
- The Mother—caretaking, redemption, devotion, fertility, fruitfulness, protection, sympathy, solitude, wisdom, spirituality, assistance [Jung, 1954]
- The Trickster—mischievousness, drama, emotions, creation, transformation, joking, divine-animal nature [Jung, 1970a, 1970b]

We have re-purposed the names, characterizations and descriptions of these archetypes in ways that we believe are more accessible and functional to the modern reader. Although this does not rework Jung's underlying meanings of the archetype, it does provide greater access to the modern sensibilities of today. This book is written with a focus on unconscious thoughts moving towards consciousness. Retrieving ancient concepts via contemporary language seems an apt parallel process to the one that Jung described. The archetype chapters that follow this section of the book provide, in great detail, the nature of the information and abilities available to fathers. Here are the modern-day names for those innate concepts:

- The Father is now renamed the Captain archetype—structure, rules, ethics, control, decision-making. This is father as leader based on his expertise in child development.
- The Wise Man is now renamed the Educator archetype— information, learning, synthesis. This is father as mentor helping the child to gain a deeper understanding of himself/herself, other people, and the world.
- The Hero and the Wounded Healer are joined into one renamed concept called the Protector archetype (the rationale for joining these concepts is described in Chapter 6)—connection, safety, empathy. This is father as "home base," the one the child turns to for consolation, but also the repository and expression of past and ongoing sufferings of the human experience (Ainsworth, Blehar, Waters & Wall 2014; Bowlby, 1969; Krumweide, 2014; Winnicott, 1990).

- The Mother is now un-gendered and renamed the Nurturer—affection, love, resources, intimacy. This is father as a source of energy able to re-charge the child in emotional and practical ways.
- The Trickster is now renamed the Jester—play, joy, rule challenging. This is father as grownup playfellow able to use humor and spontaneity to connect with his child (see Table 2.2).

Table 2.2—Comparisons Between Authors' Archetypes and Jung's Original Archetypes

Authors' Archetypes	Jung's Archetypes
Captain	Father
Educator	Wise Man
Protector	Hero/Wounded Healer
Nurturer	Mother
Jester	Trickster

Charlie Donaldson and Randy Flood created the term "mascupathy" that describes a limitation-inducing trend of some men (and fathers) who only have access to and express a narrow range of masculine qualities that are stereotypical male traits like aggression, need for control, and emotional distancing among others (Donaldson & Flood, 2014). This is Jung's Persona archetype—the perception of what society expects. In contrast, is the father who plays with his child, is involved in the practical caregiving, and is both protective and instructive with his child. This is the fathering that Jung described as aspects of a more feminine Anima. It is the merging of the two versions of fathering that speaks to our hope for fathers in the future (Jung, 1970a). Stein speaks to this hope when he writes of reaching ultimate goal of the individual—"the unification of the parts into a whole" also called individuation (Stein, 1998). For this process he writes that "at the beginning it is unconscious wholeness, whereas at the end, the sense of wholeness is conscious" (Stein, 1998).

Jung would maintain that the process of individuation is a two-step one. Using the analogy of a bird's life span as a framework, the bird grows, gains strength, and when it is ready, flies away from the nest. This is what Jung views as the first half of the process. The bird, then, creates a life for itself, procreates, and grows old—Jung's second half. Jung's concept of individuation centered on these two parts as it applies to the evolution of understanding oneself. The first is getting ready to be on one's own (psychologically, speaking) so that the second part can take place—that of working to integrate one's own ideas about the self (without the persuasive influences of one's youth) and moving oneself further toward consciousness and being whole (Jung, 1970a, 1970b). In our vernacular being whole is being more complete. This book loosely parallels the Jungian individuation process:

- First Half is comprised of the concepts of the collective unconscious, the archetypes, consciousness, individuation, and wholeness.
- Second Half is comprised of the integration these concepts as they apply to each individual father-self and how to apply and utilize it in everyday life.

In addition, integral to both parts of the process, Jung described the concept of *compensation* that exists throughout a person's life. Jung felt that compensation is required to balance the scales as one's consciousness "takes from" or reduces one's unconscious. Think of it as a form of payment for becoming more self-aware. Jung indicated that much of this compensation was in the form of (and produced by) fears, anxiety, acts of forgetting, mistakes, strange ideas, and accidents (Jung, 1970a, 1970b, Stein, 1998). He believed, as we do, that the road to building the complete father is not a smooth one. It requires levels of courage and risk taking to confront and move through what, at times, may feel like, or actually be, immense obstructions be they familial, cultural, societal, racial or historical.

Fathers make choices that need to be reconsidered and changed, say things that need to be undone and apologized for, fail to act when they could or should have. Objectively, these occurrences take place all the time within father-child relationships. Subjectively, these acts can engender consternation, pain, even suffering in both father and child. The process of being a complete, whole father has a price as it generates a lack of certainty on the father's behalf. Uncertainties (and fears) that, ironically mirror the lack of certainty of each and every child. Yet, we sincerely believe, as did Jung, that the price is "worth every penny."

Following a Jungian path, we believe that men can choose to shoulder the weight of self-exploration, go through a metamorphosis and find the treasure trove of fatherhood archetypes. In this book, we maintain that transformation is predicated on accessing the collective unconscious and its fatherhood archetypes as the route to acquiring the knowledge and skills necessary to be a complete and whole father. We believe that this transformation requires a "holding environment" and for this we diverge from Jung to the work of Dr. D. W. Winnicott, a British psychoanalyst and pediatrician. Winnicott developed the concept of the "holding environment," and described it, not as a place, but a mood and tone that creates a sense of safety, reliability, acceptance, and protection within a relationship (Winnicott, 1960).

- It is the "You can tell me anything because I love you" stance.
- It is the feeling of being loved and cared for regardless of behavior.
- It is the ability ask for advice, suggestions and recommendations at any time.

Fathering requires the creation of a holding environment that includes a sense of security, self-recognition and internal approval. This sanctuary may be challenging to build, in light of today's stressors and history's impediments, but it is attainable. And it is necessary to manage the complex and multifaceted process of fathering individuation. We believe there are inherent obstacles related to increasing self-awareness, the looking back, forward and inside, and fathers need a solid jumping off point to be successful.

The use of Jungian theories such as the unconscious self, compensation and individuation, among others, can be perplexing due to their abstract, imagery-based, and interpretive nature (Ulanov, 1999). Consequently, because accessing and expressing all appropriate fatherhood archetypes, in concert, is what ultimately enables fathers to employ a full range of emotional responses without injuring the foundations of the father/child relationship, a holding environment becomes a natural extension of this work.

Our book, in essence, attempts to create a holding environment for the reader in order to digest Jungian influenced theories and synthesize several other theories that we believe enhance Jung's theories. Interestingly, it is the same holding environment that each father eventually provides to his own child so that they may grow, develop and mature. To this end, the fathering holding environment serves as a model for the child's holding environment. One of many important accomplishments of a complete and whole father is to know that your children can seek you out when they need help, when they are having a personal crisis, or when they want to lean on someone older and wiser. This is "worth every penny"; it is simply priceless.

3

Balancing Fatherhood

Life is a balance of holding on and letting go.—Rumi

Extremes are easy. Strive for balance.—Colin Wright

Life is like riding a bicycle. To keep your balance, you must keep moving.—Albert Einstien

The proportion of the ingredients is important, but the final result is also a matter of how you put them together.—Alain Ducasse

The concept of balance is crucial to human beings as anyone who is challenged by a loss of physical balance can easily attest. Balance is a psychological phenomenon, as well. We need balance so that we can effectively manage our emotions on a day to day basis. The tightrope walkers, figure skaters, gymnasts, horseback riders, skiers on snow and water, dancers, baseball, football, soccer, hockey, volleyball, basketball, tennis, and rugby players, all need balance. So, it can be little surprise that fathers need balance as well.

As we mentioned earlier in this book, from a macro perspective, historical forces and traumatic experiences such as oppression of all kinds, immigration, poverty, and systemic inequality establish foundational imbalance in individuals over generations. On a micro level, life's crises and triumphs, can further throw fathers off balance. For our purpose here, while we will speak to some men's experience of the more significant macro imbalance, we will focus more on how becoming a father in and of itself throws a man off balance, whether it's his new biological baby, a child he adopts, fosters or acquires through a new relationship with the child's biological parent. All, inherently, can throw men off balance. The archetypes described in the Introduction and in Chapter 2, encompass a theory that ideally helps to establish balance for the varied activities of fatherhood. Each archetype provides specific resources to a father and a balanced combination of these archetypes is used to address any and all childhood needs.

Homeostasis, first used by Cannon (1915), is a term that is typically used in physiological processes or systems. We use it as the rationale that motivates fathers to focus on the realms of fathering and fatherhood archetypes. Homeostasis centers on the theory that a functional system thrives when it is in balance. Balance is defined by the extent to which each element of that system achieves an optimal operating level. Cannon was talking about the human body and all its sub-systems—the amount of water in the body, the temperature of the body, the nutrient level, the contents in the blood, etc.—but this concept has been easily applied to other systems—a society, a community, an individual, and to this we add the father-child relationship (Cannon, 1915; Bracha, 2004; Rodolfo, 2000).

Homeostasis is the checks and balances process of any system, creating changes within the system in order to maintain a functional equilibrium. From the outside, we may perceive these shifts as "good" in nature or "bad," but for the system, their subjective value is much less relevant. To the system, they are critical features that ensure its ability to survive.

For example, when a society and its people feel oppressed by its leaders or its rules and laws, the people may stay silent, hiding from danger, carrying on much of life in secret. In this way, these are protective and proactive efforts to maintain homeostasis in the society. On the other hand, the people of the society may rebel and try to forcibly remove leaders from office. This violent and hazardous approach also attempts to maintain the society's homeostasis, but through very different means. In both these cases, the goal of the system is for the individuals within the society to endure. Even under oppressive regimes, the functioning of the citizens must continue for the society to remain cohesive. If forced to further extremes—whether hiding deep underground or exploding in violence, homeostasis cannot be maintained, and the society may fall apart (Bailey, 1984; Bailey 1994).

As another example, when the human body warms up, the body sweats as a way of cooling it down. The discomfort may force an individual to also remove clothing, wear more light-weight garments, or consume cold beverages. When that body becomes too cold, it shivers creating heat. Becoming uncomfortably cold, a person may put on heavier or extra garments, consume warm liquids, or take a hot bath. By cooling itself and warming itself, the body maintains a uniform body temperature conducive to its ongoing functioning. As we know, a stable temperature of 98.6 degrees Fahrenheit is a critical aspect of the human body's day-to-day functioning; too high or too low and the body may cease to operate (Benzinger, 1969).

The push and pull of events in the life of a system create the need for course correction. The correcting function strengthens the system as it creates muscle memory for future problems that inevitably occur. "Systems cannot correct themselves if they do not stray" (Rodolfo, 2000). The statement indicates that straying or drifting or losing one's way, far from being unwanted within a system's experience, is actually a requirement. This is consistent with the imperfection of human beings, parents and fathers. Perfection is not a goal because it is both unattainable and unsustainable. Balance on the other hand means the system is not static or rigid but changes as circumstances and events warrant. In addition, there is a trial and error aspect of homeostasis. Something happens, and the system applies negative feedback as a way of sending a message that there is a need for a return to equilibrium. This critical self-adjusting mechanism is what drives the society to rebel or protest when necessary, or the body to sweat. It is also how fathers understand access to and expression of their fatherhood archetypes.

As we mentioned in a previous chapter, fathers began as hunters. Seen through the lens of homeostasis, the "choice" to hunt for game was actually a change, a form of negative feedback, in response to the increased need for protein in the family systems of early humans (Megarry, 1995; Lee & DeVore, 1968). Each subsequent change that occurred in their environment (climate, animal scarcity, population pressures, environmental degradation or increased productivity), in their fund of knowledge (technology innovations), in their cognitive abilities, and in their neurological development, created more negative feedback that required course corrections (Morgan, 2014). The hunters needed the rules and discipline of the Captain archetype and the protection and safety of the Protector archetype. The farmers needed the empathy of the Protector archetype and the affection and care for animals of the Nurturer archetype. As these changes took place, the family system's need for homeostasis demanded a myriad of flexible responses from fathers. In turn, fathers developed new skills, accessed different archetypes and expressed these archetypes in new and important combinations (Carrano, 2006).

Applying this analogy to modern fathering, we believe that the changes that a father-child relationship goes through—starting with the birth of the child and continuing thereafter through each developmental stage—requires the same homeostatic model of negative feedback and course correction. When a child is born, the homeostasis of the family is altered—(1) new person, (2) new relationships (although this one has been brewing for up to 10 months from conception to birth), (3) new tasks, and (4) new responsibilities. Each of these shifts the balance of the family system and provides fathers with negative feedback, requesting that he "consider" changes. Add to these, the homeostatic responses to the unique factors, advantages, disadvantages, and challenges from a highly diverse set of populations, societies and cultures. Requiring course corrections opens up the possibility for access to different fatherhood archetypes.

Fathers have always been aware that their role in the family is to provide for the family's concrete practical needs of food, shelter, and safety within modern economies. In recent times, this has been typically related to generating an income as a way to achieve all three of these requirements, while within premodern economies this meant hunting for food, building homes and physically defending the family from danger and attack. There are facets of fathering within modern economies that require "expanded" attention. These fit into two main categories—the physical realm and the emotional realm. The physical realm consists of all those caretaking responsibilities that require fathers to make choices about physical connection such as hugging, holding, bathing, playing, wrestling, driving, doing homework, teaching, modeling, disciplining, etc. The emotional realm centers on activities (from very basic to more complicated) that ask fathers to make decisions about emotional connection such as making eye contact, soothing and cajoling, listening, responding to distress, being supportive, providing empathy, setting clear rules and limits, praising and giving constructive input, containing emotional outbursts, having discussions of increasing complexity, maintaining perspective, etc.

In subsequent chapters throughout this book, we will read about fathers such as Steven who wants to explain sex to his shy and not quite pubescent son; Errol who feels that hitting his teenage daughter is the only way to get her to mind him; Saito who fears that his son's interest in girls will ruin his chances to get into a good college though that is many years in the future; Donald who gets angry with his son's teacher and then takes it out on his son; and Manuel who has no clue how to help his daughter manage what he believes is "just" online teasing. What these very different fathers have in common is that these situations have created in each of them a loss of balance. These fathers, and many others in the chapters that follow, will demonstrate how balance can be achieved in a variety of ways.

Operationalizing the Concept of Balance in Fathering

There is a general understanding of what is currently considered healthy eating in the United States. This topic has been constantly debated and our practices altered as research has provided new ideas about what we must eat to provide optimal sustenance for our bodies and our minds. As is common with research, studies on the same topic do not always reach the same conclusion and so "healthy eating" can be a complex topic. To this end, the President's Council on Fitness, Sports, and Nutrition, and other providers of dietary information try to offer some general guidelines. The President's Council (2016) presently describes seven points of a healthy diet:

- significant amounts of fruits and vegetables
- whole grains instead of refined grains
- fat-free or 1 percent milk
- lean proteins such as fish, seafood, poultry, beans, eggs, etc.
- limited amounts of sodium
- plenty of water
- restricted quantities of solid fats such as desserts, ice cream, fatty meat, etc.

Adapted from the President's Council on Fitness, Sports, and Nutrition, 2016.

These are straightforward suggestions. They include types, amounts, categories, and, when taken altogether, blend into what one might call a balanced diet. Because not one of these areas are more important than any other, the nutritional balance chart is no longer a triangular hierarchy of foods built on top of one another, but a series of circles reminiscent of a Venn Diagram—groups of food contributing to an overall whole dietary plan. If we take a step back from this diagram, we see that it is constructed in a similar fashion to the way that the fatherhood archetypes are related (see Figure 3.1).

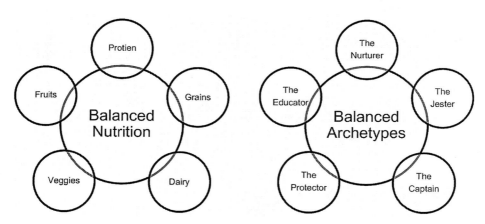

Figure 3.1—Comparing balanced nutrition and balanced archetypes.

Imagine that each of these circles can be expanded in size and decreased in size depending on the various needs of the individual. If a child needs more protein because of an iron deficiency, we enlarge the protein circle; if there is a lactose intolerance or sensitivity, the dairy is decreased or altered; and if a teenager refuses to eat meat due to a crisis of conscience regarding the treatment of animals, non-animal protein is introduced into their diet. In each of these cases, the negative feedback created by the precipitating factor would require a homeostatic response from the system, more protein-less grain, less dairy-more fruit, less protein-more vegetables. The system is rebalanced under the new regime of combinations and amounts.

Fathering, within the different realms of fatherhood and using the archetypes, follows this same format. Within the dynamics that govern each and every father-child interaction, situations always require at least two archetypes in response. Depending on how the interaction proceeds fathers may require an increase or decrease in the archetype use of any of the five. A little more Captain, a little less Protector, a greater emphasis on the Jester or a pulling back on a father's use of the Educator. This process of balancing a father's use of the archetypes becomes the back and forth that connects Jung's collective unconscious to each father in the here and now. Balancing requires an awareness and access to all five archetypes for fathers to be able to interact with their children fully and effectively.

The lack of homeostasis is communicated by difficulties in the father-child interaction which means that the combination of archetypes accessed and used is not optimally composed for that situation. The collective unconscious, containing the experiences of all humankind, fuels the fatherly need to care for one's offspring and enables fathers to have an awareness of when the father-child relationship is challenged. Sensing a bad feeling, or discomfort, connected to an interaction "gone wrong," perhaps a feeling of guilt (about something done) or regret (of something not done), or frustration (with something not working) are all versions of negative feedback indicating a loss of balance. This is analogous to the overheated body due to too much exertion or a great deal of fatigue because of poor nutrition. Based on the drive inherited from fathers of old, fathers of today will begin to problem solve with homeostatic balance as the goal (see Figure 3.2).

In subsequent chapters, we will examine the archetypes in detail and discuss the process of emphasizing, de-emphasizing, and/or recombining them and the impact on the father-child interactions. These combinations represent a father's choices, innate characteristics, historical antecedents, social pressures, cultural norms, and personal wishes/fantasies. Since this chapter is about homeostasis, using only one archetype is fundamentally unbalanced. That said, throughout this book, we will explore what one-archetype responses look like, because we believe that these types of imbalanced responses are directly correlated with the more homeostasis-challenging influences such as trauma, culture, oppression, and poverty. A father must use at least two archetypes (if not more) during an interaction with his child in order to achieve some level of balance.

Staying with the food metaphor, we may describe that each father uses a specific "recipe," or a mixture of the archetypes for each father-child interaction (see Figure 3.3). Every father has his own favored ingredients that

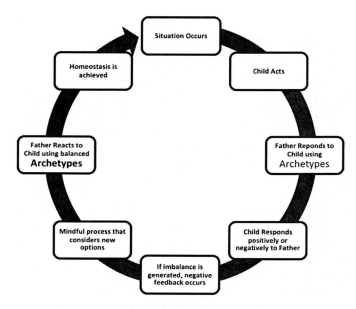

Figure 3.2—The cycle of balancing archetypes.

makes him a separate individual and different from other fathers. His own original recipes can change if he needs to be a little stricter or a little bit more permissive, more protective or less, more attentive or less depending on the situation.

Javier is a recent widower and the father of a 5-year-old boy, who is struggling with the recent loss of his mother to cancer. Javier works in the construction industry and is away from home for weeks at a time. This travel schedule existed prior to his wife's illness and continued straight through, even after her death. Javier leaves his son with his maternal grandparents. His son has been extremely upset by his mother's passing and he has become withdrawn, has difficulty sleeping and a significant lack of appetite—all obvious symptoms of grief and depression. Javier is a "tough-love" father, just like his dad, and believes that his son needs to "get over it" and that "time heals all wounds." Javier feels better when he is traveling and distracting himself from his memories. When home, Javier interacts with his son as if nothing has changed in their lives. He believes that his son needs structure in order to get over his loss, but the rigidity of this structure seems to contain both his and his son's feelings, keeping them mute. Everything he does is based on routines—in bed by 7, one book only before bed, no coming to dad's bed unless it is an emergency, no crying, no talking back, and no sugar except on weekends. These rules are important to Javier because without them he feels out of control.

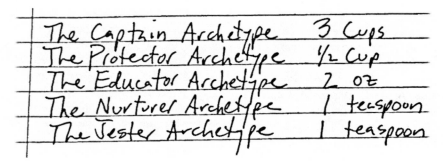

The Captain Archetype   3 Cups
The Protector Archetype   ½ Cup
The Educator Archetype   2 oz
The Nurturer Archetype   1 teaspoon
The Jester Archetype   1 teaspoon

Figure 3.3—A recipe for Javier's fathering.

In Javier's fathering recipe, the amounts of each individual archetype, as seen in Figure 3.3, describe a father who needs his space, his rules, and his structure in order to parent while coping with the loss of his wife and the mother of his child. His use of the Captain archetype with his child dominates his fathering. Most likely this emphasis of the Captain archetype was a part of his recipe prior to his wife's illness, and in terms of the homeostasis of the parent-child system, this combination worked. Since his wife became ill and died, the family system is profoundly altered—he is worried about their finances, how he is going to handle childcare and maintain the rent. Javier is more and more reliant on this archetype emphasizing rules and discipline to the near exclusion of the Educator's discussions, the Nurturer's affection, and the Jester's fun. Javier genuinely believes that he is keeping his son safe, by placing him with his maternal grandparents (a connection to his son's mother) and by making sure that his care is consistent. However, his use of the Protector archetype, while important, is only part of an adequate response to his son's grief. Javier's response lacks the necessary empathy for his son to feel less isolated and the physical affection his son needs for reassurance. With this type of recipe as his basis of fatherly nourishment in the face of the loss of a parent, Javier's son will ultimately starve. His son's grief, his need for nurturing, for play, for emotional closeness and for cognitive stimulation as intellectual distraction, are not being fed by Javier's combination of archetypes. There is an imbalance of too much Captain and not enough of the other archetypes.

Getting worried feedback from his in-laws and his son's teacher, Javier decides to seek help and advice from his friends and from professionals. With their suggestions and interventions, Javier begins to alter his interactions with his son. He stops traveling so much, decides to move in with his in-laws for a period of time, and spends significantly more time with his son. This allows for a number of new activities, including walks (increased Nurturer), going to the library (increased Educator), visiting mom's grave (increased

Protector), playing games (increased Jester) and holding and hugging (increased Nurturer). Javier begins to let his son cry in front of him and Javier allows himself to cry in front of his son. His rules are modified to allow for his son to get out of bed and see his father at night when he is distressed, for his son to express his sadness and anger, and for his son to see that there is still joy in life (decreased Captain). Javier is re-combining his archetypes by expressing certain ones more and other ones less and thus is actively re-balancing his life with his son—reaching a new homeostasis and therefore a new recipe.

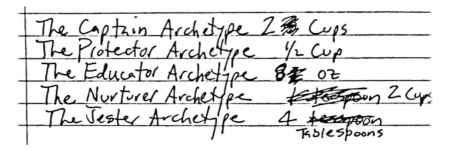

The Captain Archetype 2 Cups
The Protector Archetype ½ Cup
The Educator Archetype 8 oz
The Nurturer Archetype 2 Cups
The Jester Archetype 4 Tablespoons

Figure 3.4—A new recipe for Javier's fathering.

It is the work of this book to illustrate the inner workings of each archetype and how the expression of them contribute to men's fathering abilities, skills and talents. Fathers have the ability to fluidly use these archetypes to address everyday parenting events, extraordinary incidents and emergencies, complex and/or unjust societal patterns, typical developmental changes in their children, and the challenges of an ever-changing world. The homeostasis of a father-child relationship is not a steady state because it is a living entity of intimacy and connection that is constantly in flux. Because of its intrinsic motion, balancing the archetypes is not the end goal of fatherhood, but the means by which fatherhood is expressed.

4

The Captain Archetype

If the highest aim of a captain were to preserve his ship, he would keep it in port forever.—Thomas Aquinas

A genuine leader is not a searcher for consensus, but a molder of consensus.—Martin Luther King

A leader is best when people barely know he exists, when his work is done, his aim fulfilled, they will say: we did it ourselves.—Lao Tzu

Don't find fault, find a remedy.—Henry Ford

When your values are clear to you, making decisions becomes easier.—Roy E. Disney

Management is about arranging and telling. Leadership is about nurturing and enhancing.—Tom Peters

Throughout history, art, literature and film, the connotation of "father" carries with it an expectation of leadership. There are many families in which the mantle of leader resides with someone other than the father. We make a distinction between leadership and patriarchy as we have no intention of diminishing the leadership role of the mother, the co-father or another parent in the child's life. That said, as with all the archetypes that we will discuss in this book, we want to underscore the idea that this mantle of leadership is a role for all fathers, even ones that do not want it.

Expecting leadership as a central part of fathering may feel like an unfair burden to some fathers if the role is seen as limited to discipline, punishment and "angry" rule enforcement. This may feel especially onerous if fathers perceive that there exists within this role an ever-present power struggle centered on the child's need to challenge these rules. The idea that a perpetual state of conflict endures may feel daunting and unsettling, but as we will examine, leadership, as we conceive of it, means much more.

That said, rules are a necessary part of any family. Rules establish boundaries to contain the intense emotions, instincts, and impulses that children and adolescents experience as part of their developmental growth. As a leader, the father creates, revises and enables rules as his children grow and mature. This process of developing an overall structure, devising and implementing rules, and making modifications to existing rules have consistently been among the tasks of the successful leaders of all organizations. So too, do these tasks fall within the emotional and physical realms of "leading" a family. We call this part of fathering, the Captain.

The word "captain" comes from the Latin (head), the Late Latin (chief), and the Middle English (leader) (Merriam-Webster, 2018). We choose to use it to describe this fatherhood archetype, because it embodies many of aspects of what it means to be in charge. Walt Whitman, in his famous poem of tragedy at sea, "Oh Captain My Captain," used the terms captain and father interchangeably. To him the man who led him embodied both. The ship captain was his father. "My captain does not answer, his lips are pale and still, / My father does not feel my arm, he has no pulse or will" (Whitman, 1900).

To use the Captain archetype is to have authority and influence over others and necessitates the tapping of myriad traits and qualities that lay within us—

- Captain of Industry (from business)—thoughtful, plan-oriented, grandiose
- Team Captain (from sports)—loyal, consensus building, caretaking
- Captain America (from pop-culture)—strong, principled, selfless, moral
- Captain of the Guard (from the Old Testament)—rule-bound, duty-bound, goal-oriented

and a variety of ship captains, including

- Captain John Paul Jones (from American history)—valiant, brave, inspirational, strategic, pragmatic
- Captain Wentworth (from literature, Jane Austen's *Persuasion*)— steadfast, disciplined, loyal, ethical, giver of second-chances
- Captain James T. Kirk (from television, Star Trek)—risk-taking, courageous, imaginative, accepting of differences in thinking and feeling

The ship captain is an apt metaphor. He sets the ship's course, maintains its functioning, and creates the rules and responsibilities for those on board. More importantly, the captain of a ship thinks about the ship and its crew ahead of all else. He helps his crew anticipate problems and manage rough seas. He is loyal and dedicated and will voluntarily "go down with his ship" as opposed to abandoning his duty.

Using the ship captain metaphor helps us understand this part of fatherhood in two significant ways. First, it increases the focus on the proactive nature of this role—on thinking ahead, predicting needs, and preparing as fundamental principles for fatherhood. Second, it decreases the reliance on the reactive potentials of this archetype—moving the Captain archetype away from the "wait until your father comes home" threat of consequence, and towards aspects of guidance and control that are necessary for all types of situations from typical day-to-day concerns to dilemmas or crises that arise within families. Children want and need to know that there is clarity regarding who is in charge; that there are limits on their behavior; and that these limits will be maintained and will contain them. Fathers use the Captain archetype to display authority without being authoritarian.

The authority that we are referring to is the mandate that fathers have to help create a structure for their children's day to day lives. The structure is made up of (1) the rules, (2) the goals, (3) the plans, and (4) the ethics, that become the guiding principles that drive the decision-making process of both fathers and their children. The clarity, consistency, reliability, thoughtfulness and even-handedness of this structure becomes the foundation of children's development.

A 10-year-old girl sits on the edge of her bed, frightened. Her knees are pulled up to her chest and her arms squeeze them tight. Her father, Juan, sits next to her and looks over at the clock—9:10 p.m. "I am just really nervous," she says. "I don't know why and I'm not tired. Can I stay up with you?" She has been up for three straight nights until 10:00 p.m. doing this "I'm nervous" thing, he says to himself, getting increasingly frustrated. Bedtime had always been so consistent. 8:00 ... teeth brushing; 8:15 reading books; 9:00 in bed, like clockwork—until now. She is just not following the rules any more. Juan is annoyed. "All right, young lady, I have had enough of this, you're going to bed right now and not another word." His daughter begins to cry as he shuts off the lights and slams the door closed.

Juan takes a deep breath and lets it out slowly. He listens to his daughter weeping and feels like maybe he should relax the rules a bit until he knows what his daughter is nervous about. He re-enters the room, turns on the light, and says to his daughter, "Scoot over, let's talk. Tell me about your day and take your time, but let's stay in bed. I don't think getting up now will help you." His daughter relaxes and looks at him with tears in her eyes. "Betsy told me she doesn't want to be my friend anymore..."

This child's father knows intuitively that using the Captain archetype at bedtime is important. His daughter needs rules and routines in order to accomplish the occasionally difficult task of going to bed and falling asleep. In fact, growing up, his own father used to just send him to bed, often sternly. He would not even enter the bedroom and Juan had to put himself to bed. There was no room for negotiation. Sleep is a good example of one of those recurring situations throughout childhood that requires the Captain arche-type in order to set rules and limits that help children and adolescents go to sleep to end a day, stay asleep in order to recover resources and process the day, and wake up on time ready for the next.

Yet, so much happens during a typical day for a child and their parents that nighttime, for a variety of reasons, can be fraught with a child's and a parent's pent up emotions. Because of this, the rules that Juan's daughter has come to rely on for the purpose of going to bed, may at times run into the realities of her day. At these times, a nuanced and flexible use of the Captain archetype is essential. Like any solid captain will tell you, it's not just about being in charge. The everyday rules of running a tight ship are situational and decisions may be altered by a variety of factors including the weather, crew, cargo, or route. In this case, the weather is the stormy emotions of the daughter's feelings of rejection, loss and abandonment. The father's job is to navigate the ship through this storm. Ignoring the power of the storm and operating from a "business as usual" stance can have consequences. It is these moments in which the Captain archetype is best used in concert with other archetypes.

Rules and Responses

The father's rule-making capacity centers on some basic reasoning. Rules have several components: an objective (the what), a process (the how and when), and a rationale (the why). Each of these parts is important to the overall understanding, integration, and implementation of any rule. If the details of rule are clear and straightforward, the rule is easier for a child to follow. This holds true for any rule a father creates—about eating, sleeping, dressing, crossing the street, talking to adults. The following three examples include the what, the how, and the when in simple, well-defined language.

- Look both ways and wait for the light to change before crossing the street.
- Do your homework when you come home from school.
- Dress in clothing appropriate for the weather outside.

We believe the rationale is the most important part of any rule. It is the plan behind any rule. It is the "because" of each rule. Building rules on a shaky foundation makes them difficult to enforce. Building them on a strong foundation gives a father a sense of control and security when enforcing a rule. As we will discuss in a later chapter, providing an explanation for a rule to your child takes time, but it enables a child to integrate the rule in a more complete way. This is the joining of the Captain archetype with the Educator archetype and makes for a powerful and stabilizing combination.

- Look both ways and wait for the light to change before crossing the street because drivers may not see you and you may be injured by a car.
- Do your homework when you come home from school because when you wait until later you get tired, your brain is less efficient, you slow down, and it gets more difficult.
- Dress in clothing appropriate for the weather outside because your body has to work very hard to adjust to any temperature issues it may have based on what you are wearing.

The rationale for rules fall into several categories. These are simplified for ease of use into the following categories: (1) Health and Efficiency, (2) Safety, (3) Dependability and Reliability, and (4) Social Responsibility.

- Health and Efficiency—medical and psychological concerns, hygiene, body and mind functioning
- Safety—danger avoidance, reduction or minimization
- Dependability and Reliability—repetition, routines, structure, consistency, containment, and developmental awareness
- Social Responsibility—the recognition that other people live in the same family, neighborhood and world with their own needs and wishes to be respected and treated with dignity

Eran stands in his living room feeling frustrated with his 13-year-old daughter after he trips over his daughter's basketball uniform that is on the floor. He notices there still is cardboard and glue on the dining room table from a project she was doing the night before. He calls to his daughter, "Dina, come here." Dina enters the room. "What?" Eran looks at the stuff and points. "What's the rule?" "I don't know, pick up after myself?" Dina says with a mocking tone. "Good memory, correct," replies her father. "Now for the big question: do you know why we have this rule?" Dina glares at her father. "Two reasons: one, because I want you to be able to find your stuff the next time you need it, and two, you are part of this family and you have responsibilities, just like me. I have more than you, but you still have some and you must do them."

In this scenario, Eran is not giving this rationale for the first time. In fact, he has provided this rationale so many times that he cannot remember. The Captain archetype is responsible for describing, explaining and enforcing rules as often as necessary until the rules are integrated. Not employing this aspect of the Captain archetype may lead fathers to relying on the power differential between parent and child as rationale.

Notice that the "Because I'm your father" statement or the "Because I said so" version are not included in the categories of rationale. Rules can feel coercive by their very nature—the father is making them and enforcing them; and the child has to follow them. The Captain archetype is the part of a father that simply *is* in charge. It is not an "if-then" proposition regardless of what either party (parent or child) may feel or say. Reminding a child of this as part of a rationale is exerting power unnecessarily. Explicitly embedding this power differential between parent and child in each rule is a recipe for conflict. It can make a child feel "small" and ineffectual requiring them to "push" back in order to maintain a modicum of power. The potential power struggle that a "Do what I say because I say so" response sets up, can decrease a father's access to the Captain archetype and limit his options to resorting to a use of force.

Once the daughter puts her basketball uniform away and cleans up the table, her father thanks and praises her for being responsive to his re-iteration of the family rules. While punishment by the father provokes fear and anxiety in the errant child, praise creates a non-material reward for rule adherence. The father's use of praise is his most powerful communication especially in situations where rule enforcement has been contentious. The father's praise contributes to the on-going development of the child's self-esteem. This is explored more in Chapter 7: The Nurturer Archetype. Conversely, the overly critical use of Captain archetype depletes the child's emotional reserves and intrudes on the child's development of confidence.

Setting Goals, Creating Plans and Making Adjustments

The captain of the ship knows the destination. Ships are contracted to travel from one port to another. When the destination is reached the goal of the trip is achieved and the captain gets paid, as does his crew. The father's use of the Captain archetype is responsible for setting these destinations, or goals, for a child. But how is the archetype to know what goals or plans are appropriate, necessary, or achievable. In order to successfully accomplish this task, the archetype needs information in the form of knowledge about all aspects of children. Would we expect a ship captain to make it to a port that he has never been without navigational charts, knowledge of the currents, a sextant, and weather reports? This information is collected and synthesized by the father into the goals and plans for his child's day-to-day existence. This information comes in the form of data (see Table 4.1).

Table 4.1—A Father's Necessary Data Set

- Developmental needs (trust, autonomy, separation, empathy, defenses)
- Developmental milestones (neck control, rolling, crawling, eating, sleeping, toileting, talking, walking, grabbing)
- Effects of environment and changes (race, religion, oppression [individual, institutional and cultural], diversity, ethnicity, losses, new homes, new siblings, divorce)
- Innate qualities (temperament, cognitive attributes and processes, language, learning style)
- Stages of physical development (infancy, toddlerhood, early childhood, latency, adolescence, young adulthood)
- Stages of sexual development (response to parental touch, response to self-touch, response to affection, sensuality, desire/libido, sexuality)
- Strengths (resilience, humor, creativity, etc.)

The specifics of each child affect how that child moves through a progression of maturation. Developmental psychology is rife with theorists who articulate concepts and information detailing the growth and maturation of children from infancy and on. Vis-à-vis the Captain archetype, their ideas can help fathers' set expectations, prepare for day-to-day interactions and make sound decisions. The following is a list of some of the most renowned of these developmental theorists—along with some of their most essential concepts—that the Captain archetype may use to begin to create a database of information and possibilities for the purpose of planning and decision-making.

- Mary Ainsworth theorized that caregivers and children develop different qualities of connection with one another (labeled *secure*, *insecure*, or *disorganized*). With John Bowlby, she researched how these varying connections (1) directly affect the quality of a child's ongoing relationships with, not just the primary caregiver, but others too, and (2) can be a contributing factor of mental health problems in children including depression and anxiety (Ainsworth, Blehar, Waters & Wall, 2014).
- John Bowlby researched and identified the concept of *attachment*. He described this as the emotional bond between a child and his/her caregiver that develops from birth (and possibly earlier). He indicated that it is the primary foundation of *trust* and *safety* for a child. With Mary Ainsworth, he proposed theories on the quality of attachment (Bowlby, 1969; Krumwiede, 2014).

- Uri Brofenbrenner (1981, 2004) proposed that children are of a product of both *nature* (their innate, genetic predisposition) and *nurture* (their environment, experiences, upbringing). He indicated that to understand a child, one must examine the interconnection between these co-relative factors and that looking at them separately, or ignoring one, was not holistic enough to have achieve accurate picture of a child.
- Stella Chess and Alexander Thomas was able to identify nine attributes with which all children are born. She described the varying combinations of these attributes—activity level, rhythmicity, approach/withdrawal, adaptability, intensity level, mood, persistence level, distractibility level, sensory sensitivity level—as a child's *temperament*. Chess and Thomas were the first to categorize temperaments' three main types: *feisty, flexible,* and *cautious* (Chess & Thomas, 1990; 1996).
- Erik Erikson developed the concept of developmental crises. He proposed that a child, with the help of his/her caregivers navigates a series of stages in order to achieve certain milestones, including feeling *trust*, having a *sense of self*, developing one's own *ideas*, taking steps to accomplish tasks and gain *confidence*, and finding one's own *identity*. He stated that mental health problems, including depression and anxiety, accompanied a failure to achieve these milestones (Erikson, 1950; 1968).
- Anna Freud developed the ideas of psychological *defenses*. These defenses, or psychological protective measures, used by children and adults alike, help control any distress or difficulties that individuals may encounter day-to-day. She believed that children achieve relief by altering the feelings and thoughts associated with these stressful situations, environments and/or relationships. Some examples of defenses that children utilized are *denial* (disavowing a stressor), *regression* (returning to an earlier and less complicated state of functioning when a stressor occurs), and *acting out* (turning feelings and thoughts about a stressor into action) (Freud & Burlingham, 1967).
- Margaret Mahler focused on the concepts of *separation* and *individuation*. She indicated that each child, as they leave infancy, goes through a process of emotionally disconnecting from his/her primary caregiver and then reconnecting in a new way. This process gets spurred on by biological, physiological and neurological changes in the child including his/her language and speech, motor skills and cognitive abilities. Some theorists

believe that children go through this process over and over again throughout their development (Mahler, Pine & Bergman, 1975).

- Jean Piaget developed ideas that focused on how children gain knowledge, think, and learn. He saw all children as little scientists, testing hypotheses, using trial and error, experimenting, in order to discover how the world around them operated. He identified how children's developmental capabilities shape their ability to take in information including how the way their thinking moves from *concrete* (facts, details) to *abstract* (reasoning, making connections) (Piaget, 2001; Piaget & Inhelder, 1969).

- Robert Regoli and John Hewitt posited a theory that focused on how oppression in its various forms including exploitation, marginalization, disempowerment, and violence can have a variety of deleterious effects on child development. The concepts of their *Theory of Differential Oppression* range from a transfer of societal oppression to parental oppression, the "negative" adaptations children can undergo when confronted with a combination of oppression within the parent-child dyad and societal oppression, and how these adaptations can affect children's decision-making and their experience of choice, leading to a reinforcement of their negative self (Regoli & Hewitt, 2001; Young, 2004).

- Lev Vygotsky, like Piaget, examined how children learn and think. Their ideas differed in that Vygotsky believed that an individual child's culture and social connections significantly affects learning. Two of his main contributions are that children learn from a *More Knowledgeable Other* (MKO) and that a child learns differently when acting independently or when receiving *encouragement* and *guidance* by an experienced partner—Zone of Proximal Development (Connery, John-Steiner & Marjanovic-Shane, 2010).

- D. W. Winnicott described two important concepts that shape the way parents may understand their role in a child's life. The *holding environment* centers on the idea that it is a parent's job to "contain" a child's development by setting boundaries and structure, providing empathy and safety, and maintaining an ongoing awareness of a child's developmental needs. With *good-enough parenting*, he believed that, although missteps will occur, there are many ways for a parent to achieve a helpful and healthy holding environment (Winnicott, 1953; 1963; 1990).

- Aline Zoldbrod's *Milestones of Sexual Development* describes sexuality as beginning with birth. She believes that parental love is communicated through touch (the practical caregiving and affection of parents) and that this physical interaction is the basis of body awareness, sensuality (as the infant determines what feels good) and mutual enjoyment (reinforced by parents' positive sounds and comments punctuated by smiles and eye contact). Thus, the foundation of body image and body self-esteem begins as a reflection of how the parents interact, care for, touch and "praise" the infant's body and is cultivated, throughout childhood, by parents through their positive comments and acceptance of their child's physical changes and development (Gallo-Silver & Bimbi, 2012; Zoldbrod, 1998, 2003).

These ideas and others, together, serve as the Captain archetype's map. A child does not know these goals, milestones, stages or responses. He or she moves through life performing a series of actions dictated by biology, neurophysiology, anatomy, and environment, etc. A father's understanding of the relationship between the growing child and the child's psycho-social development allows for his ability to stay in charge and ahead of the process. The captain must know his route, ship and his crew.

Mark sits with his 7-year-old son. They are alone in a room in their new home. He has recently moved into this new spacious apartment after separating from his wife, the mother of his son. They are discussing a situation that occurred in school in the past week. Mark received a call from the school principal who reported that the boy had left class without asking and stayed out of class until the lunch hour only returning to collect his lunch box. When asked where he had gone, his son was unwilling to respond.

MARK: *"Tell me why you did that."*
SON: *No response.*
MARK: *"If you don't tell me, I am going to assume that you were trying to make trouble. You know that you are not allowed to leave class without asking."*
SON: *No response.*
MARK: *"Fine, you are grounded for a week and no movies for 2 weeks."*
SON: *(Tearing up) No response.*

Without maps and the knowledge to use them, this father is lost at sea. The Captain archetype needs information in order to prioritize, plan, make decisions, process data and help his child do the same. What information does this father have? According to child developmental theorists, this child needs to be building a sense of confidence in himself and in his surroundings. In spite of this, unfortunate life circumstances arise and he is confronted with a new family structure, a new home, new feelings and a new normal. These types of circumstances can create a loss of confidence and a decrease in one's sense of control. In terms of behavior, we know from research that overwhelming and frightening experiences (traumatic situations) can promote acting out. Acting out is a defense mechanism employed when a person is under stress (Freud & Burlingham, 1967). It works by behaviorally expressing feelings and thoughts that are too difficult to talk about. For example, an adult may have an affair because he is unhappy in his marriage or a child may avoid doing homework because she is having trouble with learning the material.

All of this information can help Mark use the Captain archetype to focus a plan around two key elements. One, the child needs a sense of control over his new life and, two, the child may be breaking rules as a way of gaining some control and communicating his distress. Punishment may be a way of enforcing a rule or responding to a rule that has been broken, but, in this case, punishment misses two important roles of the Captain—that of goal identification and plan adjustment. In this case, the punishment does not make use of any of the developmental and psychological information that the father has at his disposal. In addition, rule integration is diminished rather than enhanced by this punishment because the father's response displays uncertainty, lacks empathy and may disorient his child further. This confusion becomes the child's lasting memory rather than the rule. Having his son write (because he does not want to speak) a few sentences about how he feels about the separation and the father's new home is a more holistic use of the Captain archetype.

Structure vs. Real-Life Pressures

Creating a structure for our children to thrive is the mandate of the Captain archetype. Clear rules, appropriate enforcement, helping with decision making, planning options and choices. The pressures that fathers experience in the real world all have their place in the day-to-day structure that fathers create for their children. Here are just a few examples.

- Time Constraint
  - I have to get my child to school on time
  - I have to get to work
  - I have to do home maintenance
- Expectations
  - My child is supposed to listen
  - My child is supposed to behave
  - My child is supposed to respect me
- Shame
  - What the other parents think when my child "acts up"

- ⊙ What the teachers think when my child acts out
- ⊙ If I can't control my child, what kind of man am I?
- Fatigue
  - ⊙ I am exhausted, and I do not have the patience for this
  - ⊙ After the 10th time of reminding my child, I just want to scream
  - ⊙ My child is ungrateful for all the hard work I do

To deny experiencing them or to consider the situations that create these thoughts as failings feeds a fantasy of a perfect father. This renders a father far less flexible then he is able to be. There is no way to avoid these pressures, they are ubiquitous and therefore, fathers may accept and absorb them into the structure the Captain archetype provides.

Fathers use the Captain archetype to help their children understand that following rules is an inherent part of every society's structure; that a child is not owed compensation for adherence to rules. Following rules may also involve a recognition of compliance by the father. This, often called a "promise," is an aspect of a father's beneficence. A promise is a transaction a father offers under certain situations and conditions. It is neither a payment or bribe nor is it always a certainty. If situations change and other rules are in conflict with a "promise," the father as Captain shares the rationale for the delay with the child. This ability to re-adjust is an essential aspect of the Captain archetype, as is the guilt-free understanding that clear, consistent rules are necessary.

A 6-year-old boy stands in front of his father, Kemal, with his hands balled into fists. His face is contorted, and he is screaming, "I WANT MY ICE CREAM! YOU PROMISED IT TO ME! YOU TOLD ME THAT I WOULD GET DESSERT!" This goes on for several minutes as Kemal patiently waits for his son to finish. When the boy finally exhausts himself, Kemal says, "I am sorry, we can't have ice cream tonight. It's too close to bedtime. I don't want you to have so much sugar right before you try to go to sleep. It will keep you up." His son begins to cry. "You said we would have ice cream. You lied to me."

Promises are always part of parenting and going back on promises pushes against the pillars of trust and truth that are so important to building a solid foundation between father and child. Sometimes, however, a father is required to enforce a rule based on an unforeseen route that the ship is taking—in this case, that the ship is reaching port in the evening when the crew is tired and operating on fewer resources and adding another activity could create unnecessary consequences. The boy is angry that his father broke the promise that "Dad will get me dessert [the what] from the store today [the how and when]." Because the father is also responsible for determining the rationale for the structure and its rules, in this case, the day did not work out the way the father had expected, and it was too late for ice cream. Maintaining the structure determined by the Captain archetype may be confounded by the surge of empathy for a sad and upset child. As we will discuss later, balancing the Captain archetype and the other archetypes responsible for empathy and worry can be a challenge.

Fathers' Dilemma with Discipline: Strength vs. Weakness

We hear all the time that a parent who disciplines is strong and that a parent who does not is weak. Is a father "strong" because he feels comfortable disciplining his child? Is he "weak" if he does not? Examining discipline in this way distorts and dismantles its true nature and purpose. The Captain archetype create limits as necessary boundaries for the healthy and safe development of children. In concert with other archetypes (see Chapter 6: The Protector Archetype and Chapter 8: The Jester Archetype), the Captain accepts and understands the testing of these limits is a natural way of learning that all children employ. We know that children learn by doing and will discuss this further in Chapter 5 when we describe the Educator archetype (Piaget, 2001; Piaget & Inhelder, 1969; Connery, et. al, 2010; Shephard, 1996; Dewey, 1986).

There is always some conflict inherent in helping a child learn boundaries and limits because of all the testing that occurs. Examining one's comfort with these feelings and sensations regarding conflict is important but it is not a matter "strength" and "weakness." There can be many reasons for one's reticence to set and maintain limits.

The Captain archetype enables a father to approach this aspect of his child's developmental structure—that of providing discipline—with an eye toward achieving the goal of helping his child learn. When a child tests a limit that has been set by his father (does not follow a rule or challenges a rule), that child is actively attempting to understand something about the Captain archetype's role in his or her life. The understanding of limit testing in this way is also a function of the Jester archetype and will be discussed in further in Chapter 8.

Our interviews with several fathers produced this typical list of rule compliance/adherence situations with comments about their children:

"My son does not follow directions."
"My daughter does not listen."
"My children never follow my rules."
"I have to say things a hundred times to get them to do anything."

"I think my kid has attention problems."
"I always have to threaten to take something away."
"It's in one ear and out the other."
"It's like I'm talking to a wall."
"My child does not pay attention."
"I tell him to do something and I come back a few minutes later and
      it's not started."
"My rules mean nothing to her."
"Getting her to do anything is like pulling teeth."
"I just don't have the energy to keep telling him to do it."

When used aptly within the context of discipline options, the "strong" use of the Captain archetype centers on a father's clarity of his disciplinary act's purpose and his understanding of its ultimate effect, not his ease regarding exerting power over a child. The Captain archetype does acknowledge that providing discipline and applying limits can create conflict between father and child. There is a reason that rule enforcement can be contentious. The idea that a child would simply agree to rules is an understandable wish. That said, the conflict that limit testing creates is not considered by the Captain archetype to be an undermining of the father's authority or power at all, but a child's consistent and pressing need for the archetype's firm direction and guidance. In other words, children break rules and test limits because they want and need the ongoing reassurance that their father will be there to provide all necessary support for their impulsive behaviors, intense emotions and confusing thoughts.

Errol has told his 14-year-old daughter a million times that she has a curfew and must be home for dinner by 6:00 p.m. She is consistently late and always has an excuse and reason. Errol becomes enraged, takes off his belt and threatens to hit her with it. His daughter cries and begs her father not to hit her. Errol restrains himself, but he threatens to "teach her a lesson if she is late again."

A father can threaten to hit in order to establish his authority with his physical size, toughness and power. This dynamic in a central tenant of Regoli and Hewitt's Theory of Differential Oppression. To deconstruct this, it is important to consider the complexities that specifically shape Errol's version of the Captain archetype—his relationship to his daughter, his own life experiences as a child and as a parent, and his world view (how safe and secure he feels within the world around him). These elements, discussed in detail later in the book, have a bearing on a father's reactions and responses. Errol may be experiencing

- *fear* that he does not know that his daughter is safe and secure
  when she is out,

- *rejection* of his own authority and the fabric of his family and his family rules, and/or
- *inadequacy* related to his inability to control and/or manage his daughter's impulses and decision making.

In light of all this, the concept of "weak" with regard to disciplining one's child, centers on the absence of the Captain archetype's thoughtful, pragmatic approach to discipline and how it can be overwhelmed by external factors. Errol feels scared, angry and helpless. His choice to threaten discipline by force, to under-express the Captain archetype, was a short-term, visceral act to feel more in control. In this situation, an active Captain archetype responds to the sensations of vulnerability and helplessness by reminding this father that his daughter needs his guidance and that as she develops, she may require different types of structure, containment and boundary maintenance.

Physical Punishment and the Captain Archetype

Does the Captain archetype include the utilization of corporal punishment? According to a 2012 study of parenting choices, 70 percent of Americans stated that "it is sometimes necessary to discipline a child with a good, hard spanking" (Smith, T., et al., 2013). The rationale behind corporal punishment is that a child will alter his or her future behavior and/or decision making if a parent causes pain and fear by physically striking them or causes pain in a non-contact situation (i.e., extending arms and holding books out in front of the body for a prolonged period of time). The "correction" of behavior in this manner is supported by concepts of classical conditioning and operant conditioning—the theories and practices of psychologists like Ivan Pavlov (2003), B.F. Skinner (1966) and Albert Bandura (1969)—that showed that behavior could be modified by rewards (for desired behavior) and punishments (for undesired behavior). When experiments with operant conditioning in the form of electro shocks were used with developmentally disabled children or children on the Autism Spectrum, controversy ensued as to whether this was cruel treatment of research subjects. This controversy abated as rewards for desired behavior gained greater emphasis over punishment for undesirable behavior (Silberman & Sachs, 2016).

Errol's daughter breaks her curfew again and he hits her on her bare legs with his belt. In the confusion of his daughter trying to escape him, and his own rage and fear, he hits her arm and her neck several times. She yells that she hates him runs into the bathroom and locks the door. She remains there crying for some time. When she reappears, she goes directly to her room and goes to bed. The next day Errol is interviewed by a child protective services worker after a report made by his daughter's school. Errol is confused and angry. He tells child protective services that he received far worse beatings by his own parents, and asks how else he was supposed to control his daughter.

What one culture adjudicates as child abuse, another culture sees as typical child rearing practices. This conflict will be explored further in later chapters. The historical context of corporal punishment, however, leads one to surmise that the choice of this type of rule enforcement and its ubiquitous acceptance by certain parts of society—culturally, racially, and ethnically— is based on ingrained past experiences. It is no surprise, based on our use and understanding of the collective unconscious, that fathers are able to access the power of the Captain archetype in this way. But the Captain archetype also provides critical thinking, decision-making and impulse control. The result of the potential over-use of corporal punishment was reported by Cutty and Reeves (2014) who found that

- children who are hit regularly are at higher risk for mental health problems, including anxiety disorders, mood disorders, and substance abuse disorder.
- children who are hit regularly typically have more distant relationships with their parents in the future.
- children who are hit regularly, tend to associate violence with control, power and choice.
- children who are hit regularly have, on average, lower cognitive abilities.

In addition, Regoli and Hewitt (2003) found that the various forms of oppression and related relational dynamics (such as corporal punishment) within a family can lead on the one hand to child passivity, and on the other to acts of coercion, manipulation and retaliation against other children. The Captain archetype is a repository for many options by which fathers may provide structure for a child. As we have already stated, considering any route for rule creation and enforcement asks that a father have a clear and logical rationale for it. Physical punishment is no different.

Captain as the Compass for Ethical Behavior

Along with providing structure and rules, a father is expected to endow his child with a sense of right and wrong. Ethical awareness is an aspect of character building and, as an important function of the Captain archetype's rule making, is focused on social responsibility. As a father demonstrates ethical behavior and choices to his children, concepts of right and wrong are established in the child's mind. This process begins early in a child's life. Embedded in the rationale for each and every decision, rule, and communication that a father provides is the implicit message to his child: my way is the "right" way. A child gains the perspective that a father can be "wrong" as he/she develops and gains autonomy.

The Captain archetype serves a monitoring function for both father and child as situations arise that demand ethical consideration. With a child's typical functioning including limit testing, boundary exploration, and learning through doing, the concepts of right and wrong serve as a set of overarching instructions by which to operate. The Captain archetype's ethics-function serves as a child's long-term connection to the world-at-large by creating principles that last a lifetime and tend to transcend developmental stages.

As children develop, gain autonomy and begin to think more and more abstractly, they are confronted by complex situations that may put pressure on the rules and structure that they have learned. These situations may leave them perplexed as to how to proceed while remaining within the guidelines that they have been provided. We call these moments, ethical dilemmas. For a father, the Captain archetype's role within these complicated circumstances is to assist a child in identifying the underlying issues, problem solving and weighing their options.

Jamal's 12-year-old son goes to the park with his friends after school. One of his friends arrives with a six-pack of beer. The friend states that he stole it from his dad and asks if anyone wants to try one. Jamal's son accepts, takes a few drinks of the beer and then tells his friends that he just received a text from his mom and has to go home. They make fun of him for leaving early. That night, Jamal notices that his son is quiet and asks him if anything is wrong. His son shakes his head. Jamal persists but his son cannot make eye contact. Jamal has told him that he has to stand by his friends and family "no matter what," that loyalty is important. Jamal has also told him that underage drinking is illegal and is dangerous because of the effects that alcohol can have on a child's brain.

Three days later Jamal's son tells him, "Me and my friends were drinking beer in the park the other day." His father stares at him for a moment and tries to figure out how to respond. He is furious at his son's friends and feels like he is going to explode. Jamal thinks of drinking and driving and all the information he has heard and seen about teenage drug use in his neighborhood. All of this is complicated by his own memories of underage drinking and smoking.

Within this one situation are conflicting issues related to safety, health, relationships, and autonomy. Jamal realizes his son is struggling with balancing three conflicting elements:

1. rule-breaking and his growing need to be more in control of his choices
2. following to his father's rules and by extension honoring his family connections
3. feeling included in his cohort, being loyal to his friends, and being responsible

The Captain archetype is responsible for the "deliberate" calculations necessary to manage the "intensity" of problems such as this. After reinforcing his son's good judgment regarding sharing his dilemma, Jamal can use the Captain archetype to deconstruct and prioritize the rules related to each of these categories. He does this in order to guide his child through these types of dilemmas in which rules may conflict with peer pressure and where right and wrong plays a heightened role in decision-making. Whereas creating rules and rule enforcement require clarity and consistency, managing ethics involves the capacity to consider and balance opposing or conflicting views. The power of the Captain archetype lies in its blending of intellect and command.

The Corporal

Not to be confused with or limited to corporal punishment, the Corporal version of the Captain archetype exemplifies a rigidly authoritarian use of the role of fatherhood that excludes the tempering effect of the other arche-

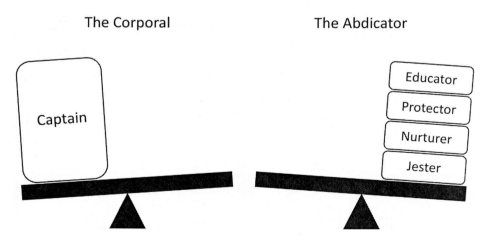

Figure 4.1—The Corporal (access to Captain archetype only) and the Abdicator (access to all archetypes except Captain archetype).

types' attributes including empathy, safety, love, affection, playfulness, or thoughtful teaching. Within a family that harbors a father as Corporal, the decisions, choices, rules, and policies are the exclusive domain of this individual. Any attempt to wrestle control away from him, intentionally or otherwise, is discouraged or stopped by the Corporal. This over-expression of the Captain archetype can include the physicality necessary to enforce his control or can utilize a more intangible menace as a way of establishing dominance. Above all, the Corporal remains in charge.

Xavier's 7-year-old daughter is running. Xavier is chasing her around the living room yelling for her to stop. He decides not to hit her when he catches her, only to squeeze her arms very tightly. She needs to be taught not to run. She is saying, "Please, please, Daddy, please, please don't." Xavier does not hear her. She escapes his grasp only to fall and scrape her knee that is now bleeding. Xavier says: "See, God punished you for not getting your shoes on and running away from me." She deserves it, he thinks. She will remember his rules after this.

The father as Corporal cannot conceive of any other way of interacting with his child but through this blunt control and power. It is the only language he speaks, and other forms of discourse often lead him to feel less in control. For the Corporal, this loss of control can be experienced as anxiety and will, invariably, increase his need for domination. A child's attempt to speak to him in a language of needs, choices or autonomy is typically met with stern rebuke.

The Abdicator

As a counterpoint to the Corporal, some fathers may see their role in the establishment and maintenance of structure within the family system as more readily accomplished by the other parent or other caregiving adult. The line "Who wears the pants the in family" is the overly simplistic (and dated) nod to a dynamic that speaks to one parental figure having decision-making authority. When a father defers this role, for reasons which we will speak to in the following section of the book, he becomes a Captain who relinquishes this authority and responsibility. We call this version of the Captain archetype, the Abdicator, and it centers on the under-expression of a father's authority, organizational role and overall leadership.

Alexander's husband, Jerry, is away on business, and he and their 5-year-old son are arguing again. His son is yelling about having to get dressed in the clothes that Alexander has pulled from the closet. As it is snowing outside,

Alexander found long underwear, a red flannel shirt and a pair of jeans. His son is refusing to put on the flannel shirt, saying that he does not like the way long-sleeves feel on his wrists and that he does not like the color red. Alexander feels extremely frustrated. For the first arguments, he tried to remain firm, but has recently begun responding to his son's protests with answers like "Fine, you'll just get sick" or "I can't argue with you anymore, make your own choices" or "It's just not worth the fight." Since this change in Alexander's stance, the school has called several times to report that his son has not been dressed appropriately. Jerry, on the other hand, errs to the other polarity of overexpression of the Captain role, expressing the Corporal to roughly force his child to wear the clothes that they pick out for their son.

The Abdicator variation of the Captain archetype is problematic in several ways.

- First, the gap in structuring a child's life is filled by someone other than Abdicator father and the child is left with the uncertainty of who is in charge.
- Second, the child runs the risk of understanding his father's retreat from the responsibilities of the Captain as a rejection or a withdrawal of love.
- Third, the child may internalize the behavior as an indication that the child has done something wrong or "bad."

That Alexander wishes none of these deliberations on his child is secondary to the reality that his son will inevitably attempt to interpret his father's archetype-based communications and choices.

5

The Educator Archetype

Only one person in a million becomes enlightened without a teacher's help.—Bodhidharma

The great benefactors of individuals and of communities are the enlightened educators: the wise-teaching, mental and moral instructors and exemplars of our times.—Dorothea Dix

Parents have become so convinced that educators know what is best for their children that they forget that they themselves are really the experts.—Marian Wright Edelman

It is the supreme art of the teacher to awaken joy in creative expression and knowledge.— Albert Einstein

I have never in my life learned anything from any man who agreed with me.—Dudley Field Malone

The mind is not a vessel to be filled but a fire to be kindled.—Plutarch

When you want to teach children to think, you begin by treating them seriously when they are little, giving them responsibilities, talking to them candidly, providing privacy and solitude for them, and making them readers and thinkers of significant thoughts from the beginning. That's if you want to teach them to think.

—Bertrand Russell

In every civilization, there have been celebrated educators. Jung calls this role within the archetypes of humanity the Wise Old Man. These individuals, embodying the diversity of humankind, are sage and knowledgeable men and women who have, through intellect and gravitas, moved their respective societies and cultures forward scientifically, spiritually, and structurally. Among them are Buddha, Confucius, Marie Curie, Albert Einstein, Benjamin Franklin, Mahatma Gandhi, Jesus, Martin Luther King, Florence Nightingale, Socrates, Pablo Neruda, Desmond Tutu, Mother Theresa, and the Dalai Lama. They are essential to the fabric of history and we cannot imagine a world in which these individuals do not exist. Can we try to imagine it? A world without the theory of relativity, real-life ideas of compassion and caretaking, electricity, methods for looking after the sick, problem solving as a skill, the acknowledgment of inequity and the need for empowerment and justice. Humanity was taught these pieces of knowledge by people. Without these wise men and women, the world would be less bright by far.

From Jung's perspective, the Wise Old Man centers on the dissemination of knowledge, wisdom and understanding in the fulfillment of the expanding self. Inherent in this archetype is powerful relationship that is forged between a giver and a receiver of matters of import. There is a security that exists within this relationship. The Wise Old Man knows what is needed and will provide it. From scientists to philosophers, from messiahs to spiritual guides, the Wise Old Man (and Woman called "Great Mother" by Jung) stand as models from whom for human beings to follow and learn (Robertson, 1995). People are drawn to them because they help us to understand ourselves and the world around us, and in this understanding, we gain a sense of mastery and efficacy and feelings of empowerment.

For our purposes, we have updated Jung's Wise Old Man archetype to the Educator. We do this for two reasons. First, Jung saw this aspect of humanity as quintessentially spiritual and psychological in nature. He believed that it is this archetype that allows for and enhances the process of moving an individual into an autonomous and complete person (individuation)—the increasingly clear sense of self that a person may achieve as he develops and matures (Edinger & Elder, 2002). We want to emphasize that this sense of self is one that makes its way into many other areas of life—sports, school, family, work, relationships, politics, social change and justice, community, etc. In addition to developing his child's sense of self, the father as Educator helps children develop into socially responsible and self-aware adults—those who participate in their societies (despite the challenges they may face) in a productive and life-affirming manner (Kenklies, 2012).

As an individual learns and integrates information in any area of experience, he or she has an increased sense of perspective, a larger base of knowledge from which to grow and thrive. The information is used to have opinions, make decisions, and think things through. And so, like Jung, we believe that this archetype focuses on building the self with fathers expanding this concept to the passing on of *all* knowledge—spiritual and otherwise, including throwing a football, advocating for oneself, writing a paper, washing hair, chewing food, telling truth to power, respecting oneself, managing anger, organizing homework, and so on.

We want to emphasize the idea that this archetype contains not just the "what" to share, but also the "how" to share and "when" to share. We see the Educator archetype containing a father's awareness of the process of providing and acquiring knowledge including diverse learning styles and different forms of pedagogy. Pedagogy is the area of educating that is focused on the method of teaching.

To this end, there are various ways that the "Wise Old Man" and the "Great Mother" pass on the information and knowledge from one person to another. Based on the environment, developmental requirements, and other specifics, the process of "educating" can take many forms. Using the Captain archetype's awareness of child development to identify the individual attributes of a specific child, the Educator archetype helps fathers select a child's optimal learning style, a suitable instructional format and the appropriate age-related timing for any given teaching moment. Recalling these from a previous chapter, they include

- a child's developmental needs
- a child's developmental milestones
- the effects of environment and changes on a child
- a child's innate qualities
- a child's stage of development
- strengths [Chapter 4, Table 4.1]

The Basics of the Educating

It behooves us to address the power differential between father and child as it affects teaching and learning. The power differential between father and child is an essential part of every archetype and develops naturally from the differences between these two individuals. By naturally, we mean as an organic interplay between (1) the individual characteristics of both father and child and (2) the way that their environment and culture has shaped them (by building them up or oppressing them) and their notions of their own power. We understand that this concept is fluid and evolving within each parent-child relationship and must be consistently reflected upon. For it is an aspect of all interactions between father and child, varying in size, intensity and importance within the breadth of a child's experience.

As the Captain, fathers attempt to utilize the power differential in an open but non-authoritarian manner, because it is inherent in a leadership role that the power differential is respected. The father as Educator, though, needs to be aware of how to modulate the power differential between parent and child. This modulation promotes the child's ultimate ability to think independently of the father. A father, who has difficulty modulating the power differential in this way, risks limiting his child to functioning off of memorization without a developed ability to analyze situations, think critically, or problem solve.

With their "power" within the relationship, comes the responsibility for fathers to identify and coordinate appropriate timing, structure, quantity and quality of the information they provide to their children—what we call the "method" of information delivery and the "form" of information. As a child grows and matures, the opportunities for teaching and learning come in every shape, size, and color. Fathers may feel more comfortable with one type of conveying information over another, but all the practices involve thought and planning based on what each child may need at any given moment. The "method" centers on the type of interaction, or relational dynamic, that the educator chooses to use. Each choice impacts the power differential in specific ways that are important to remember. Father can use any of the following interactional dynamics or types of "method" (see Table 5.1).

Table 5.1—Methods of Information Delivery (Interactional Dynamics)

- Directed Experience—the co-participation of father and child in mutual events or moments (power differential is quieted or de-emphasized for the purpose of increasing closeness)
- Discussion—the mutual verbal "back and forth" interaction between father and child. This often focuses on problem solving which is a mutual exploration and discovery of options and choices (power differential is flattened or reduced for the purpose of increasing the child's willingness to share)
- Lecture—the verbal unidirectional explanation from father to child (power differential is louder or emphasized for the purpose of having the lecturer's message take on greater importance and weight)
- Modeling—the non-verbal "showing by example" of father to child with the understanding that ultimately the recipient will copy the demonstrator (power differential is present but not overly emphasized and grants the recipient confidence that the modeler has wisdom that comes from experience)

The ways that information delivery between teacher and student, or from father to child, can be further attuned to a child's needs, is by focusing on the "form" that the information takes. This refers to the information's setting and structural components. These different teaching "forms," can be used individually or mixed together and are linked to specific types of "method," described in the following ways.

Forms of Information with Identified Method of Information

- Allegoric: Teaching through the use of storytelling (Method—Discussion)

Putting information in story form allows the knowledge, rule, or lesson to arrive in the mind of a child disguised as something more acceptable (more open to listening), digestible (more readily integrated) and accessible (more likely understood). It is also easily remembered because the information is surrounded by a richness that the characters and the plot provide. For example, the story of "The Tortoise and the Hare" in which a rabbit brags about being faster than a turtle, then winds up losing a race with the turtle because he does not pace himself well.

- Didactic: Teaching through the use of facts, figures and examples (Method—Lecture)

Sharing information in this way is meant to follow an organized method that ascends to a point of understanding. This is a passive type of learning (for the receiver of the information) that enables the child to take in one concept, one idea, and one point at a time, detail after detail. This building process allows for a solid wall of knowledge to be assembled—the wall's elements having been viewed from many different angles throughout its construction. For example, dinosaurs lived a long time ago; they do not live anymore. Some were plant eaters; others were meat eaters. Some were very big, others were small. We find evidence of them by looking at fossils. Here are some pictures of dinosaurs. In another example, children of color are targeted by law enforcement at higher rates than Caucasian children. Sadly, this means that children of color need to be specifically instructed on how to interact with law enforcement personnel for their own safety.

- Experiential: Teaching through the use of immersive activities (Method—Directed Experience, Modeling)

Incorporating information that we want a child to learn within an activity has similar benefits to allegoric teaching. The experience creates three-dimensional learning opportunities and allows for a child to use all the senses to take in the knowledge. The type of learning also allows for a child feel empowered because of the active participation in the knowledge acquisition. The child is moving toward the information as opposed to the information coming to the child. Any game, including all sports are taught experientially. Cooking a recipe together, building a model; making a puzzle; taking a trip to a historically or academically significant location (i.e., Stonewall in New York, a Southern plantation, any National Park, or any museum such as the National Museum of African American History and Culture in Washington, D.C., or the Natural History Museum in any number of cities).

- Hypnotic: Teaching through the use of repetition and suggestion (Method—Directed Experience)

Sharing information in this way allows the child to integrate the knowledge that de-emphasizes the actual give and take of the teaching process. The blurred boundary between giver and receiver, creates a possibility that the information did not necessarily come from the teacher and offers an increased sense of ownership over the knowledge. Ideas are passed from one person to another through a subtle process of repetition that feels like a consistent string of notes that one hears and unconsciously hums throughout the day. Using a word in multiple different sentences, sharing an idea in a variety of forms, gently emphasizing a specific point. For instance, "I love you. You are loved. Lovable is your middle name." Or "Black is beautiful, black is powerful, black is life."

- Metaphoric: Teaching through the use of symbolic words and ideas (Method—Discussion)

Reworking information into a form that builds on a child's existing knowledge base creating a filter through which a child can integrate concepts more easily. In addition, the idea of "putting this in terms that you already know" provides points of comparison that allow the Educator to weave together ideas. For example, "When you get frustrated, you are a pot of water boiling over; see if you can turn down the heat"; "When I leave for work and you miss me, imagine there is a rubber band connecting us; the farther we are away, the tighter it feels."

- Socratic: Teaching through the use of posing purposeful questions (Method—Discussion)

Allowing knowledge to grow and evolve by enabling information to move from posed questions through child's answers and is intended to enhance a child's ability to think critically. In this way, the child is encouraged to make associations, synthesize facts, and draw conclusions. Questions are used to pace the learning process by linking it directly to each child's unique cognitive process. The Educator watches and waits as the child thinks of answers to the questions. It is the child's sense of profound accomplishment when the connections are made that drives the learning forward. For instance, "What is it about the earth that sustains life?" "What is more important, people's differences or people's similarities, and why?"

- Symbolic: Teaching through the use of play and toys (Method—Directed Experience, Modeling)

Providing information in one's mother tongue enhances the process of learning by eliminating the need for translation. Play, and all things play, is language that belongs to children and not adults. Using toys, games, balls, or dolls, to teach simultaneously creates the safety required to learn and validates the learner. This is their world and we are willing to come to them, to speak their language. The materials of play represent ideas, relationships, words, teaching becomes a matter of "playing" the information that is to be provided. In this space, next to the world of the real, we kiss the *doll's* head at night and tell her (and therefore, the child) that everything is going to be okay. In this space, we pour and rub oil into the mitt and tie it up tight for safe keeping or we pump up the basketball and tuck it securely in the closet for the next time it is needed.

Father as Search Engine: The Process of Educating

Knowing what to teach a person, how to teach a person and when to teach a person are the three parts of the triumvirate of educating. In these ways, the Educator archetype is like a developmentally-aware search engine— it's a living Internet with the father as Google™. Following this metaphor, the Educator archetype provides fathers with an apparatus to make decisions about all types of "searches":

- answering children's difficult questions
- interpreting complex situations
- providing children with guidance
- helping children to problem solve
- building children's general fund of knowledge

After dinner, Steven's 8-year-old son approaches him, a distressed look on his face. His son asks to speak with him in private. Later that evening, Steven and his son are talking on the boy's bed.

SON: *I did something...*
STEVEN: *(Silence with eye contact, raised eyebrows in an "I'm listening" gesture)*
SON: *I looked at something bad.*
STEVEN: *What was it?*
SON: *Something on the Internet.*
STEVEN: *How come you're upset, buddy, what was it?*
SON: *(In a small voice) I Googled the word S-E-X and looked at pictures.*
STEVEN: *(Closes his eyes not knowing what to say, feeling angry, wanting to yell, remains quiet and breathes for 10 seconds, then replies in a calm voice) Well, then, you would have seen some really confusing stuff.*
SON: *(Looking uncomfortable) Yeah, it was really gross stuff. There were people and animals.... I'm sorry.*
STEVEN: *Yeah, buddy, I am sorry too. First, I want you to know that that's not really what sex is about. Second, we've not really talked about sex, how come it's on your mind?*

The Educator archetype understands the complexity of the world and helps the father enhance his child's comprehension and critical thinking. The Educator approaches the issue of sex without alarm or emotion but wants to address the issue with acceptance as a natural and normal area of discourse. The father uses the discussion method of information delivery to problem solve each "teaching" moment and breaking them down into (1) the what—

the different elements of each situation, (2) the how—the ways that would be most effective to share the information, and (3) the when—the most beneficial moment to convey the information.

In this scenario, Steven is presented with a multi-faceted challenge and opportunity. The choices he makes within this type of situation are the contribution of the Educator archetype—the deconstruction of complex situations in our own minds so that we can make them less complex for our children. Being the parent, Steven's obligation to discuss this material and his choices about pedagogy coalesces into the following thought process.

- The What

Steven has options. Because of the nature of this material and his son's initial distress, the first requirement of this father is a risk assessment—a brief evaluation of a person emotional and physical state to discern if someone is in danger. We will discuss this in greater detail in Chapter 6: The Protector Archetype. With his son appearing to be stable and in no danger, the Educator archetype helps the father break down the moment into its constituent parts. This is accomplished by examining the situation from a variety of directions, keeping an open mind, and making the determination that all aspects of the situation deserve equal consideration to start.

Steven identifies five main elements that he may address. They are (1) the nature of the Internet (anonymity of its users, on-line predators), (2) the images of sex that his child has seen (his child's feelings, ideas, fears about them), (3) his child's judgment (curiosity vs. safety), (4) his child's loss of innocence (pacing the process of maturation, managing anxiety), and (5) any age-appropriate information about sex can assuage his child's curiosity for the moment. His son has the opportunity to learn something within each of these areas without feeling any of them are out of bounds or taboo.

With the elements of focus identified, Steven prioritizes which one or ones require his wisdom. He picks and chooses based on what he believes his child needs at the moment and what his child is able to handle and process. This selection process requires the further assessment of the "how" and the "when."

- The How

At 8 years old, Steven's son is learning about many topics in school—math, history, English and science. He is an average student and does not particularly like to study. He likes class discussions and debates but does not like to read. Topics that personally fascinate him, he will connect to and want to learn more about; topics that do not, he tends to avoid or only engage with superficially. His son can be described as a child who likes to feel in charge and so, not knowing about a topic can cause him to feel discomfort.

With this in mind, Steven can use the Educator archetype's awareness of forms of pedagogy to determine that because his child already feels "small," a loss of control and alone, he may need Steven's help to feel more solid before being able to "hear" and integrate any attempts at learning about the more sensitive elements of this situation (the meaning of the pictures, the predators, pornography). In terms of the method, lecturing him may feel too isolating and punitive. Sharing a personal story may not help his son understand the gravity of the situation. A discussion may allow for his son to share some of his own thoughts and worries. As far as form is concerned, Socratic teaching with questions allows his son to pace the discussion, while using metaphors decreases the power of the already "intense" material.

- The When

Steven's son has not yet reached puberty. Developmentally, he has reached the stage in which he is curious and using this curiosity to push the boundaries of his knowledge. The Educator archetype must help balance the threads of this child's maturation that may be working at cross purposes, or at least operating unawares of one another. To that end, Steven may conclude the priorities of this moment are not about sex and pornography for his pre-pubescent son, but more likely about age-appropriate curiosity about nudity and his changing body. Steven may also surmise that this is also about social pressures and pushing boundaries, which would fit his child's developmental stage. Believing this, Steven may push off a lecture about pornography and focus on discussing his son's current needs.

SON: *I am really sorry, Dad.*

STEVEN: *It's fine for you to be curious. I don't imagine you meant to see something that upset you so much.*

SON: *No.*

STEVEN: *Do you want to tell me what exactly upset you?*

SON: *The pictures.*

STEVEN: *What about the pictures?*

SON: *Just gross, I can't explain it.*

STEVEN: *All right. So, here's the thing ... the Internet does not know who you are. It's like sending it a letter that you typed out through the mail—the post office workers can't tell who you are by the typing or the envelope. When you log on and type in a word like S-E-X, the Internet thinks, here is an adult asking for an adult topic. And so, it gives that person everything that it can find under that topic ... even the gross stuff. Does that make sense?*

SON: *Yes.*

STEVEN: *When you put that letter in a mailbox, do you think the people at the post office have any idea that it is you?*

SON: *No, not unless they see me do it.*

STEVEN: *Exactly and like the post office, the Internet cannot see you. It has no idea that you're an 8-year-old kid. It doesn't know if you are a boy or a girl or anything about you. So it will give you everything and because it will give you everything, you have to be careful. I could put security on the computer, but eventually you will find your way around it, because you are curious. So I am going to trust you and I want you to take care of yourself.*

SON: *Okay.*

STEVEN: *Does that make sense?*

SON: *Yes.*

STEVEN: *One other thing. About what you saw in the pictures, I would like to talk to you about it a bit ... if that's okay. I know about sex and you can ask me about anything you want.*

SON: *I don't want to talk about that stuff.*

> STEVEN: *There is other stuff that is not so gross ... stuff about how moms and dads*
> *have a child.*
> SON: *Okay, yeah, I am okay with that.*
> STEVEN: *Also, your friends may also be talking about stuff like this, but I want you*
> *to remember that each kid handles things differently. Not better, not worse, just*
> *different. Learning new things is like going from one place to another. Some kids*
> *run fast, some run slow, and some just like to walk. They are all perfectly fine*
> *ways of getting from one place to another.*

In the end, Steven accomplishes this teaching moment by having a discussion with his son about viewing sexual material on the Internet. He explains his points by using a metaphor and questions and answers to explain about the anonymity of individuals using the Internet and to help his child feel more secure with his burgeoning curiosity, and with setting his own pace.

To Share or Not to Share: Containing the Know-It-All Father

Fathers typically feel a sense of competence and confidence when they share information with their children. It is one of the main reasons that fathers educate—it makes them feel helpful. These teaching opportunities that fathers encounter on a daily basis are ubiquitous. In every facet of life, there exists information that a father can explain to his child. A function of the Educator archetype is to find and identify the opportune moments to teach. The right time. The appropriate instant.

Invariably, fathers know more than their children (technology aside, maybe) based on their years of experience. This fact creates an interesting dilemma. It is an opportunity (and a challenge) to the power differential. Fathers must choose to share or not share what they know with a child. When do fathers not share even though they can? When do fathers modulate the power differential (flattening it, quieting it, or accentuating it) between educator and student?

To answer this, it is important to be aware that a father who is always teaching, who always feels compelled to share what he knows, is a less effective educator. It is, at times an over-emphasis of the power differential. Educating, as is the case for each of the other parenting roles, is relational. There must be a give and take. Too much sharing can lead to a child's sense of interacting with an all-knowing father creating a distance between parent and child rather than a connection. While there may be some comfort in this knowledge for a time, a child's growing sense of autonomy and a burgeoning identity may find this to be oppressive and constraining.

A counter point to the strong pull to share all that we know with our children, is the fact we will be offered many, many instances to provide wisdom during the life of our children—too many to count. If fathers choose to skip some, there will be many more right around the corner. In fact, children revisit each of these teaching moments over and over again throughout their development.

Pedro watches his 6-year-old son set up the board for the chess match. His son has been taking chess classes after school for several months and he has asked his father to play a game. Pedro loves chess and has been waiting for the opportunity to play his son. He has asked him several times over the past few months, but his son has always said no. When his son mentioned playing this morning, Pedro is very excited. His grandfather taught him the game and he wants to teach his son.

> SON: *I am going to be white. You be black.*
> PEDRO: *Okay. What's the difference?*
> SON: *White goes first. This is the way all the pieces go. See, Pawns here.*
> PEDRO: *I see. Thank you for showing me (he places his own pawns).*
> SON: *(Places each one in turn) This is the King. This is the Queen. These are the other pieces—the Rook, the Bishop, and the Horse.*
> PEDRO: *(Picking up the knight) This is called the horse?*
> SON: *Yes.*

Pedro knows that the "horse" is, in fact, called a Knight. The Educator archetype understands that Pedro can focus on any number of elements at this moment: (1) the name of the pieces, (2) where the pieces go on the board, and (3) how the pieces move. With his son just becoming comfortable playing with him, Pedro has decided to let his son lead and maintain a sense of control. He is already choosing to pretend that he does not know the basics of chess in order to give his child the space to share his own knowledge. Now, he chooses to "teach" his son through further questions, a basic form of the Socratic method. In its more complex form, this method utilizes questions to draw out a person's understanding and ideas by requiring them to answer queries designed to stimulate critical thinking.

> PEDRO: *Got it. So now that you have taught me where the pieces go, can you teach me how they all move.*
> SON: *Of course.*
> PEDRO: *How does the Horse move? Like this? (Pedro makes the Knight jump up and down)*
> SON: *(Laughing) No Papa! (Taking the pieces and moving it) The Horse moves two forward and one side ways.*
> PEDRO: *Ohhh. I see now.*

Pedro can enjoy that his son calls the Knight a "Horse." It is funny and sweet. It is a moment in time, a good memory, and a signal of the innocence of childhood, when a person can get things wrong and it does not matter, there will be no consequence. The Educator archetype reminds fathers that gaining wisdom and knowledge is supposed to take time.

Fathering in the Age of the Internet and Information

Children, in a rapidly changing technology-driven world will ultimately know how to do things the father cannot do. This at times, may cause a reversal of roles in which the child is teaching the father. The Educator archetype reinforces for fathers the understanding that this reversal in roles is not a reversal of the power differential, but an alteration. The father continues in his role as educator by participating in directed experiences and focusing on modeling process instead of content. This includes teaching the various ways people learn: visually (seeing); aurally (hearing); or kinetically (doing). The power differential is de-emphasized, and the child is encouraged to fill the gap and share what he or she knows.

Jeffrey is told by his boss that he needs to be able to retrieve his e-mails using the new state-of-the-art iPhone that they have given him. Baffled by the new technology, he asks his 11-year-old daughter to help him. She sets up the iPhone for him within minutes. Jeffrey asks her to go back to the beginning and then move through her installation again, step-by-step, to instruct him, while he makes the correct connections to retrieve his e-mails. It takes Jeffrey a few tries, but he eventually is able to add his personal e-mail address as well. He thanks his daughter and points out that he always learns best by doing a task rather than watching someone complete a task. His daughter tells him she learns best that way too.

> DAUGHTER: *Dad this is so easy. I can't believe you can't do this.*
> JEFFREY: *I know. I'm old. These new machines are complicated.*
> DAUGHTER: *No, they're not. You just have to try and do it.*
> JEFFREY: *First, you are smart and clever. Don't even try to deny that it takes intelligence to use one of these things. I am just not going to believe you if you deny it.*
> DAUGHTER: *Okay. Fine, but you can do it.*
> JEFFREY: *I will try. But I learn by doing not by watching, so let's go back to the beginning and explain it to me step by step. Deal?*
> DAUGHTER: *Yes. Do you want me to write it down for you?*
> JEFFREY: *No, I can do that myself ... its part of how I remember things.*

Jeffrey is not diminished by asking for and accepting his daughter's help. The Educator is, after all, a life-long learner about a world that continues to change, that becomes smaller due to connectivity and globalization and that expands due to new discoveries, innovations and inventions.

The Skill of "I Don't Know"

It is reasonable and likely that fathers do not know all of the answers that their child may "ask." They may not have the experiences or the facts to be the font of all the world's wisdom. The process of finding out, by researching or asking for help from others, is part of imparting wisdom as well.

"I don't know" may seem as if it were an inadequate response to a child's question. But what if it is followed with a strategy of how to find out the answer that includes the child. Father as Educator knows that imparting knowledge is a mere fraction of his function and that encouraging the child to share their knowledge or to develop and discover new knowledge on their own is just as important.

Tarique's 12-year-old son shares that he is learning the parts of the brain in school. He shows Tarique the various structures in his high school textbook. Tarique recalls how the two of them played with his son's anatomy model when he was ten years old. Tarique indicates he is impressed and wonders out loud if his son will want to be a doctor someday. The son says he wants to be a neurosurgeon in order to help people with brain tumors or aneurysms. Tarique asks his son to explain aneurysms to him and is blown away when his son launches into a detailed lesson.

> SON: *This is what we are working on in school.*
> TARIQUE: *The brain?! Isn't that early for you to be studying something so complex?*
> SON: *No, Dad, it's totally what everyone is doing.*
> TARIQUE: *(Shaking his head) I just remember when you were around 10 and you got that invisible man anatomy model. We worked on that for days. You were so focused. It's amazing that you stayed so focused for all this time. I'm really impressed. (fist bump)*
> SON: *I just really like it.*
> TARIQUE: *I can tell. Is this what you are interested in for the future.*
> SON: *Yeah ... it's what I want to do. I want to be a neurosurgeon. I want to help people with brain tumors and other problems, like aneurysms.*
> TARIQUE: *(Smiling) Aneurysms? I have heard of them, but I'm not exactly sure what they are. Can you explain them to me?*

The Apprentice Gains Independence

Apprenticeship is an institutionalized way of learning by seeing and doing. In many ways, the Educator archetype aids a father in teaching the child how to become self-aware, curious, competent, and confident. The mixture of these creates a sense of mastery over one's place in the world and is espoused by many psychological theorists of our time including Jung, Maslow,

Erik Erikson, Carl Rogers, and others. This concept of mastery centers on increasing self-acceptance, autonomy, purpose, and control.

In concert with the other archetypes, the Educator archetype, utilizing this concept of mastery, sets a goal for each father. That goal centers on a father working to help his child acquire sufficient knowledge to move beyond the father's experience, in order to obtain a sense of self by which a child may stand independently. In the original Star Wars movie, *A New Hope*, Darth Vader antagonistically confronts his old teacher, Obi-Wan Kenobi, and says, "When you left I was but the learner. Now I am the master." What went wrong in this teaching relationship that instead of colleagues these two became adversaries?

The idea of moving beyond may seem frightening to fathers and children alike if it conjures notions of a loss of control, of loneliness and of isolation. Unfortunately, common, this type of thinking is a breakdown in the understanding of independence, and if left unchecked corrupts the process of acquiring knowledge and experience. This occurs when being independent is confused with being alone. It is the crux of the Vader-Kenobi conflict.

Ultimately, the teacher is responsible for the contentious dynamic in this relationship. For his own reasons (fear for the future of the human race, concern over the survival of the Jedi, anxiety about being usurped or replaced), Obi-Wan Kenobi is unable to modulate the power differential between teacher and student in a way that honors his apprentices' growing need for autonomy and independence. The master's fear and his sense of a loss of control within the teacher-student relationship, forces his apprentice to reach the conclusion that the only way to continue to learn is to disconnect from his teacher and become adversaries.

Children grow into adults who know things their fathers do not. Through experiences, innovation or invention, children gain knowledge and grow. It is the way of the human race. This follows the understanding that a father's wish is that his children will grow into adults who surpass him, have better lives and achieve more. This is not only in terms of economic and educational attainment but also in ability and skill. The successful father as Educator is a powerful engine for a better future for his own children and for all of human-kind.

The Squasher

A subset of the know-it-all father is the nitpicking, hyper-critical father who, for the purposes of delineating him from father as Educator, we will call the Squasher. Intentional or not, this father teaches through a process of negative learning. The child learns within an uncomfortable and, at times, humiliating atmosphere awash with shaming. The "Here, let me just do it"

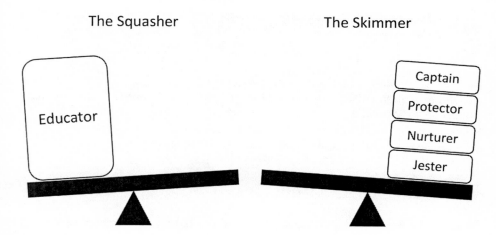

Figure 5.1—The Squasher (access to Educator archetype only) and the Skimmer (access to all archetypes except Educator archetype).

approach is a co-opting of modeling with little or no expectation that the child will ever be able to accomplish the task independently.

As we stated earlier in the chapter, the Educator archetype requires cross referencing with the Captain archetype to make pedagogical choices for a child. The Educator archetype also needs the empathy for his child afforded by the Protector archetype (see Chapter 6). The Squasher is a result of possible vulnerability, low self-esteem, or frustration and is unable to access either of these archetypes in these teaching moments. By exhibiting an overwhelming need to show his child what he knows, this father uses his knowledge and the power differential to diminish the child, creating among many other issues, self-doubt and a sense of inferiority. We will examine the etiology of this type of educator later in the book.

Hubert hopes his 14-year-old daughter can improve her grades in antici-pation of her being accepted at a top college. He checks her homework and pays particular attention to research papers and reports, as he is concerned about her ability to effectively write her college essay.

> HUBERT: *This report you wrote on penguins needs some work. Let me see what I can do with it.*
> DAUGHTER: *(Annoyed) Dad! It's fine! My teacher likes the way I write.*
> Hubert doesn't respond and busies himself correcting her paper using his favorite red pen. Hubert believes that the red will get his daughter's attention.
> HUBERT: *Here is your paper; I think it is much better. Now, fix it before dinner so I can check it again.*
> DAUGHTER: *(Sighs) I will do it after dinner.*

HUBERT: *No, young lady, you will do it now!*
DAUGHTER: *(Eyes tearing)*
HUBERT: *You know, sweetie, that I am only doing this to help you.*
DAUGHTER: *Yeah, I know.*

The potentially inspiring process of teaching and learning for Hubert and his daughter is non-existent. Hubert's conscious intentions—to help his daughter write better—are lost by his lack of empathy and the resulting disconnected relationship. He edits alone; his daughter corrects alone. The over-emphasizing of the power differential creates isolation.

The Skimmer

The Skimmer is an under expression of the Educator archetype and it is characterized by a father who does not participate in educating his child about life lessons or academics. The reasons for this are varied and can include one or more of the father's following concerns:

- does not see the usefulness or appropriateness of his participation is his child's education,
- struggles with the idea that he may be too zealous in his involvement in his child's school work,
- worries that he does not know enough to help his child learn, and/or
- has difficulty finding the time to engage with his child for moments of teach, sharing information or ideas

The Skimmer stands diametrically opposed to the Squasher in every way but one—the two archetypal variants are accompanied by a great deal of anxiety about a father's fluid role in his child's learning process.

Damon looks at his 11-year-old daughter's homework. She asks him to go over it with her and to explain how she is supposed to proceed. He says, as he always does, "No." She asks him why and he responds by saying, "Look, if I tell you how to do it, you will never learn." Damon hated doing homework as a kid; he never liked school. He believes that it is the teacher's role to teach his kids, that his role is to make sure they do the work assigned. His daughter tells him that she doesn't understand the assignment and Damon gets angry thinking about the teacher not doing her job well. "Fine, let me look at it," he barks. After a few minutes of examining the assignment, he hands it back to her. "This looks simple enough, you just have to concentrate."

The support missing from the Skimmer is the point of main concern. Learning can be anxiety producing in children—even if they enjoy the experience. Not knowing something is a one-down position meaning that one feels at a disadvantage. In these moments, the process of learning is challenging. All children are born into and confronted by a world in which they lack experience, size, and power. As the Educator archetype part of the father functions as the guide on the journey of growth for the child, the absence of this guide, the Educator as Skimmer, puts a child at a profound disadvantage. The learning experience—conducted by a disparate and varied group of teachers, coaches, friends, television, and the Internet—requires an organizing set of pathways to receive information and an understanding of oneself in order to incorporate all the information that a child receives. Damon, and the trust his daughter has in him, is the obvious choice for the person that can provide these paths. He can be the person who explains to teachers, coaches and other professionals, who his daughter is as a learner. Damon, as the Skimmer, leaves to his ill-equipped and alone daughter the tasks of accepting, processing and integrating information from her class, and more importantly, from the world.

6

The Protector Archetype

I cannot think of any need in childhood as strong as the need for a father's protection.—Sigmund Freud

Everything that irritates us about the other can lead us to an understanding of ourselves.—Carl Jung

Our lives begin to end the day we become silent about things that matter.—Martin Luther King, Jr.

We think we listen, but very rarely do we listen with real understanding, true empathy. Yet, listening, of this very special kind, is one of the most potent forces for change that I know.—Carl Rogers

We all need somewhere where we feel safe.—Emma Thompson

He will win who knows when to fight and when not to fight.—Sun Tzu

Leadership is about empathy.—Oprah Winfrey

He adopted a role called being a father, so that his child would have something mythical and infinitely important: a protector.—Tom Wolf

In modern times, whenever an individual does something brave or courageous in the public eye the word heroic is often used. "Hero teen saves 5-year-old by chasing kidnapper on their bike"—*The Daily News*, July 15, 2013. "Everyday Hero: Volunteer has comforted sick children for 40 years"—*Global News*, June 24, 2016. "Muhammad Ali: America's First Muslim Hero"—*The Daily Beast*, June 6, 2016. In 1980, Steven Stayner, after being held captive by a pedophile for almost 8 years, fled. During his escape, he chose to bring with him his captor's most recent victim, 5-year-old Timothy White. A statue commemorating Stayner's heroic act was erected in his hometown of Merced, California.

Heroes have existed throughout history crossing cultures and geography. In their actions, we see ourselves or the people we wish to be. Whether intentional or not, whether he or she consciously knows the possibility of heroism prior to proceeding, history is rife with examples that the actions of the "hero" make a profound connection between people. This connection is often so powerful that it transcends time with our heroes being remembered for decades, if not, centuries. Over time, these individuals have helped countless numbers feel less alone and isolated, because people feel less vulnerable knowing that there is goodness in the world and that there are protectors who "conquer dragons" ("The Conjunction," CW 14, par. 756).

Heroes provide a sense for all humanity that as individuals we are not alone, that people look out for one another, that there is a reason to push through difficult times. The word strikes a specific cord in our consciousness. It speaks to qualities in people that feel more substantial. These attributes often feel inaccessible to many of us which is why we may find the act of employing them daring. Courage, selflessness, inspiration conjure up a sense of magnitude and so we name these people heroes. Granted, everyday life experiences for one person may seem extraordinary to others. Individuals struggling with mental health or physical difficulties, or fighting through poverty, persecution, discrimination or oppression of any kind, display courage and provide inspiration on a daily basis, by not giving up. Heroism, then, is a matter of context and perspective and does not necessarily need to be moments found worthy of news coverage.

Jung believed that the Hero archetype is the access corridor to a person's consciousness and is represented through a conquering of conscious thought over unconscious thought, of choice over instinct, of awareness over ignorance. He believed that this is a demanding process and to accomplish it is a "triumph" (Davies et al., 1982). He felt individuals require heroic traits (their own and trusted others) to overcome the vulnerability they feel because of their inexperience, anxiety, fears, and basic impulses. And as a lasting byproduct of prevailing over these challenges, Jung held that the Hero archetype contains the people's ability to emanate safety and security to the more vulnerable, stemming from the empowering nature of fighting the battle.

Supporting the vulnerable as a central component of the Hero archetype intersects with another of Jung's archetypes, the Wounded Healer. The Wounded Healer offers an additional type of security—the sense of safety and belonging that one experiences when feeling understood. Similar to Jesus' reciprocating tradition of washing the feet of his apostles—a way of conveying his acceptance of and appreciation for them and their journey—the Wounded Healer archetype conveys the sense that each of us can truly know the other if we choose, that we have been down similar paths as human beings. In this knowledge, the archetype offers empathy—"the ability to understand and share another person's experiences and emotions" (Merriam-Webster, 2018). When Dr. Martin Luther King stated, "I have a dream," his "dream" is a shared one that, although using the pronoun "I," conveys a deep understanding of the black community and its history and provides a sense of security within those empathic words (King, 1963).

For our purposes, these two Jungian archetypes, the Hero and the Wounded Healer, are melded into one powerful fatherhood archetype. This archetype emphasizes different forms of human connection as the way of maintaining safety and security throughout the life of a child. We call this archetype, the Protector. Fathers use this archetype to strike a balance between a child's vulnerability and a child's development. This complex and often vexing position between potential danger and inevitable progress is that challenge of all fathers. The Protector archetype is the part of the father that generates the worry and concern for his children and responds to those feelings by helping the father identify and comprehend the true nature of his child's experiences. This understanding creates a closeness between father and child and functions as an empathic safety net for the child.

Through each developmental stage, children mature through risk taking and exploration by trying out new behaviors, activities and experiences. Fathers utilize the Protector archetype to craft necessary responses to issues of safety and vulnerability endemic to the maturation process of a child. Risk-taking and exploration can, at times, result in increased danger. Whether this danger exists (1) passively by a child simply exiting one's home in a dangerous neighborhood or by walking around in an area in which discriminatory practices are reinforced by law enforcement, or (2) actively by a child pushing the limits of what is safe by using elicit substances or breaking laws and/or rules, the father as Protector needs to titrate his response so that the child can mature safely without being stifled. These developmental/maturational activities range from

- pursuing separation and independence (both physically and emotionally) from caregivers (Mahler, Pine & Bergman, 1975; Bowlby,1982; Ainsworth Blehar, Waters & Wall, 2014) to
- testing limits and boundaries of one's environments and rules (Mahler, Pine & Bergman, 1975; Winnicott 1963) to
- actively seeking and acquiring new knowledge (Piaget, 2001).

Every child engages in these pursuits, gaining skills and struggling, as they participate in a wide variety of experiences from the positive to the negative. The father as Protector highlights the importance of staying emotionally connected to a child during these explorations via the empathic safety net and through active safeguarding and/or shaping of safety measures.

In addition to the child's survival, enabling the child's ability to thrive is equally important and requires the maintenance of a secure environment (Bowlby, 1969; Winnicott, 1963, Ainsworth, Blehar, Waters & Wall, 2014). Examining the details of each exploration and weighing potential challenges and risks against the possibilities of growth and maturation is the work that the father as Protector. Safety maintenance, in this sense, is influenced by the belief that while maturing, children take risks, and, at times, place themselves in jeopardy in various ways. Fathers as Protector manage this worrying reality by maintaining an overarching vigilance—looking down the road, and off on the side streets, for problems and opportunities. This safety is centered on three major areas.

- Emotional Safety—the attendance to variable thoughts and feeling states and what a child is experiencing as he/she moves through different relationships and situations. Also, the observation of a child's mind and body connection and how a child is managing the navigation of his/her developmental milestones.
- Physical Safety—the focus on the child's body integrity as the child grows and matures and how a child uses his/her body in the world.
- Existential Safety—the focusing on the preservation of the child's sense of self and place in the world and the impact of these realities on the father (May, 1967; Frankel, 1963).

Leonard's 10-year-old daughter has indicated that she may want to go to sleep-away camp. Leonard is the grandson of Holocaust survivors. His daughter's request to go to camp sets off all kinds of concerns and worries in Leonard's mind about separation and safety.

Is she going to be safe? (physical)
Is she going to be happy? (emotional)
Is this too soon to send her away? (existential)
Will she make friends? (emotional)
Will she be scared and withdraw from everyone? (emotional/existential)
Without me, who will be there for her if she is having a hard time?
    (emotional)
What will happen to her if I make the wrong decision? (existential)

Leonard feels overwhelmed by all the different thoughts and feelings he is having and how to help his daughter with this decision. Leonard's family back-ground is a factor that makes him wary of the world outside of his community. Leonard says, "No," and tells his daughter that he is not sure if she is ready for something like that. He tells her that they will think about it again next year. His daughter starts to cry.

The Protector archetype can help Leonard organize his ideas in these obviously fraught areas regarding his daughter's maturation. He can talk to her about her own safety measures, about the developmental importance of taking thoughtful and planned out risks, and about ways to stay "in touch" if she feels sad, lonely, or anxious. Leonard, the Protector, can use his own current life experiences of feeling safely separated from his own parents as a reality check to the powerful fears he feels stemming from his family's unfortunate history. Providing empathy helps his daughter feel support and connection and moves the discourse forward. It helps both father and daughter with

- identifying their individual concerns and come together on their mutual ones;
- problem solving for solutions and strategies that are based on the reality of the current situation; and
- reinforcing his daughter's sense of self (her courage and determination) and the father's role as protector.

All of these steps increase his daughter's safety and security and can help her move forward with a sense of protection.

A few days later, Leonard approaches his daughter to revisit the issue of sleep-away camp. "I have been thinking of our discussion about sleep-away camp and I would like the chance to reconsider. I get spooked by you wanting to be away from the family. It is complicated, but it has something to do with my grandparents' experiences during World War II. So, I tell you what ... let's look for a camp where we are allowed to stay in touch, so I know that you are doing okay. Even though you are growing up, I will always be interested in knowing you are okay and being there just in case you need me." His daughter cried again but this time hugged her father with intensity and thanked him. The message to his daughter is clear: I am here to protect you and be there for you, but not to hold you back.

The Danger Brain

At this point, we think it is important to understand the nature of how the brain typically interprets danger. The Protector archetype provides—from vast reservoirs of experience—an ability to identify danger and respond to it. We would like to reinforce this base of knowledge by briefly describing the current understanding of the mechanisms at work when the brain perceives a threat to the survival (a danger) of our loved ones. Based on a highly *simplified* version of the work of Bessel Van der Kolk (2014) and other researchers, there are three main parts of the brain that are involved in the analysis of and reaction to danger. They are

- the brainstem (the maintenance and action part of the brain);
- the limbic brain (the emotional, visceral, unconscious part of the brain); and
- the prefrontal cortex (the more rational, conscious, aware part of the brain).

These segments have other elements within them that are all individually important to the process, but for our purpose of examining the dual roles of the father as Protector, we will focus on these three brain structures.

When a message (a sensation, feeling, information) that a danger exists reaches the brain, it is sent to two places simultaneously, the limbic brain and the prefrontal cortex. Research has shown that the message travels faster to the limbic than the prefrontal cortex. Thus, a person's unconscious brain processes the danger first, and quickly passes the message on to the brainstem. The brainstem forces the body into chemical and physical "danger response-action" with its hormone and nervous system. The prefrontal lobes—the thinking part of the brain—receive the information after the limbic brain (albeit soon after). In this way, however, we are often physically reacting to danger before we are fully conscious of its nature (Van der Kolk, 2014) (see Figure 6.1). From this perspective, Leonard's initial "No" response to his daughter about going to camp is about action more than considered thought. He is responding the danger, viscerally, with action before truly even thinking about it.

As an important corollary, current research indicates that when children play violent video games or watch violent movies on a regular basis, this process of receiving and responding to danger may become slowed or dulled, as if absorbing all the violent material anesthetizes the brain to actual danger (Bergland, 2016). This process of numbing is also true for children of color living in poverty who may grow up communities in which they cannot escape the all-to-real violence that occurs daily in their neighborhoods (Van Der Kolk, 2014). Because these mechanisms are so important to the safety of a child, father as Protector endeavors to maintain or re-establish the healthy connections when they are compromised.

Fight or Flight: Protector Archetype's Heroism

When confronted with threat, people have a "danger response-action" also called the flight or fight response (Cannon, 1932). This stress response provides one of two options for those experiencing it: (1) avoid in order to

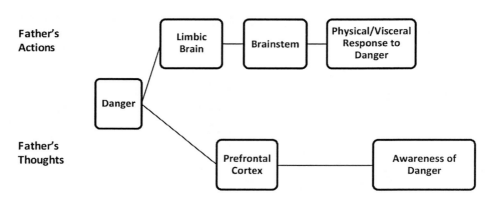

Figure 6.1—Danger information processed by the brain over time.

protect the vulnerable or (2) confront as a means of defending the vulnerable. Women may, in fact, have more choices, but for our purposes, we will focus on a father's most common responses to threat (Taylor, et al., 2000). This response is closely related to the part of the Protector archetype associated with heroism and the concrete tasks of keeping one's child safe from harm.

We believe that for fathers, this fight or flight response expands. When their child is in danger, the instinctual, unconscious thought of their own self-preservation is subjugated. In its place is the instinctual, unconscious thought of protecting their offspring. Our distinction here may be immaterial to fathers, in that protecting one's child is akin to existentially protecting oneself, however, it is not to their children. Children notice when their fathers step in to protect them and notice when they do not. Saving one's child no matter what—if it means running or hiding (flight) or doing battle directly with a threat (fight)—is the true essence of heroism to that child.

Pablo walks his 7-year-old son to school. Pablo notices that his son is very restless, jumping up and down and circling all around him as they walk. Pablo thinks about how all the teachers tell him that his son is hyperactive and that he might need medication. He worries about it, but he thinks his boy just has a lot of energy like he did—he remembers that he always used to get in trouble. His son is excited because it is Friday and his abuela is coming from the Dominican Republic for the weekend. As they approach the main street between school and home, up ahead, across the street, his son sees his best friend. He calls to his friend, but his friend does not hear. Pablo's son suddenly starts running, moving off the curb into the street. Pablo yells, "Stop!" A driver of a car sees his son and honks the horn and stops short. Pablo's son freezes in fear, four steps out into the street. Pablo reaches him and pulls him back roughly by lifting him off the ground and on to the side walk. He yells at his son and shakes him, telling him that he could have been hit by a car and killed. His son begins to cry, saying, "I am sorry" over and over again.

In this scenario, Pablo's son places himself in danger unexpectedly. Pablo and his son move into the flight or fight response. (1) Pablo's adrenaline increases, and he rushes toward the street "heroically" sweeping his son to safety (fight the danger). (2) Then, he yells at and shakes his son (fight the danger). Pablo's son has his own fight/flight response. (1) He reacts as if his father is angry with him by apologizing (flight from danger). (2) In addition, he cries as a visceral response/release to his fear of being hit by a car and his fear of his father's reaction (flight from danger).

Pablo's son's vulnerability provokes action on both the physical/visceral and the cognitive levels that we discussed earlier. His actions to rescue his son from danger occur without conscious thought. His feelings of anger about the danger, more thoughtful in nature, manifest afterward. Both are forms of protecting his son from danger. As the Hero, the Protector archetypes binds Pablo to both of these responses.

As there is no way to create an environment in which "danger" does not exist, so there is no way to avoid this fight or flight process. It, therefore, requires understanding and management by fathers via the Protector archetype. Is the father's tendency to fight or flee? Is the child's tendency to fight or flee? Does flight to the father imply weakness or good judgment? Does fight to the father indicate strength or impulsivity. Meaning is assigned—by father and by child, individually and jointly—to all such events that take place and is used as templates for future situations (see Table 6.1).

Table 6.1—A Child's Fight or Flight Decisions

Type of Danger	Fight	Flight
Physical	Defending a person who is being bullied	Telling an adult that others are bullying
Physical	Refusing to ride in a car with a driver who is intoxicated	Deciding not to have friends who drink or do drugs
Physical	Telling a friend that smoking is dangerous	Avoiding friends that smoke
Emotional	Arguing with someone over a point of disagreement	Conceding (externally) a point of disagreement to someone
Emotional	Struggling through nerves to ask someone to be a boyfriend or girlfriend	Pretending not to like someone
Emotional	Calling out an authority figure who uses a racial slur	Saying nothing about the discriminatory behavior

Type of Danger	Fight	Flight
Existential	Staying at sleep-away camp (when homesick)	Leaving sleep-away camp (when homesick)
Existential	Quarrelling with a parent	Running away from home
Existential	Requesting a safety plan in case of an emergency	Denying the need to discuss the possibility of emergencies

Before and After the Fall: Protector Archetype's Empathy

Let us refer back to the Pablo scenario. The discourse about street safety is one Pablo has had with his son countless numbers of times before the incident, yet developmentally children often require repetition in order to integrate all knowledge including safety practices. Pablo, as "hero," saves his son, but that is only half of what the Protector archetype may contribute. The other half of the father as Protector is the emotionally-oriented act of experiencing empathy for his terrified child and embracing and comforting him (the Wounded Healer). In a situation like Pablo's this occurs after the actual danger has passed. What would an extension of the empathic safety net look like if Pablo did this with his son? Pablo could be hugging his son close to him while still expelling his adrenaline by yelling. His son would clearly then realize his father was not angry with him but upset (distressed). *"Papa is not angry, but I am very scared that you could have been hurt."*

Recall that empathy is the ability to, in a way, feel and know what another person is experiencing. In practice, this ability centers on being able to truly imagine oneself in the body and mind of another person. What does it feel like to be him or her at this moment? In its pristine state, it requires the de-emphasizing of one's own feelings and thoughts in to order to make room for the other person's. Separating one's own thoughts and feelings requires self-awareness. For a father, this means trying to be in touch with his own foibles, fears, and worries from his earlier life including childhood. This is a challenging process, as it acknowledges that fathers were once (and maybe still are) vulnerable, but it is an important piece of staying connected to our children. Did our parents argue and get violent in front of us? Were we afraid of the dark? Did we not want to be alone? Was our father missing from our lives? Did we lose a family member unexpectedly? Were we harassed by the police? Did we cry on the first day of school? Did we hate to try new food? We will take a deeper dive into this aspect of fathering in the next section of the book on fatherhood characteristics.

Children begin to form their own empathic ability in infancy as their fathers, mothers and other caregivers show empathy toward them in various situations (Iacoboni, 2008). During this time in a child's life, fathers' attempts at mirroring—matching a baby's facial expression—and at responsive care-taking are both forms of parental empathy. Both are the work of Wounded Healer half of the Protector. Hearing a baby cry and trying to imagine how she feels and what she needs. Is she hungry? Is she tired or fatigued? Is she gassy and in need of relief? Does she need a diaper change?

These thoughts and questions are all early attempts at fatherly empathy. For infants, they are also forms of fatherhood safety measures. If any of these actions—feeding, sleeping, burping, cleaning—are not accomplished with a degree of competence and purpose, a dependent and vulnerable infant will be in some level of danger. As a child grows and develops, crying makes way for increasingly nuanced indicators of what he or she is thinking and needing at any given moment, including, the use of words, facial expressions, and behaviors. These will become the fabric for the empathy safety net that the Protector archetype embodies within fathers.

In short, the empathy proffered by the father as Protector has the following purposes:

1. To help a father become more in touch with his own childhood experiences of risk and risk-taking
2. To help a father become thoughtfully activated by his awareness of environmental traumas within his community, his society and his world
3. To shape a father's decision-making prior to and during his child's experiences of risk and risk-taking
4. To influence a father's verbal and non-verbal input before and after his child experiences risk and risk-taking

Let us recall Steven, from Chapter 5, and his son who Googles the word S-E-X and is upset by the images that he sees. Steven is confronted by several safety concerns. Because of the nature of this material and his son's initial distress, the first requirement of this father is a safety assessment—a brief evaluation of the child's physical, emotional and existential state to discern if he or she is in danger. This evaluation takes the form of a series of questions and responses centered on the three categories of safety that we mentioned earlier.

- Physical Safety—How afraid are you about what happened?
- Emotional Safety—How upset are you about what happened?
- Existential Safety—How worried are about what happened?

The questions are structured to elicit concrete responses that a father can easily use to determine the subjective level of threat that his child feels. For children over 6 years old, we suggest using a 1 to 10 scale (with "1" feeling safest and "10" feeling most in danger). For child under 6 years old, we suggest using a chart with three faces—a smiling face (safe), a neutral face (not sure/don't know), and a frowning face (unsafe) (see Table 6.2). Versions of these scales are used by mental health and medical professionals for pain and distress assessments.

Figure 6.2—Safe feeling assessment for children under six.

As Steven's son chooses a value of 5 (out of 10), he assessed that his son was somewhat unsure about his feelings, and, also, uncomfortable and ill at ease, but that he was not in danger. When a child is in no immediate danger, the father as Protector "slows down" the discourse and employs the empathic safety-net to address his son's fears. This slowing down is called *pacing* and allows for extra time for both father and child to think, consider options, and make decisions. One way we can do this is by unhurried, measured breathing as it decreases the sense of urgency and vulnerability and allows the rational, conscious part of the brain to take charge for both father and son (Van Der Kolk, 2014).

Empathy is something that needs to be communicated to the other person in words, sounds, facial expression, posture and other non-verbal communications. Empathy can be expressed in degrees from a minimal amount to a significant amount. The father's choice of which degree of empathy to use in any given situation is related to his assessment of the experience and his comfort level with empathy. As he comes to know himself, a father's comfort with empathy may increase (Zimring, 2000).

To understand the different degrees of empathy, it helps to explore the work of Charles Truax and Robert Carkhuff, who, in 1967, published a study about empathy and how to communicate it. Out of this work, came the Carkhuff and Truax Empathy Scale which breaks empathy down into levels and criteria for those levels (Truax & Carkhuff, 1967; Neukrug, 2014). For our purposes, we have modified their scale for use by the father as Protector (see Figure 6.2).

Table 6.2—Empathy Scale for Fathers

Minimal Empathy (father is uncomfortable with empathy):

- The father recognizes his child's feelings and responds to that feeling with a tentative demonstration of empathy.
- The father offers modest communications of empathy such as "That's too bad," "I'm sorry," or "I understand."
- The father waits to see if the child shares more before offering more empathy.

Moderate Empathy (father is somewhat comfortable with empathy):

- The father recognizes his child's feelings and reflects back what his child has expressed to him.
- The father does not change any of the child's words and repeats them back exactly as they were spoken, "You're really sorry about what happened."
- The father asks for clarification if the child's words are unspecific or ambiguous.

Maximum Empathy (father is comfortable with empathy):

- The father demonstrates an understanding of his child's feelings by adding a description of the underlying situation.
- The father amplifies the feelings expressed by the child to increase his child's self-awareness
- The father makes educated guesses about the reasons for the child's feelings beyond what the child has specifically shared.

Adapted from Carkhuff and Truax, 1967; Weiner & Gallo-Silver, 2018.

We return to Steven to demonstrate what the various degrees of empathy can look like.

> SON: *I am really sorry, Dad.*
> STEVEN: *I understand.* (minimum empathy)
> SON: *I am really sorry, Dad.*
> STEVEN: *I can tell that you're sorry.* (moderate empathy)
> SON: *I am really sorry, Dad.*
> STEVEN: *I know you feel sorry because you think I am upset with you, but I think you are more upset with yourself.* (maximum empathy)

Steven needs to consider the maturational risk-taking involved in "researching" sex; his child's autonomy (independent exploration vs. asking for help); his child's impulses and judgment (how to identify potential dangers);

and his child's loss of innocence (pacing the process of maturation vs. peer pressure, managing anxiety).

> SON: *I am really sorry, Dad.*
> STEVEN: *It is natural for you to be curious and I don't imagine you meant to see something that upset you so much.* (maximum empathy)
> SON: *No, I didn't.*
> STEVEN: *Do you want to tell me what exactly upset you?*
> SON: *Just the pictures. I didn't think they would be that way.*
> STEVEN: *What way was that?*
> SON: *Just gross, I can't really explain it.*
> STEVEN: *We can get back to that in a minute, I am more concerned that you are upset.*
>   (maximum empathy) *I was uncomfortable about sex when I was a kid because I didn't understand it. It was embarrassing, and I didn't feel like I could ask anyone. I didn't have the Internet and Grandpa didn't bring it up so I just kept it to myself and tried to listen when my friends were talking about it, so I want you to know that I am willing to talk to you about sex whenever you want because I think it's important for you not to be upset by sex.* (maximum empathy)

The Protector Diffuses Conflict

It makes sense to return to Errol and his daughter from Chapter 4 and their conflict over her not keeping her curfew. The issue devolves into his use of corporal punishment. The various aspects of his concerns about her breaking curfew are lost in the drama of child protective services becoming involved in the situation. Errol, as Protector, has options to interact with his daughter on the issue of her curfew other than those that rely heavily on his use of the Captain archetype. Errol's daughter needs to know of her father's concerns about her safety and its relationship to his knowledge of her whereabouts when she misses curfew. Some questions for Errol to consider that may generate new avenues for discourse.

- Did he have a curfew when he was a child?
- If so, why, and how did he feel about it?
- Did he experience or witness physical, emotional or sexual violence as a child?
- Is his daughter's curfew age-appropriate?
- Does she have a cell phone, so she can text him or he can text her?
- Does she know how or is she able to defend herself?
- Does she know how to keep herself safe at night using the flight reaction to danger?
- Does he know the people that she hangs out with in the evenings?
- Does he know their parents?

- Is his daughter embarrassed by his concerns?
- Is his daughter fearful her friends will tease her if they learn of her father's concerns?

The answers to these questions open up discussions that enable Errol to focus on protecting his daughter while, at the same time, being empathetic to her overall maturation and her socialization preferences. The choice of using the Protector archetype more and the Captain less is not a defeat for him. It is not a victory of lenient fathering over tough fathering. Errol is not "giving in." Rather, he is trying to communicate in a clear manner about very important issues. The empathy safety net is a mechanism of connection which Errol and his daughter need in order to maximize her safety and security.

> ERROL: *There are things I need to know before we can even entertain you going out. With answers to these questions and your understanding that your safety is one of my greatest concerns, I am willing to discuss the curfew. But I really need your help and I want to be on the same page about this stuff.*

A Clear and Present Danger?

As we discussed earlier in the chapter, the empathy that a father provides is derived, in large part, from the "Wounded Healer" aspects of the Protector archetype. Empathic abilities are enhanced by the father's awareness of himself and acknowledgment of his own experiences as a child. When a father becomes mindful and accepts his own feelings about danger and vulnerability, he increases his capacity to more objectively examine any threat to his child.

Let us recall Dan, from Chapter 4, whose 12-year-old son was drinking in the park with his friends. His son admits the transgression to Dan after several days of struggling with it by himself. While Dan is relieved that his son shares the information with him, he also thinks of all the dangers that his son can potentially face when drinking, smoking, or using drugs. He also remembers all the problems he had to manage as a teenager and how many times he faced dangers—in cars, at parties, out in the neighborhood. Dan as Protector is also reminded that his son is not him, that he never admitted any substance use to his father, when he was a child. Dan's relationship with his own child has already surpassed the one he had with his father.

The Protector archetype contains a father's ability to reduce stress-related distortions and unclutter his thinking about dangerous situations. This process—of examining one's thinking in order to appraise it objectivity—is called *reality testing*. Dan can relax a bit in the reality that his son trusts him and that his son reaches out to him when faced with vulnerability. So, fathers can draw on the Protector archetype to assist in reality testing the veracity of the danger in situations and in making decisions based on real, not distorted, child vulnerabilities. Some typical circumstances and dynamics that may require reality testing on the part of a father are:

- How much risk taking is reasonable for a child during maturation and development?
- What is the balance between a child's knowledge acquisition and the overstimulation that can take place with too much information?
- How much independence can a child have before the child feels abandoned or too alone?
- Is using corporal punishment on a child physically, emotionally, or existentially safe?

As the Wounded Healer, the Protector archetype also holds community memories of oppression, discrimination, and trauma and an empathic connection to others that struggle and suffer in this way.

Jamal's 17-year-old son wants to have access to the family car to go out on Friday night with his friends. He just received his driver's license and is extremely excited to have the autonomy. Jamal is proud of him and is also very worried. He knows that in many areas "driving while black" can be dangerous. His son has witnessed Jamal being pulled over and asked to "step out of the car" for no apparent reason. On the other hand, his son has worked diligently to obtain his driver's license. And when Jamal rides with him, his son drives safely, so the actual driving is not the problem. It's really all about how unpredictably dangerous the world can be for a young, African American teen. They have had "the talks" about police brutality, about Michael Brown and Tamir Rice; it's just the idea of allowing, of sending, his child out into that that makes Jamal's stomach tighten up. He closes his eyes, opens them, clenches his fists, and says, "Yes" and then calmly goes over "the Plan" again.

The conscious and unconscious awareness of centuries of oppression and violence held by the Wounded Healer aspect of the Protector archetype gives Jamal pause in letting his son drive alone. Sadly, he must review in detail how his son needs to behave if he is stopped by police—it's the Plan they have worked out. Empathy makes this less than a tired old lecture his son has heard before, one that might feel controlling and be based primarily on the Captain archetype, and more an aspect of Jamal wanting his son to be protected from a potentially dangerous situation. Instead of discussing this issue with the anger and indignation that Jamal feels about it, Jamal takes a more conciliatory tone. A tone that grabs his son's attention because of the anxiety Jamal is willing to show his son.

The Secret Service Agent

At times, a child receives a prodigious, overabundance of attention from father as Protector. When this occurs, the father becomes a "Secret Service agent"—evoking an expansive attention to safety precautions usually limited to a president. The Secret Service agent focuses on safety, security, danger, and vulnerability before all else and, in doing so, utilizes the Protector archetype as the basis for all interactions with his child. With this single-minded approach, the Protector archetype absorbs and recasts other important aspects of fathering contributions and tasks in the following ways:

- rule-making (shifts focus to rules and structure as strict safety measures that must remain in place due to the ubiquitous nature of threats, from within a person and from without);
- learning (shifts focus to issues with school-related separation, socialization, and educators' opinions/interactions as potentially dangerous and requiring close monitoring and control);
- play (shifts focus to play as something that needs to be rigidly managed to prevent potential harm); and
- nurturing (shifts focus to the restriction or the micro-management of other caregivers who may be tasked with providing care and comfort to the child).

Arthur and Fred's daughter is a feisty 3-year-old who pushes boundaries and tests limits on a regular basis. Arthur finds these characteristics anxiety-

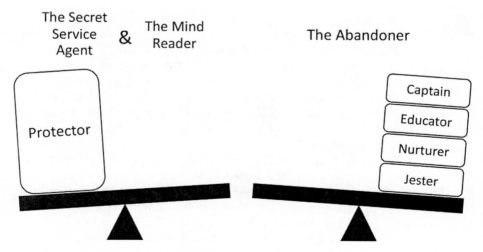

Figure 6.3—The Secret Service agent or the Mind Reader (access to Protector only) and the Abandoner (access to all archetypes except Protector archetype).

producing and is constantly punishing her. At Fred's urging, Arthur signs up their daughter for preschool—her first regular experience outside the home. She is very excited. Arthur asks for a meeting with the teachers and the administrators of the school. Perhaps knowing how Arthur can get, Fred decides not to attend the meeting. At the meeting, Arthur expresses significant reservations about allowing their daughter to start school at this age and makes several demands. He wants to be in charge of selecting her teachers, to be given information about the families of the children in her class, and to be informed when other children in school come in with colds or viruses. The school officials are unwilling to make these accommodations. When he arrives home and sits down with their daughter and Fred to explain his decision to not let her go to school, he tells them that the school is just not a safe place. The daughter runs to Fred and begins to cry. Once she is in bed, the fathers argue about Arthur's unilateral decision for "their" daughter.

Arthur as Secret Service agent has a distorted view of his daughter's vulnerability and the dangers that she faces in the world. Although the school is safe, he reaches other conclusions. The Secret Service agent finds it difficult to see any situation as anything but potentially hazardous.

When fathers over-emphasize the Hero aspect of the Protector, they simultaneously under-emphasize the Healer and its empathy. Protection without empathy can lead a child to feel stifled, immobilized, and anxious under the perpetual concerned gaze of the Secret Service agent. As we have mentioned earlier, taking risks and maturing through trial and error are fundamental pieces to the process of a child's development. Arthur's protection of his and Fred's daughter fails to grasp his daughter's other needs with regard to school and life—friendship, knowledge, fun, rules, and challenges. We acknowledge that these are complicated distinctions to make where institutional and/or cultural oppression exist. In these communities, where potential risk is not imagined or exaggerated but is, in fact, everywhere, the Secret Service agent may be an understandable use of the Protector archetype. In these situations, the counterbalance may come from empathy of the Healer in the form of an equally powerful acknowledgment that these realities are profoundly unfair for a child.

A child cannot be safe without connection to others outside of the immediate family. If no one else in the world can be trusted, children become isolated, which makes them more vulnerable. Children, as they grow and mature, always need to be able to rely on others—extended family members, caregivers, peers, friends, teachers, administrators, coaches, and, ultimately, partners. The father as Protector role helps children understand how to feel safe with confidence rather than with fear; how to ask for protection from others and to protect themselves in order lead full and rich lives.

The Mind Reader

With its connection to the empathic aspect of the Protector archetype, the over-expression of the Wounded Healer, is a version of the archetype that we call the Mind Reader. Heinz Kohut wrote of the concept of optimal frustration. This idea centers on a dynamic in which a father knows what his child needs but does not provide it immediately. Not getting what the child needs instantaneously creates an internal struggle called frustration. Allowing this frustration for a developmentally helpful period of time is what Kohut described as optimal (Kohut, 1971). The issue with this archetypal variant is two-fold:

- A father as Mind Reader finds the concept of optimal frustration too anxiety producing, not for the child, but for himself. Understanding his child's emotional state at all times allows for a level of influence and safety over his child.
- The Mind Reader also believes that sharing this empathic awareness with his child will make his child safer.

Rick is worried by the look on his 15-year-old daughter's face. "You are upset," he says. "No, I'm not," she replies angrily. "I know that you are." She stares at him. Rick continues, disregarding her look. "It's the boy, isn't it? I knew when you kept calling him that something was wrong. You called him four times yesterday, I checked the phone log. I bet your girlfriends don't like him either. Listen, you have been hurt and rejected by this guy. You feel loss. It's normal, just let it sit for a while. You can talk to me." His daughter stares at him. "Now you're angry at me, but I really think it's him that you are angry with. Sometimes we get angry at one person when we are angry at someone else." His daughter enters the bathroom, slams it shut and locks the door. Rick mutters to himself: "Ah, young love."

A father as Mind Reader expresses his lack of boundaries by not providing adequate emotional distance to allow for his child to work at figuring out how he or she feels. He also does not let his child correct the father's assumptions. It is self-protective in two ways:

- It bypasses the father's own inability to tolerate frustration as he waits for his child to process what is happening.
- It allows the father to develop a false sense of efficacy in his knowledge of his child's consternation.

This undermines a child's ability to become emotionally self-sufficient. In addition, the facetious awareness of the Mind Reader ("I know how you feel") creates emotional suppression in the child who reflexively denies feelings in order to ward off the intrusiveness of the Mind Reader.

The Abandoner

If the Secret Service agent and the Mind Reader serve as the over-protective, over expressions of the Protector archetype, then the Abandoner is their under-expressed alter ego. Although our culture seems to ridicule "helicopter" parents as being hyper-sensitive to danger and overly worried that their child will be unable to manage or cope without them, the greater concern by far of the two poles of the Protector archetype is the Abandoner. That the world, at times, can be a dangerous and potentially harmful place for children is not in dispute. Whether parents are focused on the activities of the child's burgeoning autonomy and independence, the physical realities of involvement in sport, violence, sex or elicit substances, or the complications of maturing social interaction (bullying, peer-pressure, gang-influence, sexual intimacy), the father's ability to disconnect from the inherent risks embedded in these developments is the core of the Abandoner. The desperate, wishful thinking that minimizes danger is the father's need to protect himself from anxiety and, inevitably, results in the profound under-protection of the Abandoner.

Kwame looks at his 7-year-old son and ponders his request to walk the four city blocks to school on his own. He wants his son to be brave and strong. He walked to school on his own at the same age, but he was scared. He was bullied by the older children, and on one occasion, a teenage boy flicked a lit cigarette at him, then chased him for "looking at him funny" and punched him in the back of the head. He suddenly feels down. He never wants his son to have to think about those terrible things, the violence and the fear. "Go," he says, "have fun." He tries to smile and to put the thoughts out of his head, but he cannot. He leaves the room and does not say anything else to his son about the walk to school.

Kwame's mind "runs" from even the notion of danger rendering him unable to process the real danger with his child and leaving his child to possibly surmise that there is no danger or that he must confront any worrisome thoughts or interactions on his own. This incorrect assumption leaves his child at greater risk. As the Protector archetype provides physical safety and emotional safety (in the form of empathic connection), the Abandoner's disconnect from peril holds true for both of these realms of a child's experience. Abandonment in the face of danger—whether it be the frightening *tangible* safety concerns of childhood or overwhelming *intangible* emotive expressions of children—has devastating effects on a child who needs a father's protection, empathy and support. It does not "build character" or make a child strong, rather it leaves the child unprotected from the real dangers of life.

7

The Nurturer Archetype

There are two things we should give our children: one is roots the other is wings. —*Anonymous*

Hugs can do great amounts of good, especially for children. —*Princess Diana*

Feeding my children is not like feeding myself; it matters more. —*Jonathan Safran Foer*

We've got this gift of love, but love is like a precious plant. You can't just accept it and leave it in the cupboard or just think it's going to get on by itself. You've got to keep watering it. You've got to really look after it and nurture it.

—John Lennon

Listening is where love begins. —*Mr. Rogers*

We are born of love; love is our mother. —*Rumi*

A person's a person no matter how small. —*Dr. Seuss*

When we think of the act of nurturing (especially of a child), it conjures ideas of love, affection and the providing of sustenance. If all goes well, these acts of caretaking lead to the child's growth and healthy development. As we discussed in Chapter 1, these nourishing undertakings have been, for the most part, historically the purview of mothers. Mothers carry their unborn children within them, comforting them, feeding them, keeping them warm, and caring for them. This occurs for up to ten months of pregnancy before the child gets to meet anyone else. In fact, the connection between mother's care and her child is biophysically entrenched during pregnancy with mothers sending their own cells and nutrients through the membrane of the placenta that find their way into the organs of their children (Martone, 2012). The mother retains for herself only what is leftover. The mother then provides nourishment for the newborn infant in the most intimate of ways by breast feeding.

This continuum of care, which begins at conception and continues in perpetuity, is so universally accepted as "motherly" that Jung describes it simply as the Mother archetype (or the Earth Mother archetype). In addition to emotional and physical nourishment, Jung believed that the Mother archetype contained connection to inner strength, cunning, and resourcefulness, among other attributes necessary for survival. Children's essential attributes of their mothers can also include love, support, determination, inspiration, steadiness, and loyalty. The details may change, but from culture to culture the themes remain consistent—a mother cares. In some cultures, the mother's role as nurturer is so engrained that the nurturing father receives a different title and permission to nurture under specific circumstances. For instance, anecdotally, in the southern part of the United States there is the "phenomenon" of the "MommyDaddy." This title is given to fathers who parent children on their own due to the mother's absence (through death, disability or abandonment) and takes on the nurturing functions instead of them being provided by other female relatives. The "MommyDaddy" preserves the fiction of nurturing children as a female gendered role.

In Chapter 1, we briefly discussed early nurturing activities as part of fatherhood. The early family in which all members did not sleep separately and included extensive modeling time for fathers and their children; hunting societies and the fathering and caretaking done during the intra-hunt time spent with children; and the herding societies with the father using his nurturing skills to keep his animals alive and healthy (Raeburn, 2014). We believe that ultimately, these nurturing skills are innate in all men based on Jung's theory of the collective unconscious (see Chapter 2). Today, fathers' usage of these nurturing abilities is greatly affected by the cultural and societal norms that shape the father's role in child rearing. Yet, the ability to nurture remains inside a father's psyche regardless of how much he applies it to his own children.

As the role of fathers in society evolves and social prescriptions become more fluid, fathers receive societal permission and, in some instances, societal encouragement to uncover and express the innate ability to nurture (Livingston, 2014; Levant & Wimer, 2009; LaRossa, 1997). The basis of father nurturing remains focused on nourishment—feeding his child in many different ways. The father nourishes his child with food, time, attention, praise, encouragement and support, all with the ultimate goal of helping his child learn to nourish him or herself. Many children today see their fathers in a similar fashion. To this end, we call this archetype, the Nurturer. In offering a gender-neutral form of this archetype, we want to highlight the innate ability of fathers to use this archetype to provide tenderness, affection, validation, comfort, support and love to their children.

The Realms of Nurturing and Growth

Nurturing, as we define it here, centers of the providing of emotional and physical resources to a child. These resources are based on a set of needs that each child requires to grow, mature and thrive. In Chapter 1, we referred to Abraham Maslow's Hierarchy of Needs and his contention that certain human needs were essential for survival (food, water, air) and that others were built on top of these basic needs (in a pyramid form) as a way of illustrating the prioritization of necessary resources (Maslow, 1943). For the purpose of exploring this archetype, we re-cast Maslow's human needs as met by the father as Nurturer. We place all of a child's "needs" within one of three categories or realms of growth. Each of these realms represent one specific manner that a child exists in the world and interacts with the world (see Table 7.1).

Table 7.1—Realms of Nurturing and Growth with Reference to Maslow

- MIND (a child's expressiveness and Maslow's Self-Actualization)—
  - Aiding the child to grow closer to the world around him/her.
  - Being able to speak one's mind.
  - Increasing the child's ability and comfort to express thoughts and feeling states to others as he/she engages in different relationships and situations.
- BODY (a child's physical capacity and Maslow's Love and Belonging)—
  - Increasing the size, strength, skills and awareness of the child's body.
  - Feeling confident in one's physicality and physical abilities.
  - Developing the child's body so that it may keep up with the child maturation and developmental changes.
- SOUL (a child's self-esteem and Maslow's Esteem Building)—
  - Growing closer to oneself.
  - Knowing and liking oneself.
  - Developing the child's awareness of self and evolving the quality and nature of the child's connection to his/her self [Horney,1945; Kohut,1971; May, 1953; Frankel, 1963].

Sergey is father to his 4-year-old granddaughter who is attending preschool for the first time. Sergey begins talking to his granddaughter about the first day of school several weeks prior to the date. Each day his granddaughter says that she does not want to go to school and each day appears nervous when she talks about having a new teacher and being with kids that she does not know. She wants to know what her grandfather will do while she is at school, what she will eat at school, and what she will do each day. Sergey prepares her by patiently answering her questions. He takes her to buy a special outfit, a bright pink lunch box, a book about the first day of school to read before bed, and a small frame for their family photo to keep in her cubby (MIND).

The morning of her first day of school, Sergey's granddaughter is visibly nervous and not very hungry. The night before she slept poorly, coming to his bed with bad dreams. Sergey makes his granddaughter her favorite breakfast and tells her to eat a little bit of everything, so she has enough energy for her big day (BODY).

He walks her to school, holding her hand and talking quietly with her about how nervous he was his first day of school. He tells her how normal it is for kids to be nervous and he shares with her how proud he is of her and how he cannot wait to hug her and hear about her day when he picks her up (SOUL).

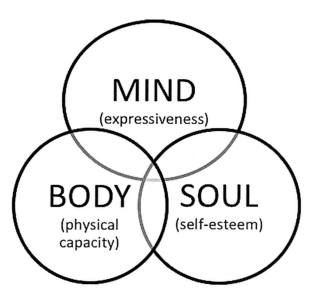

Figure 7.1—The realms of nurturing.

The childhood needs and requirements within these interconnected realms comprise a continuum of a father's nurturing responsibilities and are the focus and purview of the Nurturer archetype. To manage her first day of preschool, Sergey's granddaughter requires nourishment in all three areas of focus—her mind, her body and her soul. Her grandfather, as Nurturer, provides her with energy, attention, connection, love and praise. If Sergey omits his support in one of these realms, his granddaughter feels less equipped.

When we follow the notion that the father as Nurturer is the provider of all the physical and emotional nourishment to the child's mind, body and soul, we can use the concept of "nourishment" in its tangible form of food groups to simplify the task (see Table 7.2).

Table 7.2—Realms of Nurturing and Growth with Aspects of Nourishment

- MIND (expressiveness) requires the *carbohydrates* of undivided attention.
  - In the form of adult focus, the asking of questions and providing of answers, the creation of options and choices, and ongoing conversation
  - Leads to the development of discourse and the child's knowledge that his or her opinion matters.
- BODY (physical capacity) requires the *proteins* of unconditional affection and love.
  - In the form of smiles, hugs, kisses, tickling
  - Refills and replenishes a child's reserves which are burned and used each day to fuel the child's growth and maturation.
- SOUL (self-esteem) requires the *vegetables and fruits* rich with vitamins of admiration and enjoyment.
  - In the form of praise, encouragement and affirmation
  - Enhances the growth of the child's self by displaying to the child through parental words and deeds how interesting, powerful and unique he or she is.

The idea that fathers must nourish all these different aspects of their children may seem daunting, as actually giving children the correct diet of food often does. The interrelatedness of nurturing activities means that providing one type of nourishment often has positive ancillary effects on multiple realms. The reservoir of the collective unconscious is deep and wide in terms of nurturing children. It is the accumulation of centuries of human life; of fathers nurturing their children in myriad ways.

If Sergey gives his granddaughter affection, it not only gives her energy for the day, it also makes it easier for her to like herself. If he pays attention to her, it not only augments her ability to talk to him about how she is feeling and what she needs, it also makes her feel special. The realms overlap each other and interact constantly with one another.

The Mind

Attention is the act of validating and confirming the worth of a person's thoughts and feelings by responding to them with all the senses that one has available. The Nurturer archetype employs the active process of providing attention to a child. By active, we mean mutual and engaged. There is a back and forth within the act of paternal attention. Father to child and back to father, and so on. The father's role in attention giving centers on communicating the value that the father places on the child's abilities to dream and create. This is similar to but more expansive than the act of the more well-known concept of active listening—a strategy in which the listener reflects or repeats back what the speaker has said as a way of showing that the words have been taken in. The process of active attention consists of three forms of focus—physical, non-verbal and verbal (see Figure 7.2).

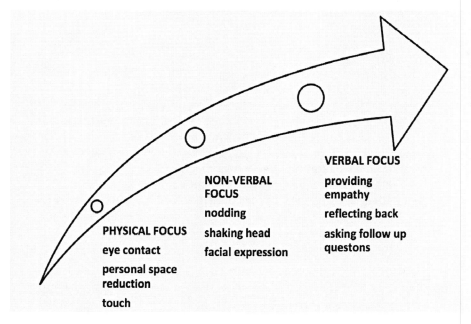

VERBAL FOCUS

providing empathy

reflecting back

asking follow up questons

NON-VERBAL FOCUS

nodding

shaking head

facial expression

PHYSICAL FOCUS

eye contact

personal space reduction

touch

Figure 7.2—The process of active attention.

In Chapter 4, when Louis responds to his 6-year-old son's heartfelt desire for ice cream with the answer "No," he does so with the rules and structure of the Captain archetype. The back and forth that takes place for several minutes with his son screaming, "I WANT MY ICE CREAM! YOU PROMISED IT TO ME! YOU TOLD ME THAT I WOULD GET DESSERT!" requires Louis to pay close attention to his child. With nods, eye contact, and closing the space between him and his son, Louis without speaking conveys to his son his undivided attention using the physical and the non-verbal foci.

In this way, the Nurturer archetype sends the message—"You can tell me what you need to tell me." This message serves a containing function— like a dam that holds back water. The father as Nurturer models for his child how to manage the dam's spill way—letting out water before it spills over the top. The active part of this process centers on the options and direction that the Nurturer archetype provides to the father. It offers different ways that the father can engage his child's mind during instances of duress or stress– knowing that for children the navigation of these moments is when true growth occurs. As Khalil Gibran wrote, "the deeper that sorrow carves into your being, the more joy you can contain" (Gibran, 1923, p. 29). During these times of challenging opportunity, a father sits quietly with his child; a father provides non-verbal indications that he is with his child and; a father engages his child with questions and statements. For the purpose of providing nourishment for a child's mind, each of these forms of attention can be successful depending on the details of each given situation, temperament of the child, the developmental stage and maturation of the child. The Nurturer archetype enables the father to use all three forms of active attention.

Verbal focus of attention includes the father obtaining more information from the child in order to increase his understanding of the child's thoughts and feelings. This requires the formulation of questions that are imbued with neutrality and acceptance of the child's responses to the questions. In order for the father to convey these feelings of neutrality and acceptance he avoids words that might sound accusatory. Questions are conceived as having three general structures (Neukrug, 2015) (see Table 7.3).

Table 7.3—The Structure of Questions

- Open Ended—a question that allows the child to answer in any form he or she chooses
  - How did you accomplish that?
  - What were you thinking about?
- Direct/Closed Ended—a question that requires a number, one word or short answer
  - Did you like what happened?
  - How many times did you do that?
- Tentative—a question that begins with a request for permission to discuss a topic
  - Would it be okay for us to discuss…?
  - I was wonder if you would be up for a talk about…?

Once the child answers a question, the father as Nurturer needs to respond to the content of the child's answer. There are three general categories of responses from a father as Nurturer (see Table 7.4). All use some form of empathy. He may provide concerned support utilizing the Protector archetype; new, relevant information as the Educator; or possible options or directions by employing the Captain. All these responses indicate that the father has heard his child and therefore communicates value to what the child has shared. Responding to his child only with additional questions does not utilize empathy and serves to separate the father's attention from the child by quickly moving on, overlooking or minimizing the child's answers and what the child has shared.

Table 7.4—Categories of Verbal Empathic Responses

- Supportive (Protector)—a statement that expresses concern for a child and a willingness to be involved
- Observation (Educator)—a statement that lends another perspective to a child point of view
- Proposition (Captain)—a statement that offers a course of action to a child

Jacob is the father of a 5-year-old daughter who has difficulty with "transitions." He tries to get her ready for bed, but she begins hitting him, throwing objects and screaming. He asks her what is wrong, and she becomes even more agitated, screams louder and cries harder. Jacob attempts to consider what his daughter's behavior may be communicating to him. He then points out (observation) that she is angry and doesn't want her daddy to leave her. His daughter looks at him and then launches herself into his arms. He suggests to his daughter that he will stay with her while she settles into bed (proposition).

The Body

Taking care of the body is the part of the father's nurturing role that includes providing "physical" sustenance to a child. This nourishment has both concrete and abstract aspects. The concrete nature of a father's physical interaction with his child is as crucial as the mother's in helping the child gain knowledge of the body, bodily sensations, and bodily enjoyment. The need for touch—established brilliantly by Harlow's monkey studies, that demonstrated the social deficits in monkeys that were not nurtured—was confirmed by the deficit studies of institutionalized infants who were left untouched by orphanage staff (Harlow, 1959). The father as Nurturer feeds his child through the somatic (physical) contact he initiates and accepts.

Toby's 11-year-old son walks over to his father and rubs his head. It is night time and Toby is working on a time-sensitive project for work. His son is heading off for bed and stands close to his father. Toby initially tenses up as he feels frustrated at being interrupted, but then he remembers what time it is. He turns to look at his boy and smiles, wrapping his son in a powerful hug as his son continues to rub his head. Toby says, "I love you," to his son, "have a nice sleep." His son puts his head on his father's shoulder.

The Touch Continuum demonstrates a progression of tactile affection from a basic tactile impact to maximum tactile impact (Maltz, 2012a, 2012b; Gallo-Silver, 2016) (see Figure 7.3).

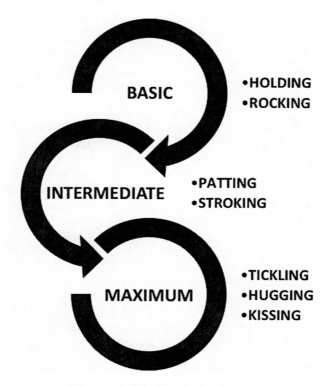

BASIC •HOLDING •ROCKING

INTERMEDIATE •PATTING •STROKING

MAXIMUM •TICKLING •HUGGING •KISSING

Figure 7.3—The Touch Continuum.

Tactile affection with fathers assists children in their psycho-sexual development (Zoldbrod, 1998). It is the way that the Nurturer helps fathers connect the father-child physical affection and contact to the physical feelings and thoughts that their children will have toward other people later in life. Let's return to Steven from the Educator (Chapter 5) and the Protector (Chapter 6) whose son watched pornography on the Internet.

STEVEN: *I wanted to know if you are ready to talk about sex.*
SON: *You mean now?*
STEVEN: *Sure, if you like.*
SON: *It was just gross. It makes me not want to grow up.*
STEVEN: *Well, sex is for more grown up people, for sure. Let me ask you something ... do you think the pictures you saw had anything to do with stuff like love and caring?*
SON: *I don't know.*
STEVEN: *Well, it does. See, right now in your life, when you want to show the people you love like me and mom and your little brother, what do you do?*
SON: *I hug you and I kiss you.*
STEVEN: *Exactly ... and I see you with your friends on the playground, you guys are always hugging each other and jumping on each other.*
SON: *That's not the same.*
STEVEN: *No, it's not exactly the same, but it is kind of the same. The people that we care about and love make us want to touch them, it's totally normal. And as we get older, that touching goes from hugs, to hand holding, to kissing and later to other things, like sex.*

In some cultures, fathers perhaps favor certain types of affectionate touch more than others. For example, tickling is often the outcome of a father chasing a child as well as an outcome of wrestling (a form of hugging) with a child, also often preferred by some fathers. The choice to use physical affection can accompany the work of other archetypes as a reinforcement or backstop to uncertainty or a perception of conflict between father and child. Let us recall the situation with Mark as Captain from Chapter 4.

Mark sits with his 7-year-old son. He has recently moved into this new spacious apartment after separating from his wife, the mother of his son. They are discussing a situation that occurred in school in the past week. Mark received a call from the school principal who reported that the boy had left class without asking and stayed out of class until the lunch hour only returning to collect his lunch box. When his son tears up from the discussion of rule breaking, Mark moves close to his son and puts his hand on his shoulder, pulling his son closer to him.

The Nurturer archetype informs fathers of the usefulness of physical closeness and the connection it has to infancy (even if children are no longer infants) when a child is comforted by holding, rocking, and stroking. As a child matures and grows, this type of nourishment is modified to accommodate for the societal norms and developmental changes around autonomy and personal space and boundaries. Fathers learn to touch in a different way, allowing their children to initiate the touch, having the touch be more jocular or informal, or having the touch, as in the case of Mark's son, be more passive (part of larger interaction).

As fathers watch their children crawl across a room, toddle down a street, scale a set of stairs, or climb a tree, the Nurturer archetype also provides the more abstract form of physical care—an awareness that these activities require strength, power and energy and a knowledge of the calorie intake required to maintain a child's health and vigor. The father as Nurturer understands the importance of balancing sleep, exercise, and food and how these change over the developmental continuum of a child's life. He makes choices about meals, has data on amounts of nutrients, and knows nutritional value of different foods. He makes decisions about bedtimes, changes in sleep cycles, and the balance of his child's studying vs. sleep needs. He creates opportunities for exercise, physical exertion, and movement, knowing that all these will be critical for his children's development as they leave childhood, move into adolescence (which requires a foundation of physicality) and then transition into young adulthood.

The Soul

Over the past several decades, there has been a great deal of debate over the benefits of praising children as more and more information about this type of child support has been studied. Some research from the 1980s and 1990s indicates that praising children can have some negative effects including creating external pressure to reproduce results, reorienting the goal of a task toward receiving praise, and generating a false sense of accomplishment defined by the praise and not by the task itself (Rotter, 1975). With this closer analysis of praise has also come a greater understanding of the mechanisms of praise and how it and other forms of admiration and positive reinforcement can create a greater sense of self-worth and self-esteem in a child (Kohut, 1971; Peetz & Wilson, 2008).

To nourish the soul of a child, the father as Nurturer, focuses the child's attention back on himself or herself. Look at yourself, enjoy yourself, the father says to his child. Fathers model this enjoyment by actively observing their children's creations and actions. This is accomplished by a father making thoughtful and sincere comments about his child's work, performance and effort—the how and what his child is doing. This is called process praise.

Process praise avoids the habit of continuous praise, praise for a mistake free activity, or for low challenge level accomplishments (Rotter, 1975; Kohut, 1971; Peetz & Wilson, 2008). Rather process praise focuses on the children's trying, attempting, persistence and resilience that are exhibited when children push themselves beyond their comfort level regardless of their level of success (see Figure 7.4). Process praise focuses on (1) the New Behavior and (2) the Level of Effort. For a New Behavior, the father praises the child using amazement: "Tell me how you did that." For the Level of Effort, the father praises the child using recognition: "I saw how hard you were concentrating."

Process praise also addresses the issue of encouragement. Encouragement centers on the father's wish that the child makes additional attempts at an activity until it is no longer a challenge and becomes part of the child's level of comfort: "Tying shoes takes a lot of focus, you can do it." In addition, affirmations are the aspect of process praise that focuses on the achievement of the once challenging activity becoming part of the child's comfort level. "You are becoming a getting dressed expert."

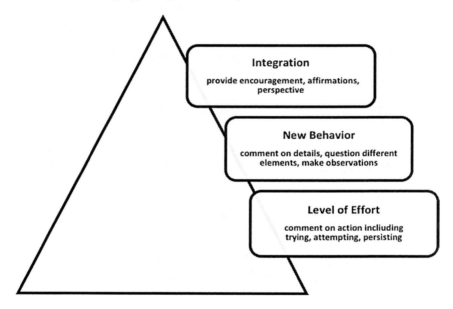

Figure 7.4—Process praise.

Transition to Fathering from Afar

There comes a time when the direct nourishment that fathers provide their children must accommodate the changing distance (emotional and physical) that stems from a child's growth, maturation and development. The burgeoning autonomy and need for control of a child who is going through the separation and individuation process calls for the Nurturer archetype to be cognizant of these changes (Mahler, Pine & Bergman, 1975). Nourishing still occurs –will always occur—but the father as Nurturer uses his creativity to maintain the realms of nurturing when he and his child are not "together."

Antoine is excited and hopeful for his 18-year-old autistic son who has made amazing strides over the years with frequent and numerous therapeutic interventions and has now decided to enroll at a college several hours from home. He is also worried about his son and gives his son lists of things to do and follow as a way of preparing him. Yet, Antoine, as the Nurturer, feels something is missing in his preparation of his son, even though his son is connected with the College's Services for Students with Autism. At the graduation dinner, Antoine gives his son a plaque to hang in his dorm room. It reads:

> *You are not alone as you have a family who loves you.*
> *If you need us, you can call home.*
> *If you have a problem that is hard to solve,*
> *you can come home as you are NOT alone.*

Antoine's son memorizes the words on the plaque and chants them softly to himself on the trip to college. The plaque with its affectionate words is Antoine's way of providing his son with a fatherly hand to hold while he is at college.

Antoine's plaque for his son and Sergey's photograph for his grand-daughter are examples of *transitional objects* (Winnicott, 1953; Ainsworth, Blehar, Waters & Wall, 2014). Transitional objects are symbolic, physical representations of the Nurturer archetype. It contains the thoughts, feelings, ideas, scent and/or memories of the relationship with a person who gives it. It stems from a shared experience between father and child and reminds a child of his or her father when the father is not present (see Table 7.5).

Table 7.5—Transitional Objects

- In early childhood, the transitional objects retain a scent:
  - an article of bedding (blanket)
  - clothing (shirt, hat)
  - a toy with a fabric element or a texture (teddy bear)
- Later in childhood, transitional objects are images or possessions of the parent:
  - photographs
  - keys
  - jewelry
  - watches

Although we talk about being apart, the changes in nurturing that take place are not necessarily a matter of physical proximity. It is more about children taking over their own nurturing responsibilities; transitioning aspects of caretaking from father to child. The child's development of these self-nurturing techniques is a continuation of the developmental arc that begins when as infants they develop self-comforting skills. The Nurturer archetype informs fathers of the need to respect the continuity of the child's developmental arc and is the catalyst for change in all three realms of his care (see Table 7.6).

Table 7.6—Developmental Changes in Realms of Care Activities

Mind
- Asking the child's opinions
  - facilitating discussions about household, community, world/political issues
- Inquiring about the child's feelings
  - balancing respect for child's need for privacy and need for the father's interest and attention
- Encouraging the child to make choices during daily living
  - accepting clothing, leisure activities, and schooling opinions/decisions
- Enabling self-advocacy skills
  - helping child talk to teachers and resolve conflicts with peers

Body
- Facilitating the child's independence in managing hunger and thirst
  - relinquishing the care of bodily needs, making healthy and reasonable food/beverage choices
- Enabling self-directed bodily care
  - accepting independence in bathing and grooming
- Preparing for bodily changes
  - managing secondary sex characteristics, puberty, and sexual responses

Soul
- Respecting the intensity of the child's feelings while maintaining family rules
  - coping with flashes of anger, irritability, and sullenness
- Tolerating child's ambivalent self-perceptions
  - validating positive self-perceptions and challenging negative self-perceptions
- Supporting child's fantasies about the future as an adult
  - accepting child's plans to use creative, athletic, and intellectual skills/interests

The father as Nurturer creates opportunities and moments that help children take the reins on their own as they mature and develop their self-nurturing skills. Typically, the father as Nurturer may not change rapidly enough to adjust to the child's maturation. When this occurs, the necessary conflict arises—with the child using either culturally approved and culturally dissonant communication styles—to remind the father that they are no longer children. We consider this conflict necessary for two reasons. One, it informs the father of the child's acceptance and recognition of growth and maturation and two, it enables the child to request an implementation of a change in the father's nurturing responsibilities. By situating the catalyst for change with the child, this avoids the child's misperception of the any changes in the father's nurturing being an aspect of his rejection or disinterest.

Jamal is excited that his daughter obtained her driver's license and gives her the keys to the car for the first time. Even so he has a tense smile on his face.

> DAUGHTER: *What?*
> JAMAL: *Nothing ... have a great time and follow all the rules.*
> DAUGHTER: *Dad, really, c'mon, do you have to say that?*
> JAMAL: *What?*
> DAUGHTER: *(Annoyed) I know how to drive, you taught me, I've driven you places so what's with the face?*
> JAMAL: *I don't have a face. I am just a little nervous. (Looking worried)*
> DAUGHTER: *I'm not a little girl riding a two wheeler bicycle for the first time. I promise not to get hurt.*
> JAMAL: *Okay, I got the message, just be careful.*
> DAUGHTER: *You're hopeless, you'll never change. (She gives him a hug)*

The Smotherer

Nurturing requires an understanding that children, at times, want to nourish themselves or want to determine what amount of nourishment they need. This idea of feeding oneself or limiting the amount of food, may feel counterintuitive, to some fathers. How can a child know what they need? They don't have the experience, the knowledge or the perspective. While on many levels this may be true, as we mentioned earlier, developmental changes and maturation often require fathers to alter the nourishing regimen. The changes in father-to-child nurturing required to manage these new dynamics necessitate a trial and error process (also called the theory of connectionism) that if done well, can provide both father and child with a sense of confidence and mastery (Thorndike, 2010).

The Smotherer is a version of the Nurturer archetype that maintains the self-referential need to determine how, when, where, and in what amount nourishing takes place. This is considered self-referential as it is an aspect of the *father's* need to nurture in a specific manner rather than the child's need to be nurtured in a specific manner. Therefore, the Smotherer nourishes because he needs to, not because his child needs it. The Smotherer is unable

The Smotherer   The Rejecter

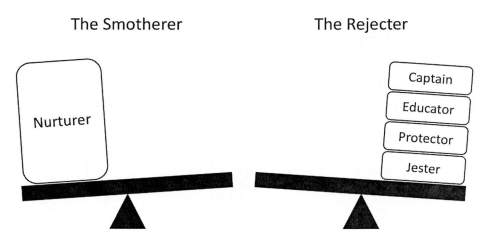

Figure 7.5—The Smotherer (access to Nurturer only) and the Rejecter (access to all archetypes except Nurturer archetype).

to change his responses in light of the child's maturation and development. The child's individuation (self-concept of being a separate person from the father) gets lost under a press of disconnected nourishment—touching, affection, closeness or food—that the child neither needs nor requests.

Jude's 11-year-old son sits right next to him. His child is upset about getting yelled at by Jude for talking back. His son runs to his room, but Jude does not think that this is what his son needs right now. His son needs to be with his father so he can understand that his father loves him and only yelled at him for his own good. Jude rubs his son's back and tells him in a soft voice that it will be okay, that he knows how he feels, that he was always upset when his father yelled at him. Jude pulls his son closer and hugs him. His son sits rigid in his arms, but Jude barely notices. Jude says, "We're best buddies, right?" and tries to tickle his son. His son quietly answers, "Leave me alone." Jude is stung and confused by his son's muted response.

As Jude's son enters puberty and then later adolescence, Jude's type of detached and overbearing nurturing risks becoming more intrusive as his son's need for personal space and privacy grows. This dynamic can occur with either gendered child and how these children manage this boundary complication can vary. Children may withdraw as a way of creating space from the Smotherer or, conversely, sons and daughters of the Smotherer may venture down the road of becoming their father's "best friend." The best friend phenomenon is the Smotherer's way of reframing the relationship in order to maintain the nurturing status quo. As children mature, receiving nourishment from one's peer-aged best friend rather than from one's father, becomes a necessary transformation that promotes the child's emotional growth. The Smotherer can co-opt this natural process.

The Rejecter

The other side of the Smotherer is the Rejecter. The Rejecter is an under-expression of the Nurturer archetype. This is a father as Nurturer who believes he has little or no role in nurturing his children. Framed in some ways by a father's personal and cultural upbringing, and made more complicated by the logistical complexities of divorced and single-parent households, this "flight" fear response from the Nurturer archetype deactivates the father's innate skill set in this area of parenting. The notion that a father does not want to nurture his child may seem far-fetched and antiquated, but for a father who uses the Rejecter variation of the archetype, his intent may seem well-reasoned and clear to him. This, certainly, may not hold true for his child. The Rejecter's rationale to justify his withdrawal from the Nurturer skill set can manifest in different ways:

- the role is better suited to his partner or other adult
- the closeness and intimacy required by this archetype is uncomfortable
- nurturing his male child makes his son soft, weak, and brands his son as feminine ("mama's boy")
- nurturing his female child is too intimate, does not have clear enough physical and emotional boundaries, and will make his daughter "confused" about her relationship with men
- prioritizing time and resources for his son is difficult with his other responsibilities

The Rejecter sends only one message to his child—"you are unloved and unworthy of being loved." Instead of nourishing his children during these all important developmental times, the Rejecter unintentionally starves his children and leads them to remain "hungry" for a father's love well into their own adulthood.

8

The Jester Archetype

Frame your mind to mirth and merriment which bars a thousand harms and lengthens life.—William Shakespeare

If you obey all the rules, you miss all the fun.—Katharine Hepburn

Respect every smile, you never know, it may have managed to makes its way through a million tears.—Ritu Ghatourey

It is a good idea to obey all the rules when you're young so you'll have the strength to break them when you're old.—Mark Twain

The cleverest of all, in my opinion, is the man who calls himself a fool at least once a month.—Fyodor Dostoevsky

For everything there is a season.... A time to cry and a time to laugh.— Ecclesiastes 3

Jung's name for what we refer to as the Jester archetype was the trickster, the fool or the clown and the rule breaker. Although our current connotation of these words tends toward the negative, Jung's trickster seemed to be more of a joker, a humorist, a dreamer and a revolutionary. Our use of the term "jester" stems from the talented, creative, and indispensable individuals from the courts of Europe, China and India. These men and women "could emerge from a wide range of backgrounds: an erudite but nonconformist university dropout, a monk thrown out of a priory for nun frolics, a *jongleur* with exceptional verbal or physical dexterity, or the apprentice of a village blacksmith whose fooling amused a passing nobleman" (Otto, 2001). It was not their backgrounds that mattered, but their abilities. They were respected and loved by the rulers and the people alike. They were the stand-up comics and the late-night talk show hosts of today—poking fun at society, satirizing, and bending the rules of propriety.

The Jungian archetype of the Jester can be found in many cultures (confirming his collective unconscious concept) with unique qualities in each.

1. Native American—the coyote, wanting to fly, challenges norms and rules of existence and conformity
2. Greek—Hermes, the god of boundaries, transitions, and thieves, the only god that is born to a mortal, the god who straddles the living world and the underworld, and the god who outwits the other gods on behalf of humanity or for his own pleasure
3. African—Esu or Eshu, a satirist, exposing the follies of men and throwing a spanner in one's plans that requires not to get too comfortable with the status quo
4. Japanese—Pig, in the story of Monkey, challenges the status quo by "tricking" and influencing authority, confronting norms
5. English—Reynard the Fox, a cowardly fox who outthinks his opponents and overcomes odds in order to survive
6. American—The Road Runner, the solitary bird who keeps one step ahead of, Wile E. Coyote, his nemesis who, with his vast resources, attempts to destroy the protagonist

Although presenting with different names, stories and appearance, each culture's Jester does share many common themes. The Jester expresses the tension between two sides of any continuum—good/bad, happy/sad, the have's/the have-nots, the power elite/the disenfranchised—able to assume the mantle of either, or to transform both. This ability to transform allows the Jester to break convention and not to be constrained by rules and norms.

There is a spontaneity within the Jester archetype. This archetype is freer than other archetypes, as its focus is not on the rules and regulations of reality (life, culture, society, family). It operates outside these constraints using the uncontained nature of creativity and imagination as its structure—trying to turn the expected on its head. Within the world of the Jester, the honest man tells a lie; the know-it-all is confounded; and the bewildered discovers the perfect strategy. The child can be an adult, the boy, a girl, the poor can be rich, the oppressed can be in charge—anyone can be anything they may conceive. In each of these ways the Jester is, in its essence, playful, yet also very meaningful. Sports, are one of those areas under the Jester's purview that is more complex than one may at first notice.

Katsuo stands 20 feet down the street, arms at his side, legs tensed and ready to move. The ball is thrown and arcs high over his head. The ball's trajectory will bring it down behind him and over to his right. He begins to run, lifts his glove and catches the baseball. "OUT," shouts his 10-year-old son, "that's three, Pirates are up." "Do you want to just play catch?" asks Katsuo. "Nah, that's boring, let's keep playing innings," says his son. "You are pitching now." Katsuo, tired from doing yard work earlier, reluctantly agrees. "When you pitch, you have to keep balls and strikes, but make sure you don't throw too hard," directs his son. "McCutchen is up." "Can you do the play-by-play, too?" he asks. The father stares down toward his son, "This is the seventh inning of a hard-fought game between these two juggernauts. The Pirates are tied with the Yankees, 2–2, and the teams have both knocked out the starters. Betances looks in and gets the sign...." His son smiles and kicks the pavement. "I'm gonna crush this."

When we interviewed fathers, many were intrigued by the Jester archetype. While it is not a common term and often conflated with a stylized silliness, fathers understood the archetype as the one who has fun with his children. It could be playing catch, or fishing, or building a model or puzzle together, or any number of types of play (make-believe or otherwise) such as the baseball game described above.

Fathers typically feel confident about the Jester and their ability to engage in activities with their children that stem from this archetype. They have the belief that they know when they are using it and when they are not. In a study conducted by the Centers for Disease Control and the National Center for Health Statistics that inquired about fathers who play with their children (aged under 5), 98 percent of fathers who lived with their children indicated they played with them "every day" or "several times a week." The percentages were lower for fathers who did not live with their children, but still remained relatively significant under the circumstances (39 percent played "every day" or "several days a week"). According to this report, upwards of 7 out of 10 children under the age of 5 played with their fathers at least several times each week (NCHS, 2013).

We find these statistics to be encouraging for fathers and their children because play is the emotional workhorse for children. That said, we are going to push the boundaries of what we see as the purpose of play within this archetype and, by doing so, embrace the "silly" father who makes his child laugh and groan. Play is where feelings are expressed that are not easily put into words and/or require more development before the child understands the words to express these feelings (Webb & Terr, 2016; Landreth, 2012; Saracho & Spodek, 1995; Axline, 1981). In light of the importance of play for a child's emotional health the Jester archetype is a critical fathering activity that enhances a child's development and feelings of being loved.

A hospital clinic is almost empty. Most of the children and their families have left for home. Billy is playing dolls with his seriously ill 5-year-old bald daughter as she waits to be admitted to the hospital. He is a rough-hewn man

from a rural state who has a small farm and augments his income with con-
struction work and logging. Yet, he is here, playing beauty parlor with his daugh-
ter. The two of them brush and style the hair of her collection of six dolls. The
beauty parlor is "real," the ill 5-year-old is a healthy "adult" and the father is
her "business partner." To the observer, her squeals of laughter at Billy's silly
hairdo, fake French accent and his enjoyment of his daughter having fun is
priceless. It is a fantasy and a wish for both of them for a future without illness
and with a continuing connection to each other. The Jester archetype within
Billy helps make precious memories even during sad and frightening times.

Understanding play in this way uses some of the concepts of psychodynamic theory. Jung and Freud began as close partners, in their drive to
develop their psychological theories of human behaviors, thoughts and feelings and lay the foundation of what we today call psychodynamic theory.
Later, working separately, their theories diverged, as they argued over the
fundamentals of their concepts. Even though these two brilliant men dis-
agreed, we choose to use their theories in tandem with one another other. It
is essential to turn to Neo-Freudian theories to understand this Jungian
fatherhood archetype. Bellack (1973), a Neo-Freudian, developed an understanding of the strengths of one's conscious mind (which Freud named the
Ego). The ego was the liaison between the internal mind—our thoughts, feelings and representations—and the external world. Among the strengths of
the conscious mind, or the ego, is the ability to play. Play is an arena (a secure
space) in which a father is able to reconcile what his child is thinking (call
them "inner questions") with what he is seeing outside (call them "outer realities") by manipulating, working with, and trying to understand each, in a
safe (and fun) way. The Jester is the part of the father who is able to enter
this secure arena and "play." When he does this, he may begin to discover,
understand and answer his child's unspoken questions and, in this important
way, help shape and reshape his child's reality. This becomes an essential
fathering function especially for children who must cope with hostile cultural
norms. Within the play these hostile cultural norms can be transformed into
new cultural norms—ones that support, empower and encourage the child.

The Purposes of Play

At this point in the history of understanding the nature and progression
of child development, all professionals who work with children or work on
behalf of children believe that play is a critical element in how children learn,
mature, and master their surroundings. There is consensus on its inherently
positive impact on emotional, cognitive and physical development. That said,

although developmental theorists, scholars and practitioners have long concluded the importance of play, the details and fundamentals of the ways in which play is used by children are myriad. Generally, play and its uses fall into a number of categories.

1. Play is a means of energy expenditure. Play is a manifestation of the surplus energy that all living things retain and must expel though some avenue of physical activity [Saracho & Spodek, 1995].

2. Play is a way of gaining confidence and self-efficacy by mastering one's surroundings (social, environmental). Lev Vygotskty believed that a child, within a specific setting (cultural, geographic, etc.), uses play to move from being an entity that is controlled by his/her environment to a being that is the master of his/her behavior within that environment [Connery, et al., 2010].

3. Play is a method for working through feelings and emotions about life. This is a widely-held belief by many and the core principle behind play therapy. Anna Freud and Melanie Klein saw play as focused on children working through their wishes and fantasies about their lives and as the means through which they attempted to reconcile these feelings with their realities [Freud, 1937; Klein, Heimann & Money-Kryle, 1955].

4. Play is a source of cognitive and physical growth and maturation. Jean Piaget believed that play was a venue to two major forms of learning and developing—accommodation and assimilation. Accommodation is the idea of copying what we see in order to do it ourselves. Assimilation is the concept of taking something we know and applying it to what we see around us [Piaget, 1952]. Karl Groos believed that play was a form of motoric practice—play fighting, chase, tag—that has its basis in the survival needs of animals, the preparation for adulthood and for taking on adult responsibilities [Groos, 1901].

5. Play is a form of relaxation and rejuvenation. Patrick contended that children, who are perpetually being asked to learn new tasks at home, in school, and among other environments, use play as a way of decreasing the stress create from these external demands [Patrick, 1916].

6. Play is a form of practicing/rehearsing for adult roles and activities through the play-acting of adult skill sets (hunting, driving, building, parenting, teaching, working, fighting, and arguing, etc.).

For our purposes, we want fathers to consider all these areas as significant because each moment of your child's play pulls from one or more of these situations.

Fathers and Play

Through the use of the Jester archetype, a father aids in his child's play—the enjoyment of life and understanding of his/her place in life. We contend that playing, both the activities of playing and the aspects of play that challenge norms and moderate taking life too seriously, require proactive tending to thrive, take hold, be integrated, and be available to the adult later in life. We believe that both are important for life success and for fulfilling parenting.

Even though we are talking all about play, we believe that the Jester archetype is the most challenging of all the archetypes that fathers are asked to access and use. On the surface it seems simple and straightforward. This archetype is the tangibly playful side of fathering—throw a ball, play with toys, dress up dolls, make jokes, enjoy a child's performance or game, watch a movie. However, its complexity is in the abstractions of the archetype:

- imagination
- rule-breaking
- rule-challenging
- limit testing
- limit setting
- humor
- developmental appropriateness
- regression

These abstractions are what create a minefield of sorts for fathers.

Ernest Kris' (1975) concept of regression—or more formally named "adaptive regression in the service of the ego" (ARISE)—is defined as a return to a more child-like state, in order to provide active relaxation for the conscious mind. An example of ARISE is our propensity as adults to play with friends by talking "trash" during a game or splashing our friends when swimming. Adults engage in ARISE when sick by climbing into bed, curling up under the covers, and to wanting to be taken care of by a caregiver. We feel smaller and, in fact, often look smaller.

Play has a tendency to create this regressive (child-like) dynamic in people. We become competitive, frustrated, excited, all in the service of our childhood experiences. As many fathers will attest, managing the tension between playing and remaining a grown up can lead to complicated moments. It is balancing these multiple vectors, at times pulling us in several emotional directions at once, all within the same archetype that creates complexity in the Jester archetype and why we find it so thought-provoking.

Hassan lies on his stomach on the floor of his living room breathing hard after completing a round of 25 push-ups. A short way off, he sees his six-year-

old son pushing small, greenish army soldiers toward awaiting tan soldiers. The tan soldiers are lined up in a neat row facing him sternly. He is saying something quietly, and Hassan picks up the words. "I am going to kill you. You are all going to die. None of you will survive." Hassan picks up a green soldier that is also lying on his stomach and moves the soldier back and forth as if it is crawling. He whispers to his son, "He is sneaking up on the enemy. He is going to surprise them." Suddenly, a yell emanates from behind the line of tan soldiers and they are forcefully pushed and hurled at the father's small charge. The green soldier is overwhelmed in a crush of tan. "He's DEAD!!!" shouts the boy, as he leaps onto the father's back. "I won, YOU lost," the son says, laughing. "He was no match for my forces."

Let us examine all that is going on during this play. First, there is the obvious content of the communication: the soldiers, killing, death, military strategy, winning, losing, yelling, laughing, and physicality. These words and ideas are the "language" of the play, what we refer to as the metaphor of the play. It is the surface story that is being told by the parties in the play. We can observe this part of the communication. For our purposes, let's call this the "tangible" part of play—its words and actions. Second, there is the underlying content of the communication: the competitiveness, power struggle, intensity, anger, anxiety, rules, attempts to control (or master) violence and death, and the limit testing. All these exist within the play. This part is unseen, and fathers can guess its nature by thinking about the possible meanings behind the play. This is the "intangible" part of the play—it's about "seeing" beyond the obvious/tangible, in order to challenge and push beyond the boundaries of reality, which is a function of imagination. In many ways it's about the mischief that jesters throughout time have played. In what reality can children kill their father, destroy their father, or overpower their father and the father be unharmed, unperturbed, and still love them? For children, mischief, the unbounded playing around with their surroundings, is filled with existential life questions—I am okay? Is this wrong? Did I overstep? Can I hurt you? Will I get in trouble for saying/doing these things? Are you going to stop me? And it is filled with possibility and promise.

The Tangible Parts of Play

The Jester archetype holds the parts of the father that engages with and responds to all parts of play. For many fathers, the "tangible" part of the play is relatively straightforward and enjoyable. Whatever the child is doing— whether it is playing with dolls, building with Legos, creating something with Play-Doh, drawing pictures, singing children songs, wrestling or throwing a ball—fathers typically have fun, ask questions, and participate in these activities. The visual and physical elements of this aspect of play are easy to think about and to see ourselves doing with our children.

A father runs a foot race in the park
A father constructs a cabin out of Lincoln Logs
A father plays on the PS4
A father sets up rooms in a dollhouse
A father plays hide and seek in the woods
A father reads a book before bed
A father wrestles on the couch
A father paints fingernails and toenails
A father shoots basket balls
A father conducts a science experiment
A father makes tie-dye shirts
A father paints Easter eggs
A father watches a favorite television show

If we see play as a basic form of interacting with one's surroundings, then all children have at least some innate ability to play. The words and actions fathers use to engage in this part of play exist in us because fathers have all been children and we have memories of our own play. The details of these memories may vary from individual to individual, from family to family, from society to society, but the seeds exist.

Obstacles to Accessing the Tangible

Some fathers can get caught up in the day-to-day responsibilities of life and the time and effort that these responsibilities require. Although this is a natural development of adulthood, it may work to alter a father's ideas about what play represents to him in his adult life and, by extension, what place the Jester has in his child's life. A father has work to do, and so do his children. Sometimes fathers may believe that play is what their children want to do when they do not want to work or be responsible. That instead of using the Jester, the father should make them do chores (the Captain archetype) or do their homework (the Educator archetype). The work and growth of the child does not (should not) have to be an either-or proposition. Work and play, can be in balance.

To this end, it is important that decisions regarding how much play and what types of play are appropriate are made with an awareness that, like a child's mind, a healthy adult mind needs to be able to enjoy play and that a healthy adult mind needs to be able to relax a "blow-off steam" (Bellack,

1973; Kris, 1975). To children, play is the work of growth and learning—it's just not the way adults do it. The Jester contains a father's memories of this fact.

Other fathers can feel that play is exclusively a vehicle for learning. In one scenario, a father teaches his child how to throw a baseball, focusing on the act of throwing, the technique, and not the mutuality of throwing a ball back and forth. Notice the word "teach" as opposed to play. Fathers teach ball instead of play ball. This is a choice of Educator archetype over Jester archetype. In another scenario, fathers focus on the rules of the play as opposed to the play itself. A father plays a board game with his child and will not allow for an alteration of the rules, will not allow for cheating, will not allow for any version of the game other than the rules on the box. This is a choice of Captain over Jester. Fathers who have some difficulty with allowing the performance part of the play to take shape according to the child, seem to retain some level of underlying anxiety about this process. Although each father may know the actual reason, it may be that using the Jester feels too immature, irresponsible, or regressive (one remembers feeling young when we play) and that this sensation feels somehow uncomfortable.

Ted walks into the bedroom and his 13-year-old son looks up from the computer screen, laughing quietly, and smiles. He asks his son, "What's so funny?" No answer. Ted realizes that his son has head phones on. "What's so funny?" he asks louder. His son, head phones still on, answers at an elevated volume "Memes! Dad, you should check these out, they are so funny." Ted sits down next to his son and his son begins to show him his favorite memes. They range from politics to potty-humor. Ted thinks some are very funny, others not so much. His son cannot stop laughing at these, deep belly laughs with snorts and his eyes watering. Seeing his son double over in hysterics is infectious and Ted starts laughing too.

Any number of archetypes could have come to fore at the moment the father entered the room.

1. The rule making disciplinarian of the Captain saying the son has gone beyond his allotted time on the computer and that he spends too much time on it or that the material is inappropriate; or
2. The realistic, learner of the Educator asking the son to explain why Vines are funny, or what types of people make Vines and post them; or
3. The concerned, environmental control of the Protector indicating that the son should be cautious about looking at memes because one cannot be sure who posted them and that some may be inappropriate.

The Jester, though, connects father and son through the joint enjoyment of the absurdity of the content, leaving the requirements of these other archetypes for another more appropriate time and place. The Jester archetype also provides the child with the temporary father as a "buddy"—the accepting, nonjudgmental friendship aspects of fathering one's child. While this, at times, can blur the boundaries between adult and child—sometimes this is what a child needs in order to feel loved.

Brandon watches his 4-year-old son put on his sister's frilly pink ballet tutu. His son then pretends to fly around the room telling his father that he is a fairy princess. Brandon feels challenged by his son's choice of play. However, he decides to play with his son and pretends to fly around the room with him as another fairy princess. This soon devolves into a game of tag that then becomes an opportunity to tickle his son. His son responds with squeals of delight and takes off the tutu so he can run faster.

Should he redirect his son's play—the Educator archetype? Should he label his son's play as inappropriate (in terms of sexual orientation or gender roles) for a boy—the Captain archetype? Should he consider his son to be gay or transgender and vow to insulate him from the world's prejudices—the Protector archetype? The Jester archetype does not overreact to the son's choice of play. Rather the father, as Jester, joins the son's play with acceptance and without judgment—knowing that his son is practicing and working through some developmental necessity. Brandon's feelings and ideas about his son wearing "girl's" clothing may be challenged as his boy grows and matures. Perhaps his son will have a fluid gender identity. In this case, maintaining father as Jester, while adding father as Educator, Protector, and Nurturer helps Brandon assist his son in managing a world that may not accept and understand him.

The Intangible Part of Play

Victor sits on his 5-year-old daughter's bed; the girl rests her head on his thigh. "Do you think Piper will like the new clothes that Santa brought her?" she asks. "Of course," he says, "Santa knows that Piper has been good, and he knows what all children want." She hands him the doll, "take off all her clothes and put on her new outfit." Victor gently removes the doll's pants and shirt. "When is Piper going to be old enough to dress herself?" he asks. His playfulness in adding a "real world" comment to his daughter's play results in his daughter yelling. "DAD!!! She's a BABY!" chides his daughter. "She is always going to be a baby." Victor puts the new dress on Piper and hands the doll back to his daughter. His daughter laughs. "You did it wrong, the snaps are supposed to be in the back, not the front." Then she looks stern. "Didn't your mom ever teach you how to dress properly?" He is startled to hear criticism. He makes an "oops" look. "You are Piper's mother, and I think she just needs you to make everything perfect." Victor waits for a moment while his daughter redresses Piper, then adds, "Life is a lot funnier, though, when things are not perfect."

Within the intangible part of a child's play, fathers use the Jester archetype to deepen their understanding of and connection to their children. The intangible part of play is more complex and subtle than the tangible. What becomes important is how a child is feeling during play. What fathers focus on is how their children understand the dynamics happening between the father and child. This aspect of play requires some detective work as its meanings must be inferred (though educated guesswork).

Rodney listens to his 15-year-old son explain about the fight that happened on the field after school. He listens with half an ear, angry about the 3-day, in-school suspension his son received. "It was nothing, Pop. Everyone's taking this too seriously. It was just a joke. Delia's been messin' around with James and Julian likes Delia and so James and Julian had to fight. No one got hurt, it's like one hit stuff, then everyone grabs them and it's over. It's just what we do. Please, don't take my phone, I already got in trouble at school." Rodney looks at his son trying to process what he is saying about fighting, girls, boys and punishments and feels confused and overwhelmed.

We understand that it may be difficult to see fighting as play, but it is. Most living creatures do this on a regular basis to develop gross motor skills, work though relational dynamics and expend excess energy. In this scenario, Rodney's son is acknowledging that there is more at work here than a straight-forward "fight" to do harm. There are relational dynamics at play—control, dominance, love, sexual attraction—intangibles that we cannot see, but can use the Jester archetype to identify. If we look deep enough we may even be able to see the powerlessness that accompanies all youths, especially those of oppressed populations.

Of course, this understanding will need to be balanced through the involvement of the Protector (safety) and the Captain (rules and consequences). Rodney as Jester, though, can safely wonder with his son who won the fight, does Delia have to go with the winner; or, even, whether Delia is pretty enough that boys fight over her? At the same time, the Protector archetype can wonder about the safety issues of son fighting and the Educator archetype can wonder if his son even knows how to fight. As his son has already been punished by the school (Captain archetype), Rodney can believe that eventually additional punishment at home may be justified, but for now, as Jester, engaging the playful, empowering aspect of his child's development is equally important.

Let's re-examine the list of the tangible parts of play from earlier in the chapter and overlay the possible meanings within the intangible realm. It is important that we look for the intangibles in any act of play:

A father runs a foot race in the park (the underlying message is a child's competitiveness and power, "I am faster than you").

A father constructs a cabin out of Lincoln Logs (creativity and control, "I don't like your ideas about the design").

A father plays on the PS4 (competitiveness and power, "I am better than you").

A father sets up rooms in a dollhouse (nurturing, creativity, "I want everyone to sleep in the same room").

A father plays hide and seek in the woods (trust and autonomy, "I want to go where no one will ever find me).

A father reads a book before bed (separation and trust, "I am afraid when you turn out the lights").

A father wrestles on the couch (autonomy and closeness, "I love when you hold me when I want to be held").

A father paints fingernails and toenails (nurturing, creativity and vulnerability, "You make me feel special and loved").

A father shoots basketballs (power and modeling, "I want to do it my own way").

A father helps to conduct a school science experiment project (autonomy, trust, and creativity "I don't care what the results are").

A father helps to make tie-dye shirts (autonomy, creativity, and choice "I want to more of one color").

A father helps to paint Easter eggs (autonomy, creativity, and choice, "I want to see what happens when I break an egg").

A father watches a favorite television show (validation and trust, "I wish I could be one of these characters").

Fathers' Difficulties with the Intangible

The intangibles of play are embedded in the messages that children send out through their play activities. Sometimes these messages, like Rodney's son's fighting, can be sad, troubling, frustrating or overwhelming to the Protector archetype, the Captain archetype, Educator archetype and the Nurturer archetype, but the Jester archetype is able to tolerate all types of messages communicated by a child's play. Participating in your child's play in some way—through direct engagement or by more passive means such as observation—creates intimacy. Intimacy is one of the major intangibles of play.

The Jester archetype enables the father to enjoy and participate in the play, while appreciating the intimacy of being playmates. Yet, fathers locked into the Captain archetype may find intimacy disruptive to their authority and rules. Fathers who depend on the Educator archetype may find intimacy distracting from their lesson plan and contrary to the correct way that the play is being conducted. Fathers focused on the Protector archetype may experience all play on a continuum of safety concerns and be hyper-aware of the play needing to be contained. The father who relies on the Nurturer archetype may find that the intimacy propels them to disrupt the tangible aspects of play with demonstrations of "affection" or "sentimentality" centered on offering many choices and being too concerned about the child's well-being.

Recall Antoine and his son from the previous chapter, from years earlier.

Antoine, a worried father, watches his 4-year-old son roll his toys from one end of the room to the other. At times, his son spins the toys while humming three tuneless notes. Just a year ago, his son played with his toys like any other child his age. He once spoke in full sentences, but now rarely speaks at all. He hardly ever sleeps more than an hour at a time. According to the specialists who examined his son these are all symptoms of Autism. He watches his son play and tries not to cry. Then, Antoine gets down on the floor, spins some of his son's toys, and rolls them from one side of the room to the other. He, too, hums the three tuneless notes. He feels closer to his son. His son does not outwardly act as though he notices his father. After a few weeks of playing next to each other, his son gives Antoine toys to spin. The son seems to smile and then Antoine allows himself to cry. His son interrupts him by offering another toy to be spun. And so, Antoine spins the toy enabling the play to continue.

Throughout history the Jester was the confidante, a person that would listen to anything. The message of the boy with autism in the example seems to be "I am present, I know you are here with me, I know you care for me and so I offer you my toys to spin, so I can feel closer to you in a way that is safe and comfortable for me." This is a message only the Jester archetype can hear.

Mischief Making and the Jester Archetype's Dilemma

As it pertains to children, mischief is defined as playful misbehavior or trouble making. As much as the world of grownups find this aspect of youth frustrating, annoying, and/or infuriating, mischief—also called testing limits—is as fundamental to healthy child development as breathing. As we discussed in Chapter 4, limit testing, rule breaking, boundary challenging are all dynamics that help children learn where their place is in the world around them.

Where the Jester archetype comes into play, is the framing of rule test-ing/breaking not as "bad" but as pleasurable and even, empowering. Con-forming to rules and structure is a serious endeavor that requires a level of control over oneself. The vigilance that this control asks of children is exhausting and so children engage in mischief—the acts of flouting rules, losing control, and generally not being serious. The Jester archetype sees this mischief for what it is, another form of play. In this case, a hybrid of Patrick's and Vygotsky's forms of play. A child feels energized and achieves a level of relief through the purposeful discounting of the structures that form his world—misbehaving.

Carmine, an annoyed father, stands out of sight in the hallway that leads into the living room as he watches his two sons, ages 11 and 7, race in and out of his view, yelling and laughing ... and throwing a FOOTBALL! He thinks, "How many times have I told them? If they break anything I am going to punish them, forever!" His older son shouts, "Rodgers drops back to pass" [he throws the ball] and hits Nelson across the middle. His younger son leaps up, catches the ball and hurls himself into the air and onto the couch. "TOUCHDOWN!" they cheer and the older and much bigger son runs and jumps on the younger child. Carmine cringes and thinks, "He is being so rough." He steps into the room to put an end to the "game" and his sons turn to him. "Dad! Did you see that, it was AWESOME!" Carmine smiles....

Of course, the sons know the rules. It just does not matter, in this moment. They follow rules at school, in the neighborhood, crossing the street, at their friends' homes, with the babysitter, but now It is time for freedom from rules and the power and enjoyment that this can bring. As the Captain struggles with running and jumping in the home, and the Protector worries about potential for injury, and the Educator contemplates how much the fur-niture is going to cost to replace, the Jester reminds all of them that there is a time and a place for everything.

Children need to test the limits that society puts on them. This skill is learned through a version of play that many in our society misinterpret as acting out or acting up. In point of fact, the art of mischief making is a first step in a line of personal development that leads all the way to self-promotion and self-advocacy. Through an understanding of these dynamics, fathers can provide their children with the acceptance and reinforcement necessary to push back. This element of the Jester becomes all the more important if we take into consideration the all-to-real biases and "isms" that exist in our soci-ety. When the rules and structures around us are prejudiced, exploitive, and unfair, it is the Jester archetype that conveys a father's acceptance to his child that challenging or deconstructing these injustices within their own limited means is justified. The child can be strong when the society tells him he should be weak, he can be the peacemaker instead of being violent, he can be superior instead of being inferior, and he can be smart instead of being "slow."

As with all the archetypes, balance is essential. When it comes to mischief making, fun and shades of gray, the Jester and the Captain must be both present and coordinated. In fact, the Jester is a useful supplement for all the other archetypes and one that we believe fathers often use instinctively. From feeding the child play ("here comes the airplane") to math games to silly faces that help cheer up a child to morality tales of Pinocchio and the boy who cried wolf, the Jester can and should have a place in everything we do with our children.

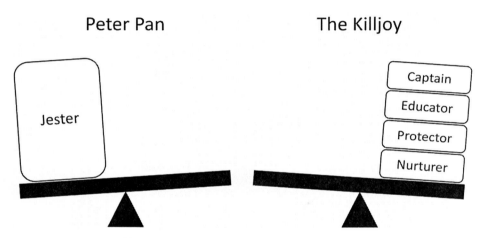

Figure 8.1—Peter Pan (access to Jester only) and the Killjoy (access to all archetypes except Jester archetype).

Peter Pan

The Jester archetype enables an environment in which rules have a bit of flexibility depending on the situation. In this way the Jester archetype demonstrates an antidote to black and white thinking; introducing a notion of the shades of gray in between. That said, the Jester archetype can, at times, undermine the rules of the household, discounting, testing, or even dismissing the rules and structure of his own family. We call this father, Peter Pan, and this is the over expression of the Jester archetype.

Kenneth and his 13-year-old daughter argue about her shutting down her electronics for the night. He has been having this debate with her for weeks now, ever since he got her the phone for her birthday. He asks his co-workers about it and they tell him to take the phone at 8:00 p.m. no matter what and plug it in for her so she has it the next day. This, they say, kills two birds with one stone: getting her off the phone and preparing her for the next day. What he wrestles with is the fact the he does not see his daughter as much as he used to because of the divorce and he wants her to have fun when she is with him. Saying no to her just ends up in a fight and she looks so happy when she is talking to her friends. The bigger problem is that he is getting angry texts from his ex-wife that their daughter is coming home tired from her stays with him.

The father as Peter Pan creates difficulties in the family's dynamics in a variety of ways:

1. The divorced father who uses the Jester to change all the rules when his children visit in order to fulfill his wish to be the "cool" parent or the more loved parent.
2. The single father who uses the Jester to justify giving his children junk food for breakfast to make-up for the missing/absent parent.
3. The father who uses the Jester because he is uncomfortable with the Captain archetype and feels like he is mean when he says "no," having difficulty setting limits and rules for his children.
4. The anxious father who uses the Jester's playful, humorous elements to deflect the inevitable seriousness of certain life situations such as errors made by his child during the course of their natural development.

The Killjoy

The Killjoy is an under expression of the Jester archetype and the alter ego of Peter Pan's frivolous stance toward life, play and freedom. The Killjoy is frightened of the chaos he believes would ensue as children become over stimulated by their fantasies, laughter and over exuberance. He seeks to contain, control and confine a child's emotional, playful expression as a way of maintaining order. This variant of the Jester archetype sees the rule challenging, play-orientated aspect of the father-child relationship as unnecessary and unwanted. In fact, this father sees the related lack of seriousness as a sign of weakness in human nature and potentially dangerous. Fathers as Killjoys are aptly named as they focus on eliminating the various forms of play in which a child obtains considerable joy. It is important to note that the Killjoy expresses the absence of the Jester archetype, not simply by avoiding play, but also by over-investment in the rules, inappropriate competitiveness and trash talk that is belittling or humiliating.

Cliff sits with his 8-year-old son playing tennis on their Wii gaming system. They do not speak except when Cliff taunts his son with jibes—"You stink. I'm totally going to crush you." "Ha, ha, you are going to have to play better than that to beat me." His son sits in focused silence with a forlorn look on his face as Cliff scores point after point. When the game is over, Cliff turns toward his son. "You should practice more. Do you want to play again?" His son says no and gets up to go. Cliff shrugs and starts the game again.

Cliff, like many fathers whose children play sports, instruments, or have other hobbies, maintains the pressure-laden stance "If you can't do it right, don't do it." This requires the abandonment of an essential aspect of childhood—that of the irresponsible, unfettered joy of being a kid. Father as Killjoy increases his child's feelings of inferiority and inadequacy and can reinforce negative cultural messages.

9

An Overview of
Fathers' Characteristics

The battle between the ideas of "nature" and "nurture" is an ongoing one in the intellectual world of the developmental psychologists, psychiatrists, neuroscientists, social workers, educators, parents, and even politicians. When it began is debatable. In the later 16th century, Richard Mulcaster, the headmaster of the Merchant Taylor School in London, was quoted as saying "treasure ... bestowed on [the students] by nature, to be bettered in them by nurture" (DeMolen, 1991). The concepts were first more widely used scientifically by Sir Francis Galton, considered to be the founder of eugenics, and a relative of Charles Darwin, the author of *The Origin of Species*. Galton (1883) focused on what traits get passed on from generation to generation. Based on his chosen field of study of eugenics, and the all-to-often tragic application of its bias-inducing and discredited research throughout history (research that led to policy horrors such as the Holocaust and Apartheid), Galton's point of view is easy to dismiss. That said, even Galton could not completely eschew the fundamental interrelatedness of nature and nurture in a human being. Although eugenicists since Galton's time have strived and hoped to understand the workings of the human being from a purely genetic point of view, Galton was forced to concede that only when peoples' internal struggle between nature and nurture was controlled for the variable nurture would there exist a set of circumstances in which nature's influence would win out over nurture (Galton, 1883). In other words, one would need to have everyone living under exactly the same circumstances to truly identify that nature was more influential in how individuals develop (West & King, 1987).

Because the playing field of human development is not even, we think it only fair to consider that both nature or nurture—to one degree or another—may influence the course that a person takes in their development. The "nature" group, focused on heredity, believes that one's overall development including thoughts, decisions and choices are most affected by biological

143

determinants (DNA and genes) and that people are born with a certain physiological makeup that guides them through life. The "nurture" group claims that one's environment shapes the way one is cared for and brought up and can override one's biological makeup. The latter idea is the hallmark of B. F. Skinner's behaviorism (Skinner, 1966, 1974). These two competing stances have remained at odds, with the idea that one or the other must be true. However, the more research is done, taking sides seems more and more shortsided and myopic. The more we know about people the more it becomes obvious that both nature and nurture have an effect on one's development (Bateson & Gluckman, 2011; Blumberg, 2005; Gottlieb, 2007; Jablonka & Lamb, 2005; Lewontin, 2000; Lickliter, 2008; Gander, 2003; Tabery, 2014; Noble, 2006; Oyama, 2000).

The impact of the area of research called epigenetics, the study of how the environment affects genes and how genes convey information within a person, has provided data that seems to conclude that nature and nurture are significantly interrelated (Moore, 2015). This scientific area of exploration indicates that genes influence one's development through the genetic "expression," while how each gene expresses itself is highly correlated to a person's environment—stress, trauma, nutrition, and environmental factors like toxins (Moore, 2015). In this way, an interplay exists between nature and nurture that can guide an understanding of people within the family structure including fatherhood.

Gordon Allport developed a theory that focused on the individuality of a person. This theory, sometimes called the Trait Theory of Personality, was devised in response to Allport's contention that the professionals within the fields of mental health, researchers and clinicians alike, were too disconnected from the realities of the individual, whether that be nature or nurture. Allport believed that each person's personality and individuality is made up of a combination of characteristics that drove that person's behaviors and thought processes and that each person has the motivation to decrease tension (generated by internal and external factors) and improve his or her situation (Allport, 1937; Allport, 1954; Allport, 1955, Allport, 1961; Boeree, 2006). He originally identified 4000 characteristics that were later culled and reworked by Raymond Cattell (Cattell, 1946, 1957, 1990). Cattell's list is as follows.

Table 9.1—Characteristics of Personality

Abstractedness	Imaginative vs. Practical
Apprehension	Worried vs. Confident
Dominance	Forceful vs. Submissive
Emotional Stability	Calm vs. High Strung
Liveliness	Spontaneous vs. Restrained
Openness to Change	Flexible vs. Attached to the Familiar
Perfectionism	Controlled vs. Undisciplined

Privateness	Discreet vs. Open
Reasoning	Abstract vs. Concrete
Rule Consciousness	Conforming vs. Non-Conforming
Self-Reliance	Self-Sufficient vs. Dependent
Sensitivity	Tender-Hearted vs. Tough-Minded
Social Boldness	Uninhibited vs. Shy
Tension	Impatient vs. Relaxed
Vigilance	Suspicious vs. Trusting
Warmth	Outgoing vs. Reserved

Adapted from Cattell & Meed, 2008; Conn & Rieke, 2004.

Allport believed that these characteristics were made up of both innate and experiential influences. He maintained that an individual could know these characteristics and work with them and change them. We see this list as a starting point; a manifest description of the way people act and/or feel.

In this section, we have created our own characteristics for fathers, pulling from many different developmental theorists, researchers, anthropologists, and historians including the Allport/Cattell attributes. Like the archetypes, this list of five interrelated "characteristics" of fatherhood is meant to provide insight into the "complete" father in a way that helps us understand fathers and fatherhood in a more complete manner. A father's access and expression of the fatherhood archetypes are influenced by these characteristics which then, in turn, drive the fathering activities of men. They each build on one another like interlocking bricks in a wall. The characteristics are

- temperament (the general overall presentation of self)
- relational dynamics (ways of relating to others)
- time orientation (past, present or future focused)
- emotional intelligence (ability to access and interpret emotions)
- world-view (perception of the world on a continuum of safety)

In these characteristics, we see aspects of both nature and nurture at work. There are genetic, heredity-based qualities of people that get passed down from generation to generation and there are aspects of each persons' life experiences that get passed on as well. Here are some examples.

- A father whose life is focused on managing Posttraumatic Stress Disorder-related flashbacks (from past traumatic experiences in wartime, or from growing up in his dangerous and impoverished community, or from the terrifying time in his abusive, childhood home) may find the Protector archetype's activities of staying present and empathic difficult to access and may over-express the Captain archetype's need for control, venturing toward the Corporal and potentially recreating the violence of his own childhood.

- A disciplined and practical father who was brought up in a home in which success in school and going to a good college was by far the most important factor to his parents, may find that the Educator archetype is comfortable and feels natural to him to express with his children. Yet, he may find it difficult to be aware of and unable to express the Nurturer archetype's need to demonstrate love for his children.
- A cautious and shy father who experienced sexual abuse as a child may find that the activities of the Nurturer archetype are too intimate and uncomfortable to access and express. Yet, he may over-express the Protector archetype's need to keep his child safe from predators and may portray the over-expression of the archetype through the Secret Service agent.
- A father who was diagnosed as mildly Autistic as a child, and who exhibited a rigidity and an inflexibility growing up, may find the Captain archetype's structure and rituals familiar and easy to maintain. However, he may find it complicated to access and express the Jester archetype's fluidity and rule changing to the extent that he under-expresses the archetype significantly and displays the Killjoy.
- A father who was raised in an immigrant family whose cultural makeup highlighted and rewarded rigid structure and rules (and dissuaded acting out) may find the Captain archetype's focus on routines and discipline extremely comforting. However, he may struggle as acculturation and assimilation dynamics affect the development of his children and they begin to make demands on him that require greater use of other archetypes that do not seem connected to his country or culture of origin.

These are just several depictions of the related nature of a father's characteristics and his ability to have an awareness of and a comfort with accessing and expressing specific fatherhood archetypes. As we go through each characteristic, we want fathers to consider both their children and themselves. A thorough understanding of these characteristics and areas of development will ultimately allow for a more comprehensive use of the archetypes. As we believe in the equal importance of nature and nurture, we view the awareness of fatherhood characteristics and the related access to the full pantheon of fatherhood archetypes as providing us with the most comprehensive access to fathering choices, behaviors and actions. The third part of our book will examine the combination and interplay of these factors.

10

Fathers' Temperaments and Impact on Archetype Access

When Stella Chess, Alexander Thomas, Herbert Birch and Margaret Hietzig began researching children's personality traits in 1956, they called it the New York Longitudinal Study. Over time, the study's researchers determined that children are born with nine identifiable attributes. These components are aspects of a child's general expression of him—what could be called aspects of one's personality. These aspects can affect a range of behaviors, choices and thoughts from how a child interacts with others to how a child eats and sleeps, to how she or he manages basic day-to-day tasks (Chess & Thomas, 1956). Following this line of reasoning, the boy who then grows up to be a father retains many of these aspects of temperament into adulthood. Maturation and life experiences, both enriching and depleting, may then alter the expression of temperament to include other new aspects of self-expression. We do not view temperament as fixed. We believe that temperament, while creating a life-long foundation to the self, can be molded and shaped through maturation, learning, life experiences, and resolve.

There are nine aspects of temperament described in the literature: activity level, adaptability, relatedness, distractibility, intensity, mood, persistence, regularity and sensory threshold (see Table 10.1).

Table 10.1—Aspects of Fathers' Temperaments

- Activity Level—how a person physically engages with his environment
- Adaptability—how a person manages the changes or transitions that occur in everyday life
- Relatedness—how a person interacts with other people on a day to day basis including children and adults
- Distractibility—how a person is able to manage external factors like sounds or smells while trying to engage in a typical task

- Intensity—how a person reacts to an everyday situation that is not in his control
- Mood—how a person feels in general about typical life events and experiences
- Persistence—how a person reacts to everyday adversity or challenges like learning a new skill or figured out a problem
- Regularity—how often, when, and in what pattern a person's every-day physiological needs (like hunger, thirst, sleep, or excretion) are expressed
- Sensory Threshold—how a person interprets the effect of external stimuli (sound, light, touch, smell) on his physical and emotional boundaries

Adapted from Chess & Thomas, 1977; Weiner & Gallo-Silver, 2018.

Each aspect of temperament can be described on a continuum—from one end to another with extreme versions at each of the poles. Based on the research on children, we have extrapolated how these aspects might be expressed by adults. Each father falls somewhere within a range of expression (see Figure 10.1).

If we examine closely these disparate aspects that underpin a father's temperament, we can begin to see trends. These trends allow us to place different aspects in group-ings with thematically similar dynamics like control, adaptability

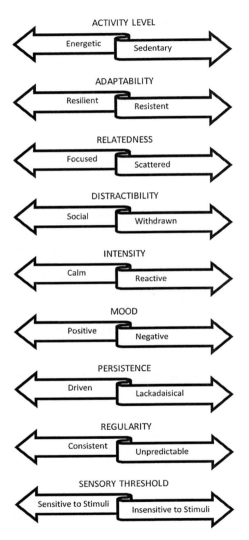

Figure 10.1—Range of expression of fathers' aspects of temperament (adapted from Chess & Thomas, 1977).

or restraint. These groupings are what Chess and her cohorts described an individual's overall temperament. She and her colleagues believed that three such identifiable temperaments existed (although they saw overlap between the groups) (Chess & Thomas, 1977). They are identified as follows:

- Feisty
  - ⊙ Energetic
  - ⊙ Resistant
  - ⊙ Driven
  - ⊙ Negative Outlook
  - ⊙ Over-Reactive to External Stimuli
- Cautious
  - ⊙ Sedentary
  - ⊙ Resistant
  - ⊙ Withdrawn
  - ⊙ Worried Outlook
  - ⊙ Avoidant of External Stimuli
- Flexible
  - ⊙ Resilient
  - ⊙ Social
  - ⊙ Calm
  - ⊙ Positive Outlook
  - ⊙ Under Reactive to External Stimuli

Thomas and Chess proposed these temperaments for childhood. The temperaments were not equally distributed among children. Feisty children made up 40 percent of the group, 15 percent cautious and 10 percent flexible. The study indicated that other 35 percent of the group exhibited some combination of temperaments (Chess and Thomas, 1990, 1996; Thomas & Chess, 1956, 1977). As we did with Jung's archetypes, we have re-interpreted these temperaments (and renamed them) for the purpose of shifting the focus to specifically address fathers and fatherhood. In this way, we can begin to understand how temperament affects a father's access and use of various archetypes. The temperaments are as follows:

- Strong-Willed
  - ⊙ Energetic
  - ⊙ Resistant
  - ⊙ Driven
  - ⊙ Negative Outlook
  - ⊙ Over-Reactive to External Stimuli
- Reserved
  - ⊙ Sedentary

- ⊙ Resistant
- ⊙ Withdrawn
- ⊙ Worried Outlook
- ⊙ Avoidant of External Stimuli
- Movable
  - ⊙ Resilient
  - ⊙ Social
  - ⊙ Calm
  - ⊙ Positive Outlook
  - ⊙ Under Reactive to External Stimuli.

For example, let us recall Katsuo from Chapter 8. Katsuo is playing a "baseball" game with his son—a game his son made up and called Innings. In this game, Katsuo is asked to forgo the recognizable features of a baseball game for his son's imaginary play.

If Katsuo has a "Strong-Willed" temperament, he would be resistant to change and have a need for things to go according to plan. He would be uncomfortable accessing the Jester archetype. The rules and regulations so much a part of the Captain archetype or the instructional nature of the Educator archetype would react negatively to his son's made-up game such as Innings. Katsuo would not play Innings with his son but insist on following the real rules of baseball even though only the two of them were playing (the Captain archetype). He may also focus on practicing his son's throwing and batting method in order to improve his skills (the Educator archetype).

If Katsuo has a "Reserved" temperament, he could be resistant to the chaos or unpredictability of a game like Innings. He may see the game's fluidity and uncertainty as overly stimulating and wish to distance himself from the discomfort and the anxiety that it creates. This temperament can lead to an over-reliance on the Protector archetype, fearing that his son will be teased by other boys for not playing a more realistic version of baseball. It may also lead to an over-reliance on the Educator archetype in order to teach his son about the importance of the rules of baseball.

If Katsuo has a "Moveable" temperament, the social ability associated with this temperament would enable him to adapt to his son's game. The playfulness represented by the Jester archetype allows for more openness to the bending of reality that are integral elements in nearly all forms fantasy and imaginary play. This temperament can lead more easily to a balanced use of the other archetypes in conjunction with his son's playful creation— the Captain to explore the new rules, the Educator to praise, note and admire his creativity, the Nurturer to create the time and attention for other opportunities to play, and the Protector to validate his son's pride.

Before we move on, we want to caution against conflating temperament with issues of power or vulnerability. While a Strong-Willed man may be perceived by others as controlling and decisive, this does not mean that he is powerful. Similarly, because a Reserved man is quiet and cautious, this does not mean that he is meek. We understand that there is always a link between nature and nurture, between an individual's innate qualities and their environment, but too easily in our society, temperament is used as a way of expressing incorrect values (and, often, pejorative ones) about individuals. A Strong-Willed man of color may be considered "uppity" or "menacing" by others. A Reserved man of any race or ethnicity may be thought of as soft, or within certain prejudiced areas of our society, may have to contend with wrong-headed typecasts centered on homophobic slurs or sexist stereotypes. A Moveable man may be seen as wishy-washy, spineless, a "squish" as politicians like to label their foes. These, and other stereotypes, substantially miss the point about temperament's role in decision-making and create additional obstacles for important fathering activities.

The Automatic Responses of Temperament

Since temperament is a characteristic based on a father's inherent nature, it often induces reflexive responses, ones that a father feels that he needs to have or is compelled to have (Ellis, 2001). A father may face a dilemma as to how to manage these automatic responses based on his temperament. The examples of Katsuo, above, theorize and illustrate that each temperament brings with it its own form of automatic response.

We believe that fathers with a Strong-Willed or Reserved temperament often gravitate toward an unbalanced use of the archetypes. Their need for control and resistance to change creates the possibility for an over-emphasis of one archetype over others. While bringing a more adjustable stance toward most fathering situations, fathers with a Moveable temperament may find it more complicated to settle on one specific archetype, if a situation demands it. Unlike the other temperaments, the "roll with it" of the Movable temperament may create some reticence about standing firm.

For our purposes, understanding the relationships between a father's temperament and the five archetypes is the first step in reducing the frequency of automatic responses. As certain temperaments rely more heavily on certain archetypes and certain expressive tendencies within each archetype, knowing these connections can aid in making alternative decisions.

When a father with a *Strong-Willed* temperament has difficulties, he seeks to manage his anxiety about not being in enough control while child-rearing.

- He runs the risk of overusing the *Captain archetype* as he feels the need to establish control with the use of rules and regulations. If the rules and regulations do not re-establish his control the father may believe he needs to use the *Corporal* and try to enforce the rules by overpowering his child using physical discipline or another method that diminishes his view of his child's autonomy.
- When using the *Educator archetype*, if he believes that the learning process is not going the way he imagined, or if he becomes frustrated with the learning process in some way, he may use the *Squasher* as a way of taking charge, increasing the academic-related demands on his child and increasing his own level of input into the work.
- When he accesses the *Protector archetype*, he may use the *Secret Service agent* or the *Mind Reader* as he attempts to exert structural control over the child's environment and intellect, in order to eliminate the possibility of danger and/or short circuit the possibility of intense emotional expression, by intrusively "guessing" what the child is thinking.
- When he tries to employ the *Nurturer archetype* he may tend toward using the *Smotherer* version as he believes it enables him to control and manage the child's ever-shifting emotional life and developmental changes by establishing a more pervasive level of closeness through overly-involved caretaking and attention.
- When using the *Jester archetype*, he may tend toward expressing the Jester as the *Killjoy* by seeing play and fun as unnecessary, too unstructured and too undisciplined. The Killjoy sees no use for rule-breaking and wants to control the play or avoid the play before it "gets out of hand."

When a father has a *Reserved* temperament, he seeks to manage the distress and pressure he experiences in having to contend with the conflict, intimacy or spontaneity of child-rearing.

- He tends toward expressing the *Captain archetype* by using the *Abdicator* as he may be apprehensive about over applying rules and regulations and the inherent tensions of limit setting. This is a father who has a hard time saying no.
- When accessing the *Educator archetype*, he may employ the *Skimmer*, only providing cursory help to his child for fear of being overbearing and not allowing the child to learn one his/her own. At other moments, he may present as the *Squasher* as he, regardless

of where his child is developmentally or academically, falls back on his own "tried and true" teaching methods that allow him to remain comfortable, while assisting his child.

- When he uses the *Protector archetype*, he may use the under-expressed version—the *Abandoner*—as he tries to distance himself from the fears associated with the physical risks and closeness of complex emotional expression that tend to accompany a typical child's developmental and maturation.
- Experiencing discomfort with regard to intimacy with his child and having discomfort that his nurturing may create even more dependency, he tends toward conveying the *Nurturer archetype* by using the under-expressed version—the *Rejecter*. This may stem from the belief or wish that there are others in his child's life that can provide these needs to his child more effectively.
- For the cautious temperament father, the *Jester archetype* may be under-expressed by using the *Killjoy* as he may be reluctant to allow for or participate in the unpredictable and spontaneous nature of his child's play, imagination, and fantasy world.

When a father with a *Moveable* temperament struggles, he seeks to manage the self-doubts about his competence and abilities in child-rearing.

- He may express the *Captain archetype* by leaning toward using the *Abdicator* when he finds it uncomfortable applying rules and regulations. He struggles with the idea that he is impeding his children's happiness with these rules and may have a difficult time setting limits. His comfort with exceptions to rules, may lead to no "hard and fast rules."
- When using the *Educator archetype*, he may tend toward employing the *Skimmer*, for fear of obstructing his child's learning in some way, believing that others may instruct more effectively. Or, alternatively, he may manifest as the *Squasher*, out of an insecurity that pushes him to get reactively involved and shape the learning process.
- When he uses the *Protector archetype*, he tends to present as the *Secret Service agent* and the *Mind Reader*, trying to consistently err on the side of caution with regard to his child's safety and well-being and being excessively concerned about the repercussions of missing something important.
- As the *Nurturer archetype*, he tends toward the over-expressing version the *Smotherer*, again, concerned about overlooking a critical aspect of his child's care and concluding that being very close and attentive is more useful, in this regard.

- For the flexible temperament father, the *Jester archetype* may be over-expressed by using *Peter Pan*, as he may be reluctant to disappoint his child or constrain his child's exuberance. This may stem from his worry that his child will not like him if he does not allow for as much "play" as possible.

None of these expressive tendencies are set in stone and all fathers can manifest any of the extreme versions of the archetypal norms. Strong-willed temperament fathers can be Mind Readers and Reserved temperament fathers can be Corporals. Moveable temperament fathers can be Rejecters or Killjoys. That said, what we have presented here are what we understand as the typical automatic responses based on a father's temperament and the logical resulting archetypal reaction. Obviously, the exact expression and structure of the archetypes that a specific father uses depend on a variety of factors of which temperament is just the first that we describe in this book.

Table 10.2—Temperament, Automatic Responses and the Unbalanced Expression of Archetypes

- Strong-Willed temperament fathers SEEK TO MANAGE ANXIETY by using
  - the Corporal as an over expression of the Captain archetype.
  - the Squasher as an over expression of the Educator archetype.
  - the Secret Service Agent or Mind Reader as over expressions of the Protector archetype.
  - the Smotherer as an over expression of the Nurturer archetype.
  - the Killjoy as an under expression of the Jester archetype.
- Reserved temperament fathers SEEK TO MANAGE DISTRESS by using
  - the Abdicator as an under expression of the Captain archetype.
  - either the Skimmer as an under expression or the Squasher as an over expression of the Educator archetype.
  - the Abandoner as an under expression of the Protector archetype.
  - the Rejecter as an under expression of the Nurturer archetype.
  - the Killjoy as an under expression of the Jester archetype.
- Moveable temperament fathers SEEK TO MANAGE SELF-DOUBT by using
  - the Abdicator as an under expression of the Captain archetype.
  - either the Skimmer as an under expression or the Squasher as an over expression of the Educator archetype.
  - the Secret Service agent or the Mind Reader as over expressions of the Protector archetype.
  - the Smotherer as an over expression of the Nurturer archetype.
  - Peter Pan as an over expression of the Jester archetype.

Fathers cannot change their temperaments, but they can establish work-arounds for a fatherhood characteristic that creates some complication for their parenting. *Slowing down* gives father the opportunity to consider (1) his innate preference—what his temperament is "demanding" of him—and (2) what his child may be asking of him. It may allow him to consider different archetypes than the one he would typically choose (his automatic response). It may offer him the option of replacing, adding or subtracting an archetype that more effectively fits the situation before him.

Let us recall Leonard from Chapter 6. Leonard's daughter has requested to go to sleep-away camp and Leonard is struggling with discussing the matter with her and initially says no. Over time, he is able to find a way to talk to her about the possibility. Let us look at how Leonard makes this transition.

Leonard's family of origin is Jewish, following a conservative faith-based system of beliefs. He grew up as the youngest of five children. He was quiet and withdrawn, very rarely speaking. His family members called him the "Mouse" and it was the joke of the family that Leonard could be in the room and no one would notice. Leonard just did not like talking and was not very comfortable with other people in general, but he never told anyone, and no one ever asked. He met his wife at a religious retreat in high school and they got married right after college. She is the social one in the family and his daughter takes after her mother. Leonard has always been quiet and careful. Although he sometimes wishes that he was different, he has taken very few risks throughout his life.

Leonard has a "Reserved" temperament as evidenced by his tendency to limit contact with connections around him, by his quiet nature and by his aversion to risk-taking. For Leonard, his initial decision to end the conversation about camp was an effort to stay away from any uncomfortable discussion (this one happened to create conflict). His daughter's request created anxiety in Leonard. His indication that he was going to delay any discussion, until she was older, was an automatic response that used the Protector archetype focuses the discussion on safety concerns related to her autonomy.

If Leonard has a "Strong-Willed" temperament, his daughter's request for camp may be similarly addressed by the Protector (and possibly even as an over-expression of this archetype). In addition, a strong-willed temperament tends to lend itself to father as Captain, so Leonard may respond to his daughter with a focus on camp as a significant increase in responsibility, a dramatic change of rules, or a complex logistical dilemma.

If Leonard has a "Moveable" temperament, he may focus on not wanting to disappoint his daughter and wanting to apply few barriers to her wishes. He may under express (1) the Captain's rules, (2) the Educator's preparation,

(3) the Protector's need for pacing, and (4) the Nurturer's stressing of appropriate boundaries by over expressing the Jester archetype which focuses on his daughter's enjoyment. Leaving her to figure out the repercussions of the decision on her own.

Goodness of Fit

In addition to the impact of the father's temperament on accessing and expressing archetypes, we also want to point out that the interplay of father and child also affects the father's access and expression of archetypes. The combination of certain temperaments can cause varying levels of conflict between father and child. These combinations can, in and of themselves, be the cause for the over expression or under expression of archetypes depending on the situation. If a child has a feisty temperament and a father has a strong-willed temperament, how does this combination affect the access or expression of specific archetypes? What occurs to archetype access and expression between a father with a reserved temperament and his child, who happens to have a feisty temperament? What are the particulars in archetype access and expression between a father with a strong-willed and a child with a cautious temperament?

This brings us to the issue of "fit." Chess and Thomas articulated the issue of goodness of fit which spoke to the responsiveness of the environment to the temperament of a child (Chess & Thomas, 1999). We are using the concept of goodness of fit in terms of fathers and their children. Not all temperaments naturally fit together. The complexity of a match may give rise to continual conflict between fathers and children. The stress created by this on-going strife may lock fathers into automatic responses, reducing the choices and options of actions to take, and diminishing access to specific archetypes (see Table 10.3).

For example, let's revisit Steven from Chapter 5.

Steven (Moveable) and his son (Cautious) work through the complications of the boy's unfortunate use of the Internet to observe pornography. After disclosing (slowly and with great difficulty) that he looked at sexually explicit material on the Internet, Steven's son needs a great deal of pacing in order to process the events. Steven (as Captain, Educator, Protector, and Nurturer) does not rush through the rules, the details, the repercussions, and the consequences, but allows his son the ability to lead. Although Steven has the strong desire to rescue his son, and the intense feeling to scold his son, his son's temperament (Cautious) requires a softer touch.

Table 10.3—Problematic Temperament Fit

Father Temperament	Child Temperament	Fatherhood Archetype Expression
Strong-Willed	Feisty	Corporal, Squasher
Strong-Willed	Cautious	Secret Service Agent, Mind Reader
Reserved	Feisty	Abdicator, Abandoner, Rejecter
Moveable	Feisty	Peter Pan, Abdicator
Moveable	Cautious	Secret Service Agent, Mind Reader

Let us look back at several scenarios from earlier in the book in order to explore this idea of problematic fit with regard to temperament.

- Errol and his daughter arguing over curfew, from Chapter 4
- Alexander and his son debating getting dressed, from Chapter 4
- Kenneth and daughter try to navigate texting and bedtime, from Chapter 8.

When we examine each of these scenarios for temperament, we can readily identify the fathers' and the children's temperaments. Errol has a Strong-Willed temperament, whereas Alexander displays a Reserved one, and Kenneth has a Moveable temperament. All three have feisty temperament children.

Errol (Strong-Willed) and his daughter (Feisty) clash, as these two individuals, invested in control and anxious without it, push each other around, physically and emotionally. There is very little compromise in their interactions as neither is comfortable with backing down. They often come into conflict. Errol often wishes that he could stop when his daughter "pushes his buttons," but he sees red when she does not listen or flagrantly breaks his rules.

These two temperaments together are a recipe for conflict and automatic responses. Their individual need for control, difficulty with adaptability and resilience make compromise nearly impossible, unless one chooses to relent. This leads to a zero-sum dynamic in which there is often one party experiencing victory and the other loss. When the child is younger, it is the father and his "You will do this my way" stance (as Corporal or Squasher) who often wins these battles. As his child matures, this reality can change, and conflict may become more intense and potentially more volatile.

Alexander (Reserved) and his son (Feisty) go back and forth over the matter of what to wear each morning. His son has very strong feelings about the color, texture, and weight of his clothing and the prolonged struggle to choose an outfit ultimately runs into the necessary departure time for school. Alexander, who becomes very tense around any conflict, has tried to reason with his son, but now often leaves the room, overwhelmed, indicating that his son should just choose. His son, left to his own devices, selects outfits that are often ill-suited for the weather. Alexander knows he needs to set firmer limits. He just feels so much pressure each morning that he has begun to avoid his son altogether.

Both these temperaments need control, the difficulty is that they require this control in different ways—the father needs calm, methodically-oriented decision making, while the son, more viscerally-oriented, needs what he wants at any given moment. The son's presentation is felt by this father as a rejection of his parenting and an emotionally distressing and intrusive. The Reserved father's retreat (the Abdicator, the Abandoner, the Rejecter) in the face of the conflict delays this conflict, sending it underground for the moment. His child is asked to tacitly accept either control (by the father) or isolation (from the father).

Kenneth (Moveable) and his daughter (Feisty) slip down a road that is very difficult to return from as Kenneth finds it highly troublesome to tell his daughter to end her evening socializing. Kenneth never feels particularly comfortable telling his daughter to stop doing something she is enjoying, which, in this case, is texting on her phone and talking to her friends until late at night. Kids are supposed to have fun especially with all the work they have to do in school, so he rarely tells her no. This dynamic has been made more pronounced since the separation and divorce that has limited his time with her. He sees how tired she looks in the morning and knows how difficult it is to wake her up for school, but he just cannot seem to reconcile the mixed roles of caretaking inside his head. The doubt leaves him stuck and mute.

The wish to be helpful that is the basis of a father's Moveable temperament, combined with the demands of a child's Feisty temperament, leave this father in a reactionary predicament. The Moveable father's flexibility and willingness to not challenge the increasingly problematic requests of his daughter (Peter Pan, Abdicator) acts as a sponge for her needs, absorbing them, but not processing their meaning, discussing their underlying difficulties, or limiting them as a way to help her grow and mature. This creates a power differential in favor of the daughter. This ultimately is unhelpful for her as it validates premature autonomy and actually leaves her quite isolated and vulnerable.

A person's temperament can be managed by a person's intellect and learning. A father can be aware of his temperament and how it limits access to the optimal expression of his archetypes. Errol, Alexander and Kenneth have the ability to make more effective choices. Errol could modulate his temperament and detour around his typical automatic response to access and express the Protector and Educator archetypes. He could then, at least, make persuasive arguments about how his daughter needs to and is able to protect herself. Likewise, Alexander's awareness of his temperament could enable him to intellectually consider ways to help his son and he could soon discover that using the Captain and Educator archetypes would help him choose appropriate clothes in a timely way. And finally, Kenneth, could realize how his temperament makes it difficult for him to help his daughter adjust to the divorce and could show her how to use healthier sleep habits by accessing the Nurturer, the Educator, and the Protector archetypes.

11

Fathers' Relational Dynamics and Impact on Archetype Access

Merriam Webster defines a relationship as "the way in which two or more people, groups, countries, etc., talk to, behave toward, or deal with each other" (Merriam-Webster, 2016). Along these lines, we see a relationship as a connection between two or more elements. These elements can be characterized as non-living or inanimate and may include relationships between a spark plug and a car engine, a hammer and a nail, World War II and the Cold War, the moon and the tides. They can also be animate or living relationships such as between two people or a group of animals, or between a person's feelings and an experience. All these relationships are dynamic and can change as the different elements, or our understanding and perceptions of the different elements, change. For our purposes, we are going to focus on the latter group of relationships—the living ones, specifically between people such as the ones below.

Manush and his wife are getting a divorce. They have two children, a son, 17 years old, and a daughter, 14 years old. They have been overtly arguing for several years and have not been getting along for much longer than that. The family tension has been growing and finally the father and the mother decided it was time to end the marriage. Manush moved into an apartment nearby several months ago and sees the children twice a week on average since then. His son plays basketball on the high school team and the father continues to go to his games. His daughter is a swimmer and Manush, who used to go to most of her morning practices with her, now goes to her competitions on the weekends.

There are two aspects of relationships between people that are important to remember and will guide the discussion in this chapter. First, the structure of each relationship has both an objective (fact-based) component and a subjective (opinion-based) one. There are facets that are non-debatable details that any cursory examination of the relationship would identify and, then, there are parts of the relationship that are subject to interpretation and may be viewed in different ways under various circumstances. In the relationship that exists between this father and the mother, from what we know, the objective aspects are

- the arguing that existed between the two parents
- the timing of separation and divorce
- the existence of two teenage children
- the father's attendance at sporting events
- the frequency that the father sees his children

The subjective components of this relationship are more multifaceted and complex in nature:

- the feelings of the two parents, now and in the past, about the marriage and the reasons and responsibility for the separation and the divorce
- the nature of the father's current relationship with his children
- the feelings of the two children about the divorce
- the feelings of the two children about their parents as individuals

The subjective components are defined and understood individually by each element within the relationship:

- the father, mother, and children's ideas of what occurred to disrupt the marriage
- the father and mother's ideas regarding his ongoing role in the family
- the father, mother, and children's feelings about the amount of time the father spends with his children
- the children's sense of their father's altered participation in their lives
- the father, mother, and children's notions of the father's ongoing connection to his children

The differing beliefs, and views of each element within the relationship exist side by side and add to the richness and complexity of the connections. Unlike the objective components of the relationship, there is no identifiable absolute right or wrong within this construct of subjectivity, just perceptions that require examination and understanding. One can decide to take the mother's point of view or the father's or the children's or one can resolve that each has merit from the perspective of that person.

Dieter's 16-year-old son is nervous to learn to drive. His son has not said so outright, but he has not signed up for driver's education even though all of his friends are already signed up. Dieter's son has always approached new tasks by avoidance and delay. He is a boy with many fears and worries. Dieter talks to his son about his fears, concerns and worries about learning to drive. He acknowledges that driving can be dangerous, and adds that it can also be safe, fun, and important for being able to do more with his friends. Dieter offers to teach his son how to drive as a way of helping his son feel more in control— even though it means he will miss some hours at work to accomplish this. Dieter's son protests, feeling that he is making trouble for his dad at work. Dieter makes it clear that he loves his son and would do anything to help him. Being able to drive is necessary to have a full range of experiences—what Dieter believes would be considered a good life. His son acquiesces and hugs his father.

Dieter's offer to help his son is objective. His son's feelings of ambivalence and gratitude at being more at ease because of Dieter's offer is subjective. His son could also have found his father's offer intrusive, overwhelming, infuriating, or inappropriate depending on a variety of factors. It is the perceptions within the relationship of each father and each child that are the crux and foundation of our examination of a father's relational dynamics. Utilizing the subjective reality of each relationship, we will illustrate the two elements that together define the relational dynamics between all fathers and children. They are

- *availability*—the extent to which a father is "open" to his child's flow of verbal and non-verbal information through the varying developmental stages of his child, and
- *responsivity*—the extent to which a father is able to use the verbal and non-verbal information he receives from his child and act upon it in a helpful and productive fashion.

The reason that we have placed these areas of focus within the realm of the subjective is that availability and responsivity are not absolutes. The achievement or struggle that fathers can have in these areas stems from a vast continuum of possible responses that depend on myriad factors from the temperament of a father and his child (which we discussed in the previous chapter) to a family's structure (such as a father who works nights) to unforeseen experiences (like the father who suffers years of grief after losing his co-workers in the World Trade Center on 9/11). There is no one way to be available or to respond. As D. W. Winnicott put it, it is really a matter of being "good enough" (Winnicott, 1953).

Amir works very long hours in the family's moving business. As this is physically draining work, when he is between jobs he tends to stay at home relaxing, which usually entails watching movies or sports on TV. His children, three girls ages 5, 7 and 9, come home from school and want to talk to and play with their father. Although Amir does not want any of his friends to know, he plays dress up, house, tea party and other imaginary activities with his daughters. They often want to paint his toe nails and braid his hair which are his daughters' favorite activities. Amir is available to his daughters. There are other things he wants to do. His muscles are sore, and he enjoys the quiet of not having to cope with anxious or demanding customers, yet his daughters feel that he is accessible to them. He is there for them in ways that help his girls feel loved.

Gabe is not comfortable being left alone with his six-month-old son, but his wife works nights and he takes care of his son while she is away. Gabe works during the day, but he reasons that his wife knows best how to take care of a baby. When his son cries, Gabe is never exactly sure what to do, and frequently calls his wife at work for help. Whenever he calls, he puts his wife on speaker phone because he feels best when he holds his son with two hands. Although he has insecurity about his own decision-making and believes he must reach out to his wife for assistance, Gabe has already provided his son with the most important intervention—he is responsive to his son's cries by holding him while determining what else he might need. Even as an infant, and knowing Gabe is not the mother, his son knows he can count on his father.

Attachment as Availability/Responsivity

A life is conceived, and a fetus grows over the course of months into a baby. As this growth occurs, relationships begin to form, develop and evolve between that unborn child and the individuals participating in his or her life. Each of these relationships has objective components (in utero nourishment, doctor's appointments, talking, humming, discomfort, home preparations) and subjective components (feelings, fears, hopes, wishes, fantasies). When the infant is born, these details of both the objective components and subjective components continue to change. The changes to the relationship center on the evolving development of the child and how the child and the caretakers perceive and understand this developmental process.

Recalling from Chapter 4: The Captain Archetype, John Bowlby named this earliest connection, attachment, and based his theories on his work at a school for children with behavioral difficulties and his research and work, as a child psychiatrist, at various clinics (Bowlby, 1969; Bowlby, 1982). When joined at the Tavistock Clinic in England, by Mary Ainsworth, another developmental psychologist, these two child development pioneers created a strategy to measure attachment and a method to categorize a child's attachment with their caregivers. Ainsworth, trained in Security Theory and its contention that children require a secure connection with a caregiver in order to be "launched" into an unfamiliar world, brought to the discussion the concept of "secure base" (Krumweide, 2014). Based on the oft-deprived child populations that they worked with, both theorists were captivated by the way children respond when they are not given the warmth, consistency and closeness that all children need to thrive and develop in a health manner (Krumweide, 2014). They called this Attachment Theory.

Attachment Theory frames our discourse on a father's availability and responsivity. It can provide an understanding of this part of the parent/child relationship from the child's point of view and from the parents' point of view. The four primary functions that Bowlby (1969; 1982) and Ainsworth (Krumweide, 2014) identified, that exist in all attachment relationships (the objective components to the relationship) are described as follows.

- *Proximity Maintenance*—a father chooses to remain physically near his child for the purpose of creating a sense of well-being and safety. His child feels safer being near his/her father. Likewise, the father feels the world is safe because his child is safe when his child is near him. The well-being he feels is feeling loved and needed by his child [Carrano, 2006; Genosi & Tallandini, 2009; Gray & Anderson, 2010]. Amir and his three daughters are an example of this.
- *Safe Haven*—a father chooses to offer himself as a refuge for his child when his child is distressed. The child's distress is mitigated by the father's presence when problems arise. Both child and father find a level of comfort and safety knowing that seeking out the father is an option for his child when there is "danger" [Carrano, 2006; Genosi & Tallandini, 2009; Gray & Anderson, 2010]. Gabe and his infant son are an example of this.
- *Secure Base*—a father chooses to serve as a resource and a jumping off point in order to help his child experience new situations and grow. The child grows and explores under the "watchful" eye of the father and feels safe and protected knowing that he or she can return to the father at any time. Both father and child feel safe and comforted knowing that while the father is "launching" his child into the world, the door back home is always open [Levant & Wimer, 2009].
- *Separation Anxiety*—a father is aware of his child's increase in emotional expression when he and his child part and chooses to engage in organizing and structuring the good-bye. The child loves and needs the father and therefore conveys upset (sometimes significant amounts) in the moments after his departure. Both child and father miss each other when apart and, while the

emotional expression may be more acute for the child, the
father, also, has feelings about the farewell [Erikson, 1950; 1968].

The rules are embedded in each of these relational functions. The offering
of protection, provision of safety, and aiding in growth and experiences can
be identified as objective components. This makes clear that according to
Attachment Theory, the father is essential. How the father actually provides
these functions and how the child perceives what the father is providing is
an equally important part of the attachment relationship; these are the subjective components. Another one of Ainsworth's contributions was a measure—she called it the Strange Situation—by which she could assess and
categorize the overall nature of the attachment between father and child by
taking into consideration both the objective and the subjective components
of the relationship (Krumwiede, 2014).

Since his sister and her husband died in a car accident a year ago, Matthew
has full custody of his 3-year-old nephew. Matthew is responsible for dropping
his nephew off at preschool in the mornings. It is his nephew's first experience
in school and Matthew believes the child is nervous. Each day the boy cries and
says he does not want to go to school. In addition to the transition into school,
the death of his parents, and living full-time with his aunt and uncle, he just
became a big brother in the past month with the birth of Matthew's daughter.
When they arrive at school, the crying increases and Matthew holds his clinging
nephew. The teachers try to take the boy, but uncle and nephew cling to each
other. A few times, the teachers successfully get the boy to participate in a morn-
ing activity with other children, only to have Matthew announce loudly that
he is leaving. This prompts his nephew to begin crying again and run to his
uncle. At least 3 days a week, Matthew takes his nephew home without leaving
him at school and delays his own arrival at work.

Matthew's attempts to take his nephew to school and drop him off there
are objective components of this relationship, yet with all the consternation
within both Matthew and the nephew, it is apparent that an examination of
the subjective components is required to establish an accurate understanding
of this relationship. These are

- feelings about transition into an unfamiliar environment like
  school,
- ability to assuage the child's agitation (associated with grief), and
- closeness and security because of the change to the child's family
  structure and dynamics.

Matthew attempts to listen, understand and act on what his nephew is communicating and needs. In this scenario, Matthew's availability and responsivity

are intertwined and the connection to his nephew is compromised—he wants his nephew to feel safe, to feel loved and to have a sense of belonging—and he is unsure what to do. Unfortunately, this difficulty results in his nephew experiencing feelings that range from upset and frightened to sad and angry. The coordination of a workable and comprehensive response to his nephew, that enables Matthew to go to work on time and his nephew to begin pre-school, requires Matthew to find support that will allow him to add levels of availability and responsivity.

Ainsworth and Bowlby proposed attachment types for childhood. From the child's perspective, these attachment types were described as Secure, Inse-cure and, later, Disorganized (Krumwiede, 2014; Mahler, Fine & Bergman, 1975). As we did with Jung's archetypes, we have re-interpreted these rela-tional connections for the purpose of shifting the focus to specifically address fatherhood. In this way, we can begin to understand how attachment and the quality of the father-child relationship affects a father's availability/respon-sivity and his access/use of various archetypes. The following are the three fatherhood attachment styles.

- Accessible—Tends to move fluidly between archetypes and has access to each archetype to one degree or another creating comfort and security within his child. This is accomplished based on to the following qualities.
  - ⊚ Consistency
  - ⊚ Empathy
  - ⊚ Resiliency
- Preoccupied—Tends to fixate on one or two archetypes based on comfort and familiarity creating reduced expectations and increase worry within his child. This result occurs based on the following qualities.
  - ⊚ Distractibility
  - ⊚ Irritability
  - ⊚ Withdrawal
- Intense—Tends to select archetypes that are ineffective for a given situation creating confusion and disorientation within his child. This is created based on the following qualities.
  - ⊚ Impulsiveness
  - ⊚ Over-Reactiveness
  - ⊚ Control

Returning to Matthew and his nephew, we can determine that Matthew's attachment style as Intense. Matthew is impulsive in his decision making about his nephew, he is over-reactive to his nephew's distress, and he is con-trolling as he presents himself as a barrier to his nephew's teachers. While the circumstances of what amounts to a new father/child relationship are tragic, Matthew's attachment style gives his nephew the impression that pre-school is an unsafe space, that separation from his uncle risks losing him forever, and that Matthew is the only adult left on Earth to console and comfort him. These are not intended messages, but they are the messages nonetheless. Matthew's use of the Secret Service Agent version of the Protector and his use of the Smotherer version of the Nurturer, instead of other archetypal expressions, are choices predicated on his attachment style.

Developmental Context and Availability/Responsivity

It was Erik Erikson, a German developmental psychologist, who gave these fathering connections life when he described the developmental mile-stones and developmental stages necessary for a person's healthy maturation and growth. Erikson believed that each parent assists children through a series of stages which he called crises. The beauty of Erikson's crises is found in its construction and application. It states that if a child is provided with sufficient support, that child moves through the developmental crises—trust, autonomy, initiative, industry, and identity—building, maturing and growing in mastery and confidence (Erikson, 1956). We can further apply this construction to fatherhood. For a father, if he is open (available) and empathic (responsive) to the evolving and changing communications and needs of his child, there is a parallel process that occurs within that father as his own sense of self, accomplishment and wholeness grows in conjunction with his child (Searles, 1955; Weiner & Gallo-Silver, 2015).

Erikson's inter-connected and progressive crises of maturation and development have one additional wrinkle that it is important to mention. While a person navigates the goals of these crises successfully, that person continues to flourish. However, there is a possibility of a father struggling to navigate these crises. In these cases, a father may become "derailed" within one developmental crisis (for any number of reasons). When struggling within a stage's crisis, the father finds it increasingly complex to navigate subsequent stage's crises (Erikson, 1956).

Using Erikson's developmental progression as a model, we track how a father develops as his child moves through the various developmental stages. In this way, we can assess fathering through a father's connection to his child and the requirements of his child's continued growth. The father's confidence in his fathering abilities expands as he travels from one stage to another or, rather, one crisis of confidence to another (see Figure 11.1). Perfection is not the focus of resolving these crises. Instead, we prefer the concept of "good enough" (first coined by D.W. Winnicott, 1953, 1990) to acknowledge the imperfection of the human condition. This is not a "low bar" of meager accomplishment, but a recognition of the complexity of parenting as part of the parent's inner (emotional) and outer (concrete tasks of adulthood) lives.

Table 11.1—Fatherhood Availability/Responsivity Crises of Confidence

Father Confidence Level	*Infancy*	*Toddler-hood*	*Early Childhood*	*Late Childhood*	*Adoles-cence*
Flourishing	Engagement vs.	Patience vs.	Curiosity vs.	Participation vs.	Flexibility vs.
Struggling	Inadequacy	Intolerance	Inhibition	Inferiority	Rigidity

Adapted from Erikson's Nine Stages of Psychosocial Development (Erikson, 1956; Erikson, 1997; Weiner & Gallo-Silver, 2018)

These crises are situated around a developmental moment for the father. They build on one another similar to rock climbing—as the stability of the previous step enables one to move to the next step (see Table 11.1). For example, if the crisis of infancy ends with a father competently *engaging* his child, he will feel better equipped to provide a good enough level of *patience* when his child reaches toddlerhood. On the other hand, if a father finds himself feeling overly *inadequate* during his child's infancy, accessing *patience* for his toddler will be a far more complex task for him. More likely, he may become frustrated and *intolerant* of his child's "terrible twos" behavior. A father's "flourishing" or "struggling" within the crisis of availability/responsivity is inexorably linked to his access to and expression of the archetypes.

At varying moments, each and every one of the five archetypes is required to be accessed and expressed in order for a father to gain a sense of efficacy and wholeness within a given developmental stage. The father's availability/responsivity crises are resolved by a fluid and shifting expression of the archetypes. Fathering and the access and expression of the archetypes are quintessential multi-tasking. Some expressions of archetypes are listed below by developmental stage. They are listed in the following order—Captain, Educator, Protector, Nurturer, Jester—for the purpose of clarity only and are not in any order of importance.

- Child's Infancy and the Fathering Crisis of Engagement vs. Inadequacy:
  - gathering information and creating a biological, psychological and developmental road map for making decisions and altering course (Captain)
  - modeling consistent responses and creating rituals including bedtime, eating, bathing (Educator)

- using empathy to understand and respond to the non-verbal communications of crying, physical discomfort, sleepiness, and hunger (Protector)
- providing nourishment, hygiene, affection, soothing, comforting and closeness (Nurturer)
- finding time to stimulate cognitive processes by being playfully engaged with sounds and touch (Jester)
- Child's Toddlerhood and Fathering Crisis of Patience vs. Intolerance:
  - beginning to employ and use different types of rules, procedures, and repercussions associated with new skills and abilities including toileting (Captain)
  - modeling and assisting in new verbal skills and new motor skills such as picking up, chewing, crawling, standing, toileting and walking (Educator)
  - enabling a secure process of separation and individuation (Protector)
  - offering encouragement, praise, and, the inevitable, first aid in response to crawling, first steps, and novel experiences (Nurturer)
  - providing a warm acceptance of the intense emotional expressions and need for control associated with a burgeoning sense of self (Jester)
- Child's Early Childhood and the Fathering Crisis of Curiosity vs. Inhibition:
  - processing new avenues of feedback as school begins and assisting in integrating new rules, rationales and repercussions from this new environment (Captain)
  - enhancing creativity and ideas by asking questions, prompting discussions and following up on lines of inquiry (Educator)
  - providing a more nuanced set of safety measures to manage developing gross motor skills and abilities and offering increasing levels of empathy in order to contain more complex social interaction (Protector)
  - shifting caretaking responsibilities from the individual to groups including friends and schoolmates to address increases in socialization and shifting caretaking stance from proactive to reactive in response to growing autonomy (Nurturer)
  - playing and creating in all its forms (Jester)
- Child's Late Childhood and the Fathering Crisis of Participation vs. Inferiority:

- ◉ assisting in the processing of information and feedback provided via interactions with other sources including teachers, coaches, the media, the Internet, friends, and other parents
- ◉ enhancing the acquisition of knowledge through involvement in areas of study, creating opportunities for learning, and debriefing when requested and/or when necessary (Educator)
- ◉ providing safety measures of physical and emotional boundary awareness and maintenance and increasing levels of empathy to contain more complex and challenging information and experiences (Protector)
- ◉ transferring the father-child relationship including time, companionship, and affection beyond the bounds of the home into different areas of interest including school, hobbies, social opportunities (Nurturer)
- ◉ minimizing the consternation, struggles and ups and downs of early relationship building, wins and losses, and attempts at mastery building by reinforcing the idea that life does not have to be too serious (Jester)

- Child's Adolescence and the Fathering Crisis of Flexibility vs. Rigidity:
  - ◉ providing a meaningful awareness and understanding of the ups and downs of puberty, the pull of independence, risk-taking behaviors, social pressures, and the underlying fears during the modification and subsequent enforcement of rules, rationales, and repercussions (Captain)
  - ◉ transitioning into a more mutual partnership in the learning process by being the student as often as being the teacher and by shifting the responsibility for learning and studying to the child (Educator)
  - ◉ establishing the importance of empathy and compassion during times of distress and creating a more complex set of safety measures that incorporates a growing need for autonomy and responsibility (Protector)
  - ◉ acknowledging the ambivalence within the maturation process, the moving towards/away, progressive/regressive nature of growing into early adulthood and sensitively and non-judgmentally providing love, affection, intimacy, feedback and other resources (Nurturer)
  - ◉ providing understanding and playfulness to counter the gravity of the boundaries and rules that are being tested, challenged or broken (Jester)

Relational Dynamics of Fathers

When we speak of relational dynamics, we are referring to the union of availability and responsivity. How available a father is, dictates to what extent and how successfully he is able to respond to his child. Put in the language of the archetypes, the more awareness a father has in choosing and expressing the archetypes, the more he can deliberately and effectively respond to his child's needs. Let us recall Jacob, from Chapter 7 and his 5-year-old daughter, who is resisting going to bed.

Jacob tries to get her ready for bed, but she begins throwing objects and screaming. He asks her what is wrong, and she becomes even more agitated, screams louder and cries harder. Jacob attempts to consider what his daughter's behavior may be communicating to him.

We describe Jacob's relational connection as accessible. He is calm and resilient in the face of his daughter's tantrum. It is his relational connection that allows Jacob to move through the archetypes one by one, touching on the Protector's empathy, the Captain's understanding of his daughter's fear and her need for structure, and the Nurturer's tenderness and comfort with closeness. Having built up over the course of her development his own skills of Engagement, Patience, and now Curiosity, Jacob is able to respond by posing to his daughter a question in the form of a statement with positive results.

He then points out that she is angry and doesn't want her daddy to leave her. His daughter looks at him and then launches herself into his arms. He suggests to his daughter that he will stay with her and read her another story while she settles into bed.

If Jacobs's relational connection is preoccupied, let us imagine how this scenario may change. This type of availability limits the father's access and movement between archetypes. Under these circumstances the father typically selects the archetypes or archetypes that he is most familiar with. Depending on what his child actually needs within a given moment, this restricted use of archetypes can lead to the over-expression of one archetype or the under-expression of another.

Jacob tries to get her ready for bed, but she begins throwing objects and screaming. He yells at her, "What is wrong with you?" and she becomes even more agitated, screams louder and cries harder. Jacob attempts to consider what his daughter's behavior may be communicating to him, but he is angry and cannot think straight—only that it is bedtime and that she is supposed to go to bed because she is tired.

Jacob is closed off to the Protector and Nurturer archetypes and is relying on the Captain. This leads inevitably to his over-expression of the Captain archetype. Without the balancing effects of the Protector and Nurturer, we hear the Corporal respond to his daughter's distress. Jacob's response is one of intolerance of his daughter's communication (and the lack of effectiveness in addressing the difficulties further inhibits him from exploring other options). Jacob may have navigated his daughter's infancy well, honing the skills of engagement, but toddlerhood and early childhood seem to have challenged him and he is off course and feels "lost" in these moments of conflict.

Examining the third form of relational connection, like Matthew earlier in this chapter, let us imagine Jacob as intensely related. Jacob, being impulsive and reactive, chooses whatever archetype or archetypes he can access in the moment without thinking things through. As many situations require a balanced combination of archetypes, he also runs the risk of over-expressing or under-expressing archetypes based on this chaotic process of connecting to his child.

Jacob tries to get her ready for bed, but she begins throwing objects and screaming. He asks her what is wrong, and she becomes even more agitated, screams louder and cries harder. Jacob attempts to consider what his daughter's behavior may be communicating to him and decides that she needs a hug, which he provides without saying a word. His daughter pushes him away and he says, "C'mon, let me hug you, I love you, you're so funny when you're angry, come heeeeeere...." He pulls her close and she wriggles to get away. "Leave me alone!" she yells.

Jacob as Nurturer, in this moment, is over-expressed in Jacob as Smotherer. His choice of Nurturer without the Protector's empathy and his choice of expressing the Jester in an unsuccessful attempt to lighten his daughter's distress, is an ineffective response to the situation. Jacob's intense relational connection has made it very difficult to build the necessary experience with his daughter over time to navigate the crisis of Engagement vs. Inadequacy. Jacob throws archetypes at the wall and sees what sticks. In this way, he is the absence of availability and responsivity to his daughter's emotional needs by displaying a lack of empathy, intuitiveness, or self-awareness.

Managing the Impact of Socio-Cultural Expectations and Stereotypes

It is beyond the scope of this book to review all of the many socio-cultural norms that affect fathers. Yet, it is important to address the powerful impact these expectations place on fathers. For this, it is helpful to introduce the concept of intersectionality (Crenshaw, 1993). Part of feminist literature, for our purposes here, intersectionality means that all of us have multiple identities (Hankivsky, 2014). Each society/culture has expectations for each of our identities. Understanding that we all have more than one "self" helps to both become increasingly aware of societal/cultural expectations as well as manage the impact of those expectations.

Staying with Jacob, we can list his many identities. He is a man, a father, a husband, a son, a brother, a member of a specific religious group. He has an ethnicity and a specific profession and is of a specific race. He is a member of a neighborhood, a city, a county, a state and a country. As long as this list is, it has not described all of Jacob's identities. Jacob is one person, one self, with many parts. Jacob might consider certain identities more important than others. As authors of a book on fatherhood, our bias is that a critical part of Jacob's identity is as father. We believe this because Jacob's identity as father (in all its diverse possibilities) is the most crucial to his children's health and well-being. That said, what specifically defines Jacob as a father is unique to Jacob. As we have discussed thus far, some of the identities will be his choice, others may be identified for him and still others will remain in flux throughout the life of his children. We feel it is imperative that these identities get passed on from father to child in meaningful and helpful ways. Within the context of relational dynamics and taking into consideration the complexity of availability and responsivity, we advocate that fathers thoughtfully consider how to pass on this important contribution to their children in a balanced and useful fashion.

Numerous research studies of children in the United States indicate that children with involved fathers are healthier and more successful (Levant & Wimer, 2009; LaRossa, 1997; Knox, 2016) With effort and self-awareness, Jacob can choose to take charge of his identity as father, at varying moments agreeing with, insulating, compromising, or tangling with the socio-cultural expectations placed on him. Similar to African American men pressing to define what it means to be a man within a society of racial oppression, to identify what African American men can accomplish, and to push back on barriers and obstacles in order to achieve the freedom to self-define themselves (and not be defined by historical, white-dominated, racist concepts), Jacob can do the same.

There is an important relationship between the concepts of intersectionality and archetypes. How a father cross-pollinates his identity with his choices as parent impacts the nature and scope of his fathering. We believe that Jacob, Matthew, Gabe, Amir, Dieter, and any fathers who choose to, can decide and take action, both internally and externally, to strive to be the type of father (available and responsive) that arises from full access and expression of all his archetypes. This requires awareness of self, for it is a slippery slope to take a path of least resistance and allow identity to drive decision-making.

At one end of the continuum, fathers may just "go along" with unfair and inaccurate stereotypes as tacit confirmation of their society's notions (prejudiced or not) of race, ethnicity, or gender roles. Not pushing back can create an underlying dynamic of guilt or shame, over wrongs unchallenged. At the other end, of the continuum, fathers may pose an ongoing pitched "battle" against these same stereotypes as visceral rejoinders of a society's inequities and bias. This steadfast approach can result in one-issue fathering, eliciting anger and sadness, over injustices unresolved. While we do not take exception to either of these stances, we do want to reiterate that each, in their own way, challenge a balanced approach to parenting. This is a reality, not a criticism, as we believe that a father's thoughts and feelings, including their anger, fear, shame or sadness, will always affect availability and responsivity.

Miguel's five-year-old daughter starts kindergarten and happens to be the only child of color in the class. She tells her father that she does not like school because none of the other girls will play with her. Miguel becomes furious that his daughter is subject to discrimination and decides to visit the school and meet with the principal. The principal invites the teachers to meet with Miguel. The teachers explain to the group that some of the girls in the class have been together since pre-kindergarten and have formed relationships. Miguel listens, but is still angry. He tells the teachers that if the girls have formed cliques then it is their responsibility to make sure that all children are included in play. The principal agrees with Miguel and the teachers say they will take steps to address his concerns. But this only mollifies Miguel slightly and he continues to worry at home, with his wife and his daughter, about how this school is ever going to handle his daughter's healthy racial identity formation. He vows to remove her from the school if he does not see a rapid response to his demands. Meanwhile, his daughter senses the upset in the household about school and refuses to go to school without a great deal of coaxing. She often feigns being ill to avoid school.

Miguel is seeing red. He is incensed that this school is not addressing his daughter's developmental needs sufficiently. Miguel knows that this is a critical time in his daughter's identity development, but Miguel as Protector is overcome by his fear that she is suffering from discrimination and bullying. In this powerful moment, within Miguel, this archetype is not in balance and is not collaborating with other archetypes to temper the intensity of the situation—the Educator to calmly share the history of his people, the Captain to problem solve relationship issues that his daughter will face throughout her life, or the Jester to create play opportunities for these burgeoning friendships. It is often the loud noise of expectations that circumvent the full access and expression of fatherhood archetypes. This elevated volume risks rendering fathers less available and less responsive in their efforts to rear their children. If the father role and all its innate gifts, is valued, then where intersectionality meets individuation, the true work is to quiet and focus the mind in order to enable identification of the most efficacious mixture of archetypal abilities to act on the needs of children. This stance moves the father role into the present, with-grounding and definition, which can help hold it steady against the oppressive currents and eddies of norms and expectations.

12

Fathers' Time Orientation and Impact on Archetype Access

There are really four dimensions, three which we call the three planes of space, and the fourth, time.—H. G. Wells

Time is the longest distance between two places.—Tennessee Williams

What times existed which were not brought into being by you? Or how could they pass if they never had existence? Since, therefore, you are the cause of all times.—Saint Augustine

How does an infant tell time? Jean Piaget, a Swiss child psychologist, believed that children generally cannot comprehend the passage of time accurately until around six or seven years old (Piaget, 1927). Prior to this age, a child's concrete thinking makes it impossible to use time as benchmark as adults do. To navigate challenges such as, trying to figure out how long until the family reaches grandma's house, attempting to manage the moments until mom or dad gets home from work, staring at the bedroom door in anticipation of father's scolding, estimating when the "timeout" will end, or experiencing the hunger that only a bottle of milk will quench, children are required to use a different method of information gathering and processing instead of time to gauge these periods.

Without the use of time, young children experience these periods of "waiting" as angst and frustration associated with the attainment (or not) of their needs (Freud, 1954). Prior to being able to understand the concept of time, children use a visceral, emotional sensation—that increases in intensity over time—to denote the interval of waiting rather than an intellectual understanding of seconds, minutes and hours. The more emotional a young child

176

becomes while waiting, the more "time" they *feel* has passed. The correlation between emotion and actual time is relevant to the subjective experience (positive or negative) of the child.

Time is also an influential mechanism in relation to adult psychology. Memories, fantasies, daydreams, wishes and hopes are all functions of how time connects one's past, present and future. Peetz and Wilson (2008) theorized that an individual's identity in the present is comprised of the individual's past and also the individual's future identities. In this way, both children and adults perceive and use time in different ways depending on their perception of events and resulting emotional states. In fact, temporal appraisal theory research has found that with regard to events from the past, pleasant events feel closer in time to an individual, while more difficult moments are experienced as further away and more remote (Wilson, Gunn & Ross, 2009). Thus, time is malleable and a useful tool in the care of one's psyche.

Linking time, emotion and behavior becomes important in understanding the ways that individuals, in our case fathers, employ time to protect themselves, organize and manage their feelings, and make decisions within their relationships—what we call *time orientation*. There are three distinct time orientations that fathers can employ that we are going to expand on in this chapter—past, present and future. Within the parent-child responding/receiving dyad, a father's time orientation leads to yet another way of understanding the father-child relationship as it affects his archetype access, selection and expression. As we begin to deconstruct this concept, let us begin by stating that time orientation's impact on the fatherhood archetypes centers on its "influence" over (1) how a father understands (or distorts) the developmental importance of certain situations for his child and (2) how he chooses to prioritize and respond to these moments.

Gary accidently walked in on his 14-year-old son masturbating. Gary has a history of childhood sexual abuse and this has made him overcautious and overly concerned regarding his son's growing sexuality. Gary is embarrassed and not sure what to say to his son. His son is mortified. When they see each other again at the dinner table, Gary says to his son: "I am sorry I invaded your privacy, I apologize, and I'll knock on your bedroom door when it is closed. You did nothing wrong and nothing to be ashamed of so are we okay with each other?" Gary's son gives him a relieved okay sign.

Between the time that Gary closes the bedroom door in embarrassment and the moment he sits down at the dinner table, he arcs through a variety of thought provoking encounters, both internal and external. The event has brought his troubling past forward into his present and has generated apprehension about damaging consequences for his (and his son's) future. This process of interpreting experiences and parent-child interactions from a variety of temporal perspectives is a natural aspect of parenting.

In this case, Gary's initial reaction is to scream inside his head. These are feelings linked to the accidental intrusiveness of this moment with his son and the unfortunate connection it has to his own childhood abuse. Once he has stopped feeling overwhelmed, he talks to his wife and calls his close friends to ask whether he has done anything wrong. This is a needed reality check that Gary has learned to request due to the fact that his views on the matter of sexuality and boundaries are compromised and distorted by his history. Over time he formulates a measured response that focuses on his son's needs. Gary could have responded in a number of ways given his history but chose to put his discomfort aside and address his son in an empathic manner.

In order to grasp time orientation in a meaningful way and its impact on fatherhood archetypes we need to first examine object relations theory. This psychodynamic theory is organized around the notion that, in each person's life, there are individual "objects," or important and influential people who are powerful influences on the child. The details, interactions and other underlying dynamics of this influence on the child becomes the foundation—a template or a road map—for all the other relationships in the child's life in the present and future (see Figure 12.1).

The theories of Melanie Klein and Ronald Fairbairn focused on the idea that people derive definition and purpose out of being connected to another person (Klein, 1932; Fairbairn, 1954; Fairbairn & Scharf, 1994). These relationships or connections provide the interactions, interest, caring and love that a person needs to grow and develop. As formative elements in a person's life, understanding the quality of the connections and the nature of the relational interplay becomes another means by which we may understand how people feel and react when they become adults. With regard to fathers, object relations become an additional window through which to see and understand their parental beliefs system.

Nicholai's 27-year-old daughter is getting married. He feels so very proud of her as he watches her move around the room at the rehearsal dinner. She smiles and talks to the guests. He is struck by how similar she appears to her mother in her mannerisms and the way she moves her hair out of her face, even the way she holds her fiancé's hand reminds Nicholai of his wife and himself when they first met. His friends are always telling him how his daughter has his sense of humor and his ability to tell a story—the way she can keep a whole room of people on the edge of their seats. This makes Nicholai smile as he remembers the way his father used to tell stories at bedtime and how Nicholai never wanted them to end.

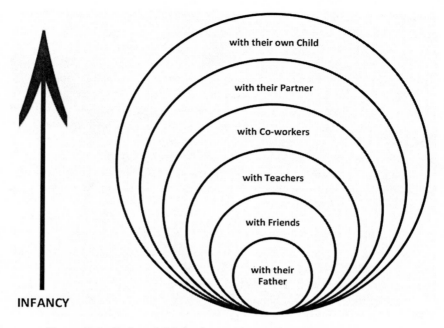

INFANCY

Figure 12.1—Father-child dyad as a relational template for the child.

It may seem obvious, but Nicholai's relationship with his daughter and his relationship with his own father are entwined. How his father felt about him is an intrinsic part of how he sees, feels and thinks about his own child. How his father related to him is the template for how he relates to others, including his own child.

Karen Horney, a German psychoanalyst and a student of Freud, was an object relations theorist who believed that, starting from childhood, a basic "way" of relating to other people is constructed within each individual. She called these ways of relating "trends" and believed that these trends were developed through relationships with caregivers. Horney felt that the primary purpose of an individual's trend was as a vehicle to get one's needs met. She divided the trends into three classifications—moving towards, moving away, and moving against. We believe that each of these trends correspond with a specific time orientation:

- past with moving away
- present with moving against
- future with moving towards

Fathering, as a general set of tasks and responsibilities, may be a standard role within the man's culture, but as a role, it remains highly distinctive for each specific man. In taking on this role men seek the familiarity of their own fundamental and foundational ways of relating to the people in their world. In light of this, we know that a father's Horneyan "trend"—the relational dynamic that he developed since his own childhood—will connect with the way he relates to his child, or as we call it, his time orientation.

We unify these two concepts in acknowledgment that the way we were cared for has a direct impact on how we care for others. The concept of time orientation operationalizes this caretaking connection and, in doing so, increases a father's awareness with regard to any "The way I was raised…" parenting. The identification of a fathering trend shines light on his path and allows a father to determine whether or not it makes sense for this specific father-child connection or situation, eventually making room for the possible access and use of different archetypes.

Table 12.1—Adaptation of Horney's Relational Trends

- Moving Toward (Future-Focused)—anxious to obtain the approval and affection from others. Yet, also has a fear that his needs, if expressed, will send everyone away and create isolation.
- Moving Away (Past-Focused)—preference to be alone and be emotionally self-sufficient. Belief that closeness will create dependency on others.
- Moving Against (Present-Focused)—needing to be in control of one's life and emotions. A belief that people are angry and challenging. He is often highly competitive and has a need to triumph.

Adapted from Karen Horney, 1945; Weiner & Gallo-Silver, 2018

Horney and other theorists go into great detail regarding how an individual arrives at a specific relationship with the world, called a world-view, yet we would prefer to devote a separate chapter to that topic (see Chapter 14). Relational trends and world-view are generally connected to the type of care people received as children. This care, though, is not only an aspect of family relationships, but also of life experiences, the impact of culture, and group history.

The goal of optimal development, Horney believed, is for people to be capable of fluidly moving between the trends in various combinations depending on the life situation at hand. That said, she understood that based on one's object relations, individuals typically adapted a relational template as adults using the trend that most closely fit their childhood relationships. In reality, Horney believed that individuals who struggle may find themselves using one trend to the exclusion of all others. "It is more common for [these people] to streamline … [attempting] to suppress permanently and rigidly oneself and be exclusively the other" (Horney, 1950, pg. 190). We consider a definition of streamlining to be a person being overly comfortable with and committed to using one of these trends to the exclusion of all others. In our view, to be overly comfortable with one of these trends is equivalent to being unable to access certain archetypes. Depending on a father's level of streamlining his access narrows to several over-expressed or under-express archetypes (see Table 12.2).

Optimistically, Horney maintained that people could have access to all three trends. She believed that being mindful, making thoughtful, conscious choices and prioritizing could help all individuals, including fathers, obtain the most productive benefit from each individual trend. We use time orientation to connect each trend to the way it influences a father's perception of his child's needs and his resulting parenting responses. We will describe both the benefits and the difficulties of each time orientation. As we present these, we want the reader to keep in mind that that just as with Horney's belief that fluid movement between trends was possible, we believe that a father's use of all time orientations is also achievable.

The concept of time orientation is connected to relational trends in its link to how a father chooses to provide for his child's needs and the motivation for these choices. Each father begins with his own understanding of how needs are met. He, then, applies this understanding to his own child. We believe that this application comes in the form of an emphasis on the past, the present or the future of a father's life. These different time foci are multi-determined, affected in large part by a father's own history of being parented, but also by his temperament, his relational dynamics, and his world-view.

As a father interacts with his child, with other caregivers or with child-related institutions (academic, medical, social, etc.), he is continuously asked to identify and evaluate his child needs and to make decisions about how to involve himself: wait, act, control, respond, defer, avoid, etc. Depending on his unique qualities and circumstances, he may see these moments as opportunities, hardships, frustrations, reprieves, missteps, or necessities. How a father chooses to "move" and involve himself in difficult moments is the crux of time orientation and, because of the dependent nature of the parent-child relationship, is significant in the relational messages it sends to his child. As Fairbairn writes, "the persistence of the child's original resentment toward the caregiver [centers on the parent] as the individual holding the power to gratify the need or not and if failing to do so, casts the child in the role of captive" (1943, 114). A father may not feel comfortable with the idea of classifying his child as "captive" to his choices, yet it is important to acknowledge a child's inherent reliance on a father's participation. In the case of Gary, he could have addressed his son masturbating with the shame and inhibitions he feels about sex in general. In that way, his son would need to carry the burden of his father's unfortunate history.

A Moving Toward Trend Leads to a Future Time Orientation

A father with a moving toward trend is swayed by his early object relationships to be a person who feels the need to stay connected to others, including his children. The influence of this trend can create worry in this father as his children begin to develop and display more autonomy. Because of the developmental pull (away) that it produces, issues related to maturity create a heightened intensity that lead the moving toward father to question himself existentially—how he is going to stay connected? Because of the perception of distance that is created through conflict, these fathers can often be ambivalent and uncomfortable with the typical tension that comes from establishing structure, setting and enforcing limits, and managing frustrations. He just wants everyone to be happy.

As he feels his child "move away" developmentally, he can feel overwhelmed by simply raising a transforming child because of what these changes represent for the future—a decreased connection. How is he going to cope with his child changing (intellectually, socially, emotionally, and behaviorally)? Dominated by thoughts of the future (and its perceived connection to being alone), everything becomes extensions of this unwanted future, with day-to-day tasks becoming inextricably linked to preoccupations about what may be.

In response to this uncertainty, the nature of this relational template shapes this father into a help seeker (whether from the internet, books, other fathers, his partner or, at times, from his children). Help seeking serves as a way of keeping him close to others, especially as his children develops. In this way, moving toward fathers engage in what they consider helpful parenting action by asking for advice and looking for suggestions. If my child fails a test, how will that impact her academically? If I let them do this, how will I be able to say "no" next time? If my child does not get into the "right" college, will he not get a good job? If my child is not with children like her, will she be scarred for life?

As a moving towards person, this father tries to shield himself from feeling alone. The result is an unfortunate paradox. Instead of being in the here and now and truly being connected to current moments with his child, this father dreams about the relationship's future. His thoughts drift to what his child could be, would be, or should be. Focusing on the future becomes his armor and protection. It is the way that these fathers distance themselves from the realities of their developing child. This is what we describe as future-time orientation. It is the pre-occupation with what may occur.

Solomon worries a great deal about his family and is constantly focused on the possibility for a better tomorrow. Solomon became a father rather suddenly when he fell in love with a woman widowed by 9/11 with three young children, twin four-year-old girls and a seven-year-old boy. She was pregnant with her daughters when her husband died. Solomon is 15 years older than his wife and never thought he would get married or have children. After he married their mother, he legally adopted the children. His daughters readily accepted him as their "Daddy." His son will not address him as father and insists on calling Solomon by his first name. He accepts this from his son. That said, he still worries about how he can connect better with him regardless of what his son calls him. He often feels at loose ends and reads every parenting book he can find. He asks friends and relatives for advice on how to help his children. He is often tentative and inconsistent with the children, which causes difficulties with his wife. He is reluctant to explain or enforce any rules without her and uncomfortable talking to his children about the loss of their biological father.

In this scenario, we see Solomon expressing the Captain archetype as the Abdicator and the Educator archetype as the Skimmer. As loving as Solomon wants to and tries to be, his dedication to his children is undermined by his forswearing of his leadership role in his family. For Solomon, his anxiety is about "saying the wrong thing" or "doing the wrong thing" and what could happen if he does. The fear of future repercussions within his relationships from a misstep in the present renders him silent and uncertain in the face of his children needs. In addition, all the loss and grief that this family has suffered heightens the intensity of the relationships for Solomon. He does not want to do anything that may jeopardize his relationships with the family. The under-expression of the Captain and the Educator archetypes are other ways of remaining close to his children, while not creating conflict or stress. In this case, the streamlining of a future time orientation adds a great deal of anxiety and distress to a traumatized family that needs a rudder—someone who feels safe and secure enough in themselves to take charge.

Moving Away Trend Leads to a Past-Time Orientation

A father with a moving away trend is shaped by his early object relationships to be a person who feels that it is important to be self-reliant in order to get things done. Moving away fathers tend to share the belief that they can help their children have a better, more successful and happier life than they did. This is grounded in their lack of trust in others. Their object relational template propels these fathers into being individuals who meet their own needs, come up with their own solutions to problems, and try not to rely on others. This self-reliance creates a sense of competence in these fathers.

The moving away trend establishes a tendency toward maintaining distance and boundaries (emotionally, intellectually) from those "others" who this father believes may turn out to be unreliable or unhelpful. The influence of the trend can create discomfort in this father as his children display an ongoing need for dependence of all kinds—affection and intimacy, help with separation, learning rules, among many others. Generally, issues of child development connected to dependence and reliance feel more intense for this father and he may pass these responsibilities on to others, downplay them or attempt to rush his children through these moments (i.e., time to man up, toughen up, be a man, etc.)

Being a moving away person, the ongoing day-to-day realities of fathering can lead this father to push away the needs of others (adults and children included) as a way of controlling and managing his feelings. This can come in the form of becoming involved by "taking over"—addressing problems that come up by fixing or repairing them himself. "Here, just let me do it." This distancing can also take the form of "minimizing"—addressing issues by re-characterizing the size and nature of the difficulty based on his own point of view. "Don't make a mountain out of a mole hill." To an outside observer, these may look like moves toward his child, but for this father, it is a pulling away, as it is based on a unilateral decision and is not be typically consistent with his child's needs.

For this fathering trend, the pull of his child's perpetual, albeit evolving, need for a relationship, creates a significant level of tension. The issues of dependence and independence that shape so much of child development are like a minefield for him. They shout connection at him, which unlocks his residual feelings about not wanting to trust others, to connect to others. Being more comfortable with moving away from people. He has been let down in the past and these past relational dynamics define him now. This is what we describe as past-time orientation. It is the pre-occupation with what occurred in one's past.

Sebastian uses the present to fill what was missing in his past. Sebastian grew up in multiple foster homes, and never felt he was part of a family. When he aged out of foster care, he joined the Army and attended college. He became a pediatric nurse and married a woman who was a doctor in the hospital where they worked together. Once they had children, Sebastian stayed home with their son, while his wife went back to work. Sebastian insists that their 3-year-old son sleep in bed with them even though it disrupts his wife's sleep. Sebastian also carries his son everywhere even though he can walk. The two are rarely separated. When his wife insists that their son go to school and that Sebastian go back to work, Sebastian becomes upset and yells at her. He tells her that she has no idea what it means to be a father for him, that she cannot imagine what it is like to have had a life like his, and that she does not have their child's best interest in mind when she is making these parenting decisions.

It is clear that Sebastian had an emotionally impoverished childhood. It makes sense that he wants his son to know that he is loved and is seen as an important part of the family. Yet, because of what was missing from his past, Sebastian expresses the Nurturer archetype by accessing the Smotherer version of the archetype, focusing on his own need to be loved and diminishing his own sense of separation. Because of his past, the urgency and determination that he experiences in relation to his son's "best interest" lead him to express the Protector archetype by accessing the Secret Service Agent. This is in an attempt to retain a level of security and control over his son's experiences, something he did not receive. For Sebastian, no one cared. From the self-reliance demanded of him by his neglectful past, we can see Sebastian's belief that no one, not even his wife, can understand what his son needs and that only he can provide for him.

Moving Against Trend Leads to a Present Time Orientation

A father with a moving against trend is shaped by his earliest relationships to be a person who must lead and be steadfast in this stance toward others. From this father's perspective, the word "against" is synonymous with "stand up to" and represents his belief that there exists a correct and proper method of meeting a person's requirements. This father has a boldness and uses his power to provide his children with all their needs in a timely, helpful fashion. He tends to have very specific ideas of how children should behave, learn, listen and show discipline. This can create a sense of safety and security for children.

His stance is not necessarily strict, so much as unvarying and consistent. When interacting with his object relationships during childhood, the connection required this father to strive and work hard to get what he needed (and now applies this to how he relates to his children needs). His relational template stems from an experience where nothing came easy for him whether because of chaos, neglect, or ignorance. In adulthood, he can be very organized and helpful as he directs and structures his child's many routines including bedtimes, bath time, getting to school on time, homework, and curfews. His children's developmental changes, needs and requirements are orchestrated by this father with little or no feedback required or solicited from others. Input from others that is accepted is done so with a catch—it is filtered through this father's assertive point of view.

The moving against father has a tendency towards rigidity, does not typically negotiate (with others), and may present black and white thinking—meaning that mitigating circumstances, missing information and situational nuances may be lost on him. This father is firmly grounded and focused on what he believes his child's needs are in this moment. The future is too abstract and uncertain for him to focus on. The past is concluded and, therefore, out of his control.

That the moving against father has a child whose maturation and development may produce disparate opinions and ideas from his own is secondary. His child's autonomy is not a priority unless it can be used to accomplish the goals he has laid out. He manages most parent-child tension by taking an adversarial position such as "You live under my roof, you follow my rules" or "When you can pay, you can make the decision." Connection for this father centers on a set of requirements that he must fulfill. The long-term impact of his methods is less relevant. This is what we describe as present-time orientation. It is the preoccupation with what is needed now and a discounting of the importance of the past or the future.

Stuart believes that firm management provides a sense of security for everyone involved. He tells people that he learned this from his parents who drank themselves to death by the time he was 15. He loves his children and wants what is best for them. His wife feels he is too strict with their two boys, ages 13 and 15. Stuart believes that the boys must be as responsible as adults are and so he has given each of them chores that are to be completed on certain days and certain times. If the 13-year-old has a basketball game planned, but also has homework to do, he must finish his school work first. Any homework needs to be completed before Stuart comes home from work, so that he may check it after dinner. When the 15-year-old wants to come home later than his weekend curfew in order to go to the movies with his friends, his father always says no.

Stuart is intently focused on the moment-by-moment lives of his children. Providing them with the tools they need to be functioning adults is his main purpose—the method he relies on is control. If his past, filled with the chaos caused by two alcoholic parents, has taught him anything, it is that one must take what one needs. Waiting for others (like his sons figuring something out on their own) or relying on others (like his wife providing leadership in the family or teachers sharing their opinions of his son's performance) are unpredictable and therefore anxiety-inducing stances. He believes that we control our own future by the decisions we make now. His rigidity, less obvious when his sons were little, is now an overly confining and, unintentionally, punitive. Stuart expresses the Captain archetype by accessing the Corporal version of the archetype. As his sons get older, they may resort to using increasingly bold forms of acting out or even risk-taking behaviors in an effort to break away from their father's grip on their lives. Stuart expresses the Jester archetype by accessing the Killjoy version. He views play (here, in the form of sports) only as conditional compensation for the completion of, what Stuart sees as more important tasks. Unfortunately for Stuart, because of his focus on the present, he has difficulty seeing that play, whether it is organized sports, dancing, or creative arts, is one of those activities that provides benefit to a child's mental health (Erlandsson, Dsilna, Fagrberg & Christensson, 2006).

Fathering in the Past, the Present and the Future

All three men are filled with "good intentions" and want to be the best fathers they can possibly be. However, being overly committed to any specific time orientation limits them (see Table 12.2). As we have seen in previous chapters, the archetype expression of men who find themselves confined to one way of fathering typically leads to under expression of certain archetypes or over expression of others. While this in and of itself may not pose a problem for father and child in any given situation, a single time orientation for all decision-making limits fathers' ability to connect completely with their children and substantially decreases their potential sense of empowerment. If a father only wants to or is only able to respond to his child's needs in one way, what happens as the child develops and matures, as situations demand different or nuanced responses, as the father ages, as the environment and circumstances around father and child evolve?

The potential for under-involvement by a moving toward father stems from his attempts to avoid potential conflict with his child (and create the perception distance). An exclusive focus on the future keeps this father engaged but obliges him to sidestep important fathering responsibilities. As we see with Solomon, archetype expression in the form of the Abandoner (under-involved Protector) and the Abdicator (the under-involved Captain) keeps the father-child relationships from becoming too intense for the moment and maintains the fantasy that all will be happy and well. It is, of course, understandable, that Solomon dreams of a future that would not include the realities of 9/11 and its traumatic effects on him, his family, and their relationship. That said, the choice to move into the present by expressing more Captain archetype or the Protector archetype can be helpful to fathers, like Solomon, and their children. Imagine Solomon using the Captain and the Protector in the following manner.

Solomon says to his son that that he is so very sorry that he has lost his father and that he knows that he can never replace him (the Protector's empathy). He continues by saying that he also knows that boys need people in their lives that can help them grow and mature into strong men (the Captain's structure) and that he is going to prove to his step-son that he is that person (the Protector's safety). Solomon tells his step-son that there are going to be times that they struggle with each other, but that that is part of how fathers and sons figure things out (the Captain's rules). His step-son does not say a word during the whole conversation and walks away afterward. Solomon tells his wife about the "conversation" and they agree that he will keep saying this to the boy. They believe that their son's lack of response is really based on a question ... will this father leave me too?

Pushing himself to have this conversation with his step-son creates a different type of father-child connection and allows for Solomon to provide different needs to his son—affection, structure, empathy. With only a future time orientation Solomon provides his son with space, autonomy and quiet, and but these can morph into isolation and depression without other types of fathering support. Compensating for a future-time orientation, fathers can move toward the present, focusing on the here and now and being in the moment.

Table 12.2—Streamlined Trend/Time Orientations and Archetype Expression

- Moving Toward/Future-Focused Only
  - Abandoner
  - Rejecter
  - Abdicator
  - Skimmer
- Moving Away/Past-Focused Only
  - Peter Pan
  - Smotherer
  - Secret Service Agent
  - Mind Reader
- Moving Against/Present-Focused Only
  - Corporal
  - Squasher
  - Killjoy

The past-focused father's tendency toward connection management takes a different approach to conflict avoidance than that of the future-focused father. As opposed to side-stepping, this father attempts to create a world in which the amount asked of him is limited. This, of course is a fantasy as children always make demands, pushing on their parents and parents must provide structure and set limits that contain their children. The moving away father's orientation to his past is one that requires an attempt to wall himself off from others. He attempts to establish a father-child environment in which he acknowledges the connection yet prioritizes his emotional separateness.

By expressing the archetypes of Peter Pan (the over-involved Jester), the Smotherer (over-involved Nurturer) and the Secret Service agent (the over-involved Protector), this father inserts his own needs into the relationship as he works to vicariously repair his own past father-child relationship. While he stays "involved" with his children, he simultaneously skirts mutuality and, consequently, limits the connection between two people. Peter Pan, while being very playful, does not set limits; the Smotherer, while meeting all needs, does not allow for requests or disappointment; and the Secret Service agent, while maintaining total safety, does not make room for injuries or comfort. While completely noble in his efforts to care for his child's needs in this way, a past orientation is incomplete because of its lack of connectedness. Past-oriented fathers, like Sebastian, are well served by looking to the present for some reciprocity for all their hard work. Imagine Sebastian using the Captain, the Protector, the Nurturer, and the Jester to help his son work through a big life transition:

Sebastian listens to his wife tell him that he needs to go back to work. He reluctantly agrees. The next day he and his wife tell his son that they are going to make two changes in the family (the Captain's structure). One, that they have decided to get a baby-sitter for him because Daddy is going back to work and, two, that they have decided to send him to school (the Captain's structure, the Nurturer's caretaking). Sebastian looks at his son whose eyes are wide with what Sebastian believes is fear. "Oh, buddy … Mom and I are so proud of you. You are growing up so big and strong. I promise you that I will take you to school every day and be home every night to eat dinner and to put you to bed. We will play and have a great time and you can tell me all about your day and I will tell you all about mine" (the Protector's safety and empathy, the Jester's playfulness). He picks up his son and hugs him. Sebastian has tears in his eyes and his son sees them and asks him, "Daddy, why are you crying?" Sebastian wipes his eyes and says, "'Cause I am going to miss you."

Sebastian's sadness is provoked by connecting to his own sense of loss that lives in the memories from his past. Moving his time orientation beyond exclusively the past gives him access to his emotions related to the longing to be connected to his child. Acknowledging that his son needs some autonomy and providing him with the opportunity is a gift to his son and to himself, as he will soon discover. Being in the present and defining what a child needs in the moment, creates a grounding for fathers focused on their pasts. For Sebastian, the separations and the resulting reunions that he will experience with his son will help him feel a greater sense of family than the dread he felt clinging to his child for safety. And he may just begin to heal some of the emotional wounds he suffered moving from foster home to foster home.

For moving against father, over-involvement in the structuring and managing of his child's day-to-day world is a perfect solution to the concerns he has about his child's well-being. His stance stems from experiences that confirmed that needs are met, and potential conflict is controlled by a deep and unyielding commitment to exactly what is required. Uncertainty cannot be abided. This strongly influences him, in the here and now, to be in charge of his own (and his child's) destiny. He inevitably narrows his expression of archetypes to ones that focus specifically on a father's structuring responsibilities—teaching and learning (the Educator), rule making and enforcing (the Captain) and rule acceptance and following (the Jester). By accessing these archetypes using the Corporal (over-expression of Captain), the Squasher (over-expression of Educator) and the Killjoy (under-expression of Jester), he retains a strong level of control over the provision of his child's needs. As understandable as this is because of his history, this father feels an immense and never-ending pressure to get it right that is very likely exhausting. In the world of a moving against father, the show must go on. There is no understudy. What can benefit this father's present time orientation, is the wherewithal to shift his focus to the past or the future by initiating some separation (emotional and physical) between his child and himself. Imagine, Stuart using the Captain, the Protector, the Nurturer, and the Educator archetypes to move the onus of meeting his child needs to others (even temporarily).

Stuart observes the reaction he gets from his sons when he talks to them about their responsibilities. He sees how they tense up and look away from him (the Protector's empathy). Stuart knows he has high expectations for his boys, but his alcoholic father had the same expectations of him to take care of things more like a parent than a child. Although he believes that he is raising them to be good, upstanding boys, he cannot help but feel a sense of emptiness each time he has to reprimand them or raise his voice because they have not followed his directions. This emptiness has been lasting longer and longer lately and so Stuart asks his wife about it (the Nurturer's additional resources). She tells him that he is missing out on his sons, that they don't need a boss, they need a father. Stuart tells her that he does not know any other way but will defer to her about certain aspects of the boys' life and that maybe he can see what she is talking about (the Captain's review of structure). Stuart's wife takes over homework responsibilities. The sons go to Stuart only for help with special class projects (the Educator's learning assistance). When they do, Stuart begins to feel needed by his sons and recognizes that it is a new feeling.

Stuart has made the realization that, although working extremely hard to help his sons be responsible young men, he finds it discouraging that his sons resent him. The present time orientation can create a false sense of security by over-emphasizing the father's importance in active helping. Passive assistance requires a father (by avoiding jumping in to direct) to wait for his children to make mistakes, to reach their own conclusions, and to try to find their own solution first. This stance is antithetical to the present-focused father's lack of trust in allowing others to provide for one's needs and can create a great deal of anxiety. This is understandable in light of Stuart history with his own ineffectual parents. That said, shifting his time orientations can offer a level of relief from the pressure that these fathers experience every day. One, truly relying on others such as partners, teachers, other caregivers (moving toward or future-focused) or two, letting his children figure problems out themselves through trial and, more importantly, error (moving away or past-focused) allows these fathers to experience and, then, model a vulnerability that, when achieved, empowers their children to ask for help when they need it.

Fathers make many sacrifices for their children. One of these sacrifices can be to choose to be uncomfortable by fluidly using each type of relational trends and time orientations when needed. Sometimes they can ask for help; sometimes they can take charge; and sometimes they can step back. Fathers need to be able to dream about the future, repair the past and direct the present in various combinations as the fathering situation demands. By doing this, they can expand their options and opportunities in relating and reacting to their children and will be increasingly enabled to access and express all of the archetypes in their most helpful forms.

13

Fathers' Emotional Intelligence and Impact on Archetype Access

All learning has an emotional base.—Plato

Emotional competence is the single most important personal quality that each of us must develop and access...—Dave Lennick

Let's not forget that the little emotions are the great captains of our lives and we obey them without realizing it.—Vincent Van Gogh

For news of the heart, ask the face.—West African saying

When dealing with people, remember you are not dealing with creatures of logic, but with creatures of emotion.—Dale Carnegie

Research indicates that intelligence is not only the measure of content knowledge and problem solving, but also the ability to be aware of one's own emotions and the emotions of others (Gottman, Declaire & Goleman, 1998). The idea of emotional intelligence was first coined by Michael Beldoch in 1964 and was made more widely known by John Goleman's 1996 book, *Emotional Intelligence*. For our purposes, the concept of emotional intelligence is defined in two distinct ways: (1) as being able to identify, process and administer one's own emotions and (2) as being able to identify, process and affect the emotions of another person (Beldoch, 1964; Lerner, 1966; Salavoy & Mayer, 1990; Goleman, 1996). "People who have developed skills related to emotional intelligence understand and express their own emotions, recognize emotions in others, regulate affect, and use moods and emotions to motivate adaptive behaviors" (Salovey & Mayer, 1990, p. 200).

Mapping emotional intelligence in people and characterizing its contribution to their relationships and interpersonal dynamics has become a significant part of ongoing research and study. Increases in emotional intelligence are characterized by a calm outlook on life and an inner peace (Salovey, 1990; Goleman, 1995). There are several key aspects of the concepts that have been recognized. Each of these contribute to the overall gestalt of emotional intelligence by affecting one's inward examination, outward connections and general mindfulness. They are:

- Self-Awareness—the capacity to know oneself including one's thoughts and emotions
- Social Regulation—the capacity to control one's emotions and feelings
- Motivation—the capacity to delay gratification (long-term thinking) and to manage one's emotions related to this experience
- Empathy—the capacity to experience and feel others' emotions and thoughts
- Social Skills—the capacity to relate to others, to interact with others in an emotionally sensitive way

Gottman, Declaire & Goleman, 1998; Salavoy & Mayer, 1990

One cannot overestimate the importance and impact of emotions on everyday life. These feelings can drive a person's thoughts, choices, behaviors, actions, ability to focus, sense of well-being, and even physical vitality. That said, awareness of this aspect of the self and acknowledgment of it in others is an oft overlooked and disregarded component of people's day-to-day functioning. We believe this discounting of emotions has a two-fold etiology. First, our society—from a need to portray strength and toughness—has rendered the concept of being "emotionally" expressive as somewhat pejorative—labeling individuals with an obvious connection to their feelings as sensitive or fragile or hysterical. An off-shoot of this stance is the wishful "what's in the past no longer affects me" understanding of mental health. Second, there are numerous populations—especially those of color—that believe that for security reasons one's emotional state should remain private. We understand this reticence as an extension historical oppression and the importance of maintaining a level of control over one's vulnerability. Living in these oppressive environments, emotionality can be life threatening owing to the negative and violent reactions by those in power. At times, this results in the rejection of any help-seeking activities—ranging from asking for advice from family and friends to seeking/accepting help from professionals.

The skills to understand and interact with emotions originates in the ability parents have to understand their pre-verbal infant. For fathers these skills exist in the collective unconscious and were the same ones used by early herders and farmers to understand their livestock and crops as they pulled together an understanding of non-verbal communication (sounds, movements, textures, color) in order to determine how to respond to injuries, illnesses. insect attacks, poor soil, and dehydration (Hewlett, 2004; Kraemer, 1991; Belsky, 1981).

The incubator of emotional intelligence begins with parents taking in and processing their child's communications, then, through their modeling serves as a conduit to build up and reinforce the child's own emotional intelligence. The importance of this connection becomes apparent as an increasing number of research studies confirm the far-reaching effects of these emotion-based aspects of the parent-child relationships. "Numerous studies have shown that parents' interactions with their children … have deep and continuous consequences in their emotional life and provide the ground for their achievement or failure in different fields of life. Recent findings indicate that appropriate emotional rais[ing] of children is an important factor which affects their future achievements…. Emotional intelligence enables [a parent] to correctly exhibit suitable amounts of different emotions such as rage, fear, love, happiness … in his/her behavior, proportional to the situations and time. Moreover, it enables them to know about others' emotions and act accordingly" (Naghavi & Redzuan, 2011, pg. 558).

Understanding people's feelings and sentiments as communications requires the ability to take into account tone of voice, facial expression, body posture, hand movements, word choice, behavior and context. Acknowledging the infant's cry, sounds, facial expressions, and body movements are all part of discerning the infant's communication. As children get older and develop, their ability to communicate their emotions and ideas becomes more complex and nuanced. They begin to gain advanced motor skills and language and learn to use these to convey messages and meaning (Panscofar & Feagans, 2010). At the same time, the receiver of information (often caregivers and teachers) attempts to keep pace with the changing forms of communication.

Over the course of their maturation from infancy into adulthood, children typically use four different forms of communication independently or in combination. They are:

- Affective (feelings/emotions)—this is emotional expression and is most often non-verbal. Displaying feelings outwardly, children express anger, sadness, happiness or fear in emotive communication that includes: a smile, frown, cringe, cry, scream, laugh, or silence. They may express with their body language or appearance an affective stance such as quiet, animated, down, anxious, emotional or withdrawn [Weiner & Gallo-Silver, 2015].

- Symbolic—this is play in which children act out their communications in the form of games, imaginary play, and artwork, by displaying both non-verbal and verbal messages. Described as symbolic, this early form of expression is constructed with representations of ideas as children learn to conceptualize, organize, and convey their ideas. Play allows children to communicate the nature of their complex world before they are equipped with the enough words to sufficiently describe this world [Weiner & Gallo-Silver, 2015].

- Kinetic (energy level, action, behavior)—this is communication through actions and behavior. This form of expression can be both verbal and non-verbal and is derived through a child's activity level, choice of movement, and energy. This version of communication is used throughout the developmental continuum from infancy (flailing, arching, and rolling) to early childhood (continuing activity when asked to stop, getting out of bed, not sitting still, running away) to adolescence (drinking, skipping homework, choices of friends) [Weiner & Gallo-Silver, 2015].

- Verbal—this is communication with words. Starting simply with monosyllabic words such as "no" and "yes," this form of communication becomes more complex as children's lives and the related requirements increase. The burgeoning language develops as a response to their ever more complicated and multi-faceted systems including social, biological, neurological, and environmental.

These forms of communication in and of themselves have two levels—a manifest and a latent. The manifest level of a communication is the observable part. The latent level is the underlying part, what cannot be seen and must be inferred or intuited. If we use the metaphor of an iceberg, the manifest part of the iceberg is that small amount that juts out above the waterline. We know from the Titanic disaster, that a significant amount of an iceberg exists below the surface of the water, this is the latent part of the iceberg. Using an infant as an example, a baby's cry (manifest communication) can mean over-stimulation, hunger, fatigue, gas, pain, stool or urine (latent communication) and one must consider each in figuring out how to response in a helpful manner.

Being able to identify the latent part of a communication takes effort and commitment. We want to acknowledge the potential for what we call the "fatigue" factor. This occurs due to overwork, single parenthood, poverty, racism and numerous other life conditions that sap our emotional strength. The fatigue factor speaks to the idea that this added level of analysis may, at times, seem like just too much or overkill. Sometimes, we may want to understand a behavior as just a behavior because there is simply no time or energy for anything else. Fathers may deem the processing of latent communication as a lower priority as they attempt to allocate their finite resources to other aspects of fathering. In response to the fatigue factor, we offer this metaphor for consideration. We believe that understanding the latent communication of children is equivalent to putting WD-40 on a sticky door hinge. It is not that the sticky door will not work, it is just that it takes a lot more effort to open it. And since we have to open the door anyway, taking the extra time now to treat the door makes opening it, in the future, easier.

If they choose, fathers have the ability to push past the obvious, by employing all the aspects of emotional intelligence. This is an essential aspect of all the archetypes—the Nurturer, the Protector, the Educator, the Captain and the Jester—each which embrace various aspects of emotional intelligence.

- The Nurturer archetype provides fathers with the ability to be keenly sensitive to non-verbal communication which includes facial expressions, posture and body movements. It is the skill that enables the father to look at his child and know by the way his child is moving that the child is feeling ill.
- This acuity of observation is further supported by the Protector archetype that aids fathers in being cognizant of the non-verbal cues related to emotions including of sadness, anger, fear and nervousness that activate the empathic functions of the archetype. The Protector archetype can inform the father that the child is frightened and when stepping in is the correct move.
- The Captain archetype's awareness of child development helps fathers (1) be aware of and (2) set expectations about often-times subtle developmental/growth-based changes that his child is exhibiting. For fathers who see their children daily, slight changes can be difficult to discern.
- The Educator archetype provides fathers with an instinct for the timing of teachable moments. In addition, it offers fathers the ability to work in concert with the other archetypes to help find the means to explain to his child what the child's thoughts, behavior or feelings may mean.
- The Jester archetype's awareness of the nuances that exist within the give and take of play, presents fathers with the rationale to

understand the underlying purpose of his child's testing of limits and pushing of boundaries.

Manuel has a 15-year-old daughter who is crying about what her "best friend" wrote about her on Instagram. She says to her father that all her friends are going to see it and that no one will talk to her ever again (manifest communication).

Trying to speculate what his daughter's latent communication, including the Captain's knowledge of child development, the Protector's understanding of safety and empathy, and the Nurturer's awareness of intimacy and comradery, Manuel considers the following:

- His daughter is feeling vulnerable (struggling with adolescent identity, how she identifies herself and how she is identified by others).
- His daughter is feeling worried (fearing isolation from her friends).
- His daughter is feeling angry (perceiving betrayal by her friend).
- His daughter is feeling sad (experiencing the situation as a loss).

In addition to their developmental drivers related to maturation, each child develops a unique set of preferences related to her or his forms of communication. Based on a variety of factors (including temperament, attachment style, neurological characteristics and cognitive development), these predilections to certain forms of communication over others ask parents to (1) adapt ways that they receive information from their child and (2) create methods to pass on information on to their child in order to maximize the child's ability to understand and respond.

As a way of operationalizing these preferences, we can place children into one of two tendencies in connection to their communication style. Generally speaking, children can be more "external" meaning that they tend toward *letting out their feelings* to others (verbally, kinetically) or more "internal" meaning that they tend to *keep their feelings inside* themselves communicating their feelings through subtler means (symbolically, affectively) (Weiner & Gallo-Silver, 2015).

Just like their children, fathers maintain a preference with regard to how they communicate their emotions and how they process their children's communications. Using the internal and the external preference as a jumping off point, we find that fathers fall in one of three groups. If you are a fan of psychoanalysis (as we are) these groups also loosely follow the Freudian triumvirate of the Id, the Ego and the Superego. Freud's concept of the workings of the human psyche involved the interaction between the Id, which included all a person's raw instinct, impulses and emotions, the Superego, which housed a person's moral compass, ethics, and sense of right and wrong, and the Ego, which functioned as the go-between for the Id, the Superego, and the outside world (Freud & Strachey, 1990). As we connect emotional intelligence to the act of fathering, our three types of fathers are as follows:

- Cerebral (Internal)—this father thinks first and feels second, if at all. Like Freud's Superego, he considers all possibilities, tends to perseverate (overthink) about decisions, and finds taking action anxiety producing. Because of these characteristics, a Cerebral father's emotional intelligence has limited connection to actual emotion. He may very well be able to identify emotions in himself and his child, but only on an intellectual level. He remains unsure how to react and showing empathy is difficult for him.

Manuel (a Cerebral father) has a 15-year-old daughter who is crying about what her "best friend" wrote about her on Instagram. She says to her father that all her friends are going to see it and that no one will ever talk to her again. Manuel sees how upset his daughter is and he feels that her friend did a terrible thing by writing about his daughter on the Internet (what he considers "teasing"). He says to her that her "best friend" is not her friend at all, and that she really is not a nice person. He says that she shouldn't let her friend's words get to her, that they are just words. His daughter gets angry and shouts, "You just don't understand!" Manuel sees his daughter is angry and is confused as to what to do next. He thinks that his daughter is overreacting and that she should be angry at her friend, not at him.

- Visceral (External)—this father feels first and thinks second, if ever. He is all Id, impulsive, head strong, and passionate. His automatic responses rule his reactions and he allows them to drive him forward in any situation and at any time. The Visceral father's emotional intelligence has limited connection to himself or others. This father finds it difficult to stop long enough to consider how his outbursts affect the people around him. Because of this, he thinks displays of empathy are weak and exceedingly out-of-his comfort zone.

Manuel (a Visceral father) has a 15-year-old daughter who is crying about what her "best friend" wrote about her on Instagram. She says to her father that all her friends are going to see it and that no one will ever talk to her again. Manuel sees how upset his daughter is and starts to yell, "That little bitch, I never liked her. She's a bully. Give me her number, I'm calling her parents and tell them just what I think of their daughter. I never want you to see her again!" Manuel feels rage and cannot see his daughter through the fury. He hears her shouting in the distance but cannot make out the words. He continues to rant and rave unaware that his daughter has run off and left him alone without giving him her friend's number. He is embroiled in his own feelings of having been teased and the various ways he has sought revenge.

- Mindful (Internal/External)—this father has the ability to think and feel at the same time. He is able to strike a balance between his feelings, his thoughts and his actions, rolling them into a cohesive reaction to his child's needs. He personifies the functioning Ego, the ability to assess situations and develop a measured response. He knows that whatever he says, his contributions are just part of a larger process that includes those around him having their own reactions. Sometimes he speaks, sometimes he listens, sometimes he takes charge, and sometimes he hangs back. He does not always get the balance right but is able to notice when he has over-responded cerebrally or viscerally and tries to course correct. The family looks to him as a barometer for the nature of any given situation. In this flexibility, he is able to display empathy, strictness, guidance, affection, and/or humor.

Manuel (a Mindful father) has a 15-year-old daughter who is crying about what her "best friend" wrote about her on Instagram. She says to her father that all her friends are going to see it and that no one will talk to her ever again. Manuel sees how upset his daughter is and sits down next to her. He wonders to himself what she needs to hear from him at this moment. He is very angry and wants to tell her that a friend who would do this is not a friend at all but waits for her to speak. She continues to cry, and he puts his arm around her. After several minutes he says, "It is really hard when the people closest to us hurt us. I think these are the moments that hurt the most. I am really sorry about all this." She leans against him and continues to cry. "I just don't know what to do," she says. "Maybe you don't have to figure it out right now," Manuel offers.

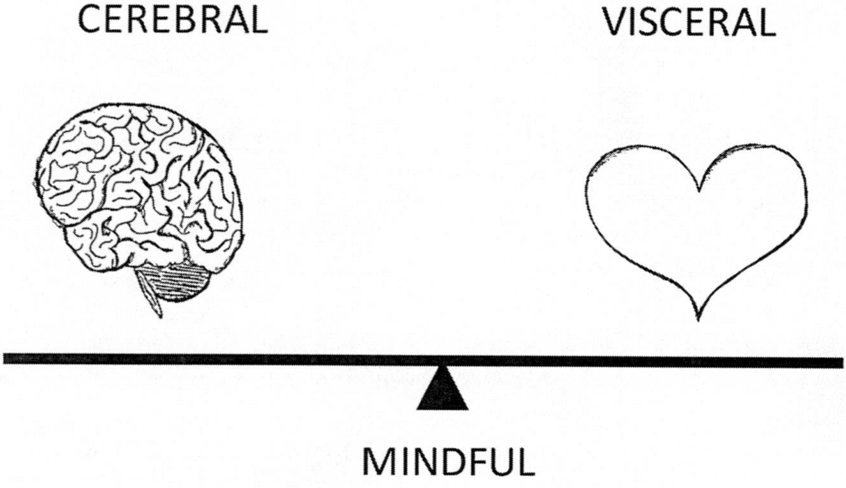

CEREBRAL

VISCERAL

MINDFUL

Figure 13.1—Emotional intelligence and the three types of fathers.

The Cerebral Father and His Archetype Expression

The archetypes that lean toward thought—the Captain and the Educator—tend to be the typical choices of the Cerebral father. This father finds accessing and expressing these archetypes to be more comfortable based on his fundamental focus on rules and data (albeit the more rigid and pedantic versions of the archetypes). These are the concrete archetypes of straight lines, correct answers and clear boundaries. They are not dependent on emotion and, in fact, may be expressed without it.

The Cerebral father's partiality toward these archetypes does not preclude his use of other archetypes. However, it makes access to these archetypes more complicated. Managing this impact on his emotional intelligence require this father to be vigilant for over expression of the rule-oriented archetypes and the under expression of archetypes that ask him to feel. The Protector archetype's requisite connection, worry, and empathy, the Nurturer archetype's demonstration of love, affection, and intimacy, and the Jester archetype's association with vulnerability, fun, and interactive play, all may challenge this father in that they necessitate a level of externality with which he may struggle.

As he communicates more and more of the concrete aspects of these archetypes without the counter-weight of the emotionally-connected archetypes, over-expression of archetypes for the Cerebral father can include

- the Corporal version of the Captain (a fixation on the rules and rule maintenance),
- the Squasher version of the Educator (hyper focus on the content of learning), or
- the Secret Service Agent of the Protector (a zealous adherence to safety protocols).

Continuing this trend, he may under express the emotional/empathic elements of certain archetypes deploying (1) the Abandoner version of the empathic elements of the Protector, (2) the Killjoy version of the Jester or (3) the Rejecter version of the Nurturer, limiting the emotional closeness that his child requires.

The Visceral Father and Archetype Expression

The archetypes that lean toward feeling—the Nurturer and the Protector—tend to be the typical choices of the Visceral father. This father finds accessing and expressing these archetypes to be more comfortable based on their fundamental focus on the expression of emotion. These are the archetypes of big feelings and behaviors. The issue is that the Visceral father may struggle with the delineation of boundaries that clarify family roles.

The Visceral father's partiality toward these archetypes often preclude his use of other archetypes as he becomes caught up in his own feelings and can lose contact with the situation at hand or the people around him. Managing the impact of his emotional intelligence requires this father to be vigilant about the automatic responses that overtake his ability to make more reasonable, thoughtful choices and remain emotionally connected to his child.

As he communicates more and more of his own needs to the exclusion of his child's needs, over-expression of archetypes for the Visceral father include

- the Smotherer version of the Nurturer (an inability to consider the needs of others and a focus on one's own need for attention, affection and devotion),
- the Mind Reader version of the empathic elements of the Protector (a belief that his thoughts and the child's thoughts are the same, and/or anticipating the child's needs based on imaginary knowledge of the child's thoughts), or
- the Secret Service agent of the safety elements of the Protector (a zealous adherence to safety protocols and a rage when they are broken).

The Visceral father may under-express certain archetypes, using his upset to withdraw from necessary contact with his child. He can do this by deploying the Abdicator version of the Captain, the Skimmer version of the Educator, or the Killjoy version of the Jester, without thought or awareness of how he his stance is putting the child in danger and abetting a sense of feeling uncared for.

The Mindful Father and Archetype Expression

The Mindful father is able to access the full range of fathering archetypes. This does not render him perfect, but it does mean he is thoughtful, self-aware and sensitive. Most importantly the Mindful father is able to observe himself and, therefore, is able to discern through his own feelings and his child's reactions when he has made an error. He is able apologize to his child and make amends. This display of human imperfection helps his child to be less critical of his or her own foibles, instills a willingness to try to do better the next time, and helps teach the important lesson of forgiveness.

Mindfulness and Its Effect on Emotional Intelligence and Archetype Expression

Ellen Langer, a social psychologist and professor of psychology at Harvard University, states that "virtually all the world's ills boil down to mindlessness" (Langer, 2014, p. 50). With this in mind, let us define the concept of the counter-agent to the "world's ills," mindfulness. Mindfulness is one's undertaking of actively noticing one's external and internal reality at any given moment, considering one's long-held beliefs and altering them to address new realities, and, finally, attempting to take actions based on any new observations (Lazar, et al., 2005; Lutz, et al., 2008; Davidson, et al., 2003; Tang, et al., 2007; Carson, et al., 2004; Barnes, et al., 2007; Hutcherson, et al., 2008; Singh, et al., 2007; Beddoe & Murphy, 2004; Shapiro, et al., 2005). Alexander calls the positive effect of mindfulness, "mindstrength" (Alexander, 2009). We like this word as it conveys the constructive force that can help men feel more empowered to make fathering decisions that feel more personally honest, conscious and complete.

Mindfulness is in essence the building of skills to control one's brain waves and in doing so enhance one's ability to think, feel, and make conscious choices. We have heard people say "Slow down" or "Relax" to someone who is upset or hyped up. Even though we are told that this does not typically help people to hear (because it usually lacks empathy), this is what these phrases are referring to—the alteration of one's mind-set as a way of helping someone to think. To aid in our understanding of how this all works, we can examine a list of brain waves and their overly simplified descriptions (see Table 13.1).

Table 13.1—Brain Waves and Mindfulness

- Theta waves—the pulses of one's typical sleep and the access point to learning and memory. They are the connection to Jung's collective unconscious.
- Alpha waves—the cadences of the rest. They exist as the brain's ability to be in the moment, to stay calm, to be watchful and aware.
- Beta waves—the rhythms of one's day to day waking life. These are critical for an individual's solving of problems, displaying judgment, maintaining impulse control, making choices and identifying options.
- Gamma waves—the fastest waves of one's highest brain functioning, including sharing information between parts of the brain.

With brain waves in mind, we can begin to see how mindfulness may help with emotional intelligence. Moving the mind from using beta waves (faster) to alpha waves or theta waves (slower) may help move Visceral fathers from action to thought, from doing to considering, from energy usage to energy conservation. An awareness of these waves and the wherewithal to gain control over the connection between mind and body may allow a Cerebral father who is typically using alpha waves (slower) to use beta waves (faster) becoming more active and involved. Promisingly, research has shown that mindfulness exercises can accomplish just this endeavor.

For the purpose of fathering, employing mindfulness can provide fathers with fuller access to their emotional intelligence. Coming from a more fluid point of view, one that mindfulness allows for, fathers can experience effective access to all the archetypes and wield this expanded archetypal use with more thought and intent and less instinct and impulse. This consciousness supported by mindfulness creates the ability to separate out two realities—the father's from that of the child's. A thoughtful separation slows the process of parenting down to the point where fathers are able to (1) side step instinctual, emotional responses (automatic responses) and (2) galvanize themselves into action that may be outside their nature. Most importantly, mindfulness enhances fathers' innate ability to "notice" the latent communication of their children whether conveyed through words, emotion, behavior, or play. This creates an increased number of choices and options for more effective fathering.

Toward the end of a parent-teacher conference, Donald and his wife receive information from their younger son's 3rd grade teacher that she and the school administration believe that their son has Attention-Deficit Hyperactivity Disorder. His wife can tell as she translates for Donald that an explosion is coming. Donald communicates to the teacher using American Sign language. His wife translates for the teacher with a good deal of embarrassment: "This information is provided to us without any warning and without any evidence of behavior problems prior to this school year and you call yourselves professionals? Did you get your teaching degree with the lowest grades in your class?" His wife makes their apologies and maneuvers her husband out of the school. She knows that she has to let her husband calm down on his own. Donald just keeps on signing to his wife furiously: "These people are idiots!" "They are going to blame him because they can't teach! Behavior problems?! Behavior problems?! I am going to call the superintendent of schools. I am going to get that woman fired … no one talks about my kid that way!" He completely obliterates all of the nice things the teacher has said about his son.

Donald is obviously a Visceral father. While the teacher uses poor judgment in presenting a diagnosis that she is not qualified to make, Donald takes her comments as a personal insult. It is as if the teacher purposely decides to insult him. Donald, a member of a language minority has experienced his fair share of rude behavior. His wife understands this since she is the hearing daughter of parents who also are members of Deaf culture and communicate using American Sign Language. His wife just hopes that Donald will take a moment to take time to think before he speaks with their son about the conference.

Donald enters his son's room, still agitated, and signs, "Do you know what they said about you?! Do you know?! I have never been more embarrassed in my life. Never! You will listen to your teacher! You will sit still! You will concentrate! You will not get out of your seat! Do you understand me?" His son sits, stunned, staring at his father with tears welling in his eyes. His wife enters the room, tells Donald to leave the room and then comforts their son.

Donald realizes almost immediately after leaving his son's room that he has made a mistake. If he has any doubts, his wife's look of reproach confirms this to him. He is filled with remorse, but still feels his heart beating quickly and the overheated discomfort from sweating through his clothes. He knows if he takes several deep breaths, he will cool down both emotionally and physically. He follows the instructions from the book on guided imagery he has on how to relax. He breathes in while pushing out his belly making room for the air, then he breathes out deflating his belly. He slows his breathing down, especially when he breathes out. While he does this, he imagines himself walking through the forest near his childhood home. The book told him to think of all the tension leaving his body whenever he breathes out. Gradually, he feels cooler and stops sweating, his heart beat slows. He gets out of his chair and walks towards his son's room. His wife blocks his way. He gives the signs that his is calmer and she kisses him.

He finds his son at his desk doing his homework. He signs: "I am so sorry. Your dad can really be a jerk sometimes. I had no right to yell at you like that…. I was totally wrong. I broke a ton of my own rules and I apologize." He waits for a moment for the apology to sink in and then continues. "The teacher told us that you are a great kid and that she really enjoys teaching you. We want you know that is the most important thing for you to remember. We also were told that you were having some difficulties focusing and sitting still and that the teacher is a bit worried about you. Your Mom and I will help you figure out what is going on, and we can talk all about that tomorrow. Tonight, I just want you to know that I love you very much, even when I make mistakes … and this was a big one. I had a lot of trouble with teachers because, I had a chip on my shoulder as a kid. I guess I still do. Do you know what that means?" His son nods. "Anyway, I am sorry … everything is fine. You okay?" His son smiles and signs: "Dad, can you do me a solid? Next time, do that breathing stuff before you come into my room and freak out?" Donald pretends to make an angry face and then kisses his son on the top of his head.

This is the more Mindful version of Donald's emotional intelligence. He employs an apology for his actions (the Protector), an acknowledgment of his own rule breaking (the Jester and the Captain), praise for son's study habits (the Nurturer), an explanation of what the teacher shared (the Educator), an assurance of parental help to face any problems (the Protector and Captain, again) and affection and intimacy before bed (the Nurturer, again). For Donald, this ultimate fathering response to his son represents a significant level of emotional intelligence and a thoroughly complete archetypal communication.

Mindfulness does not come naturally to Donald at this time. Perhaps in the future his visceral reactions will not automatically overtake him. His son cannot not wait for that day. He needs a more mindful father now. The deep breathing exercise—often called a grounding exercise—helps put Donald into the present, the here and now, where his son lives, and not stuck in the past where Donald struggled with his own teachers. This is also Donald as a Strong-willed father (Temperament), an Intense father (Relational Dynamics), and a moving against father trying to maintain a sense of control (Time Orientation). We will add more to our understanding of fathers like Donald in the next chapter about world-view. For now, the central message is that Donald is able to admit his mistakes to his son, ask for forgiveness and learn an important lesson. His son knows him better than he thinks and loves him as the imperfect father that he is.

Behind the theory, research and practice, are the ideas that Mindful emotional intelligence is about a father trying to use as many appropriate archetypes as possible for any given situation or interaction with a child. Even if they have the proclivity toward a certain type of emotional expression, stemming from any number of factors or fathering characteristics, we strongly believe that fathers can transform. If they choose to slow down and be thoughtful, or if they choose to speed up and access more emotion and urgency, fathers are capable of moving along the emotional intelligence continuum and become more complete fathers.

14

Fathers' World-View and Impact on Archetype Access

He continued to behold towers and quadrangles, and chapels through rose colored spectacles.—Thomas Hughes

I saw everything through rose colored spectacles.—Pauline Mettrenich-Sandor

Some dads because of the way they were treated by their parents ... if it was a bad way ... they treat their kids like that.—Nathaniel Owen Weiner

In the quote above, 7-year-old Nathaniel is expressing his precocious understanding of the impact of his friend's father's world-view. In his example, the father's responses have a connection to the man's past. In our effort to enumerate the factors, or characteristics, that affect (1) the relationship between father and child and (2) a father's alternatives with regard to access and usage of specific archetypes, we chose five—temperament, relational dynamics, time orientation, emotional intelligence and, now, world-view. This last characteristic is a synthesis of the previous four. For our purposes, world-view is defined as a person's general and persistent outlook on the world and life (Merriam Webster, 2016).

This individual perspective, or way of thinking, flows from and is constructed by a father's experiences and notions, starting from infancy and moving forward (Sullivan, 1953). The notion of childhood, life experiences and perceptions shaping one's life track and outlook is not a new one. It revolves once again, around the consideration of nature versus nurture, and in this case, views nurture as preeminent (Ridley, 2003). The practice areas of psychology, psychoanalysis and social work have been operating under this assumption for decades. However, until scientific research began confirming this idea, the connection was theoretical and its substantiation anecdotal. One theorist who was in the vanguard of this type of thinking was Harry Stack Sullivan, an American psychiatrist who helped develop psychoanalysis and psychotherapy in the United States. He believed that people develop their own individual sense of "reality" from a collection of early experiences and early relationships (Wampold, 2010). For our discussion in this chapter, we would like to use the metaphor of glasses (that a person wears in order to see more clearly) as representing one's reality.

To confirm Sullivan's theories, there have been many scientific studies that have focused on determining what factors affect the trajectory of one's life and one's related outlook. For our purposes, we are focusing on what happens to, and around, a man during his lifetime (before he is a father and when he is a father) and how these experiences—whether positive or negative—shape him.

In 1975, the Minnesota Longitudinal Study of Risk and Adaptation began as an attempt to discern what and how life experiences influence people's risks, strengths, and overall life routes and outcomes. In 2005, Drs. L. Alan Sroufe, Bryon Egeland, Elizabeth Carlson and W. Andrew Collins published *The Development of the Person* which details the findings of research collected over 36 years of 267 first-time mothers. Among many conclusions, researchers found that the quality of the early relationships with both parents and with friends is correlated to how individuals will interact with their later relationships (significant others and children) when they reach adulthood. "Positive parenting in the first generation correlated ... with positive parenting in the second generation; negative parenting in the first generation correlated ... with negative parenting in the second generation" (Sroufe, Egland, Carlson & Collins, 2014, p. 292). The areas of caregiving included levels of supportive attention, the nature of the assistance, the level of hostility, and the type of boundaries that were maintained, with impacting factors of note involving level of education, financial wherewithal, and cognitive processes, among others (Sroufe, et al., 2014).

In 1998, Drs. Vincent Felitti of Kaiser Permanente Health Centers and Robert Anda of the United States Center for Disease Control published a study entitled *The Adverse Childhood Experiences (ACE) Study*. Their study of 17,421 men and women indicated that childhood experiences of violence and other traumas could result in risky life-style choices, chronic medical conditions, diminished potential, disrupted relationships, and early death (Felitti, Anda, Nordenberg, Williamson., Spitz., Edwards, Koss. & Marks, 1998). The ACE studies and other subsequent studies, demonstrate that a person's ideas about life, identity and the self, and the world, when shaped by traumatic and/or oppressive experiences such as maltreatment, racism, poverty, sexism, or other abuses of power, can create thought processes that lead to poor decision-making and deleterious automatic responses (see Figure 14.1).

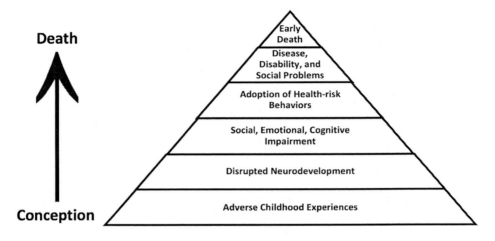

Death

Conception

Mechanisms by which Adverse Childhood Experiences Influence Health and Well-Being over Lifespan

Figure 14.1—Possible effects of adverse childhood experiences (adapted from Felitti and Anda, et al., 1998).

Sroufe and his colleague's (2014) use of terms such as "positive" and "negative" parenting pull our discourse toward the idea that regardless of the specifics, there exists a constellation of factors that can move the needle in one direction or another with regards to how a person experiences early life. While Felitti and Anda et al. (1998) might use different words like "adverse" or "favorable" to describe the way someone experiences being parented, any of these characterizations—from positive to negative, adverse or favorable, good or evil, punitive or kind, normal or not normal—will influence a father's overall understanding of his environment. Drawing from how they were parented and a variety of other factors which we will discuss below, fathers maintain this sense of "the way the world is"—what we call world-view—and incorporate this outlook as yet another characteristic that shapes their access and expressions of fathering archetypes.

The father's world-view is often a fixed entity within each man and is one of the driving forces behind his decision-making and thought processes (Langer, 2014). This world-view exists as the synopsis of all the files stored on the father's computer hard drive—his brain. The files contain his memories, feelings, ideas, thoughts, and wishes that are part of his childhood and beyond. This includes his life as an infant, child, adolescent, young adult, and adult (see Table 14.1). For the purpose of organization, let's place these files into separate folders.

Table 14.1—Files of a Person's World-View

- Relationships with his parents, his siblings, other family members, other adults and friends in addition to the stated and unspoken rules (family, religion, cultural, and societal) that governed these relationships;
- Experiences at home, in school, at work, and in his community;
- Fixed ideas about the right and wrong ways of eating, sleeping, spending, working, studying, playing, yelling, crying, laughing, and being angry, sad or scared;
- Events (that he has witnessed), situations (that he has participated in), trauma and losses (both resolved and unresolved that he has experienced), and instances of oppression including varied forms of violence, danger, exploitation, marginalization, and powerlessness (that he has encountered) (Young, 2004);
- Memories, fantasies, wishes and fears related to all the above categories.

These five folders hold the details that shape a father's world-view and influence all his thought processes in addition to how he understands his life. A father who believes that his life is a certain way—positive or negative—bases his conception of his reality on the analysis of the files pulled from these folders. We call this analysis—his perception. Perception is a powerful, yet underappreciated, tool of the brain. It allows fathers to understand their "external" reality in many different ways (Lanza & Berman, 2016). In addition, we believe that perception is made up of both nature and nurture elements that work in concert without any meaningful boundaries between the two. Specific experiences affect neurological development, shaping how one's neurobiology processes future experiences. It is a loop without a detectable beginning or end (Stern, 2004). It should be clear, then, that no two fathers can have exactly the same world-view as no two fathers can share life experiences or identical neurobiology. Yet, because of the existence of historical trauma affecting groups, communities, cultures, religions, and whole populations, there are often common elements or themes among fathers' perceptions and, consequently, world-views (Graff, G., 2014; Murdoch, 2009; Meierhenrich, 2007; Bell, 2006; Sotero, 2006; Eyerman, 2001).

In returning to Sullivan's writings, he believed an individual's own brand of reality was fixed (for instance, "rose colored glasses"). When a father's fixed sense of reality is challenged by new ideas, experiences and relationships that do not "fit" into his sense of reality, that father is left to deny, avoid or undo the new information as a way of preserving his special brand of reality. Gazing though his own rose-colored glasses of perception, a father may re-interpret or distort what he sees, struggling with the idea that there may be an alternative to his rose-colored view. The other option that Sullivan suggested is for a person to change his/her perception of reality to include these new experiences and relationships. In this way, a father may decide that the rose-colored glasses need to be traded in for a different shade or color. If a father chooses the latter, he may now experience reality in a different way, accompanied by a change in his expectations of and assumptions about the world in which he lives and altering the perceptions and understanding of all of his relationships from the past and to the present (Sullivan, 1953).

As we have done in previous chapters, we feel it necessary to simplify the concepts for the ease of application and use. Synthesizing all the files, we place a father's outlook, or world-view, on a continuum. Depending on how he processes and integrates the material in each of his folders and what long-term impact this has had on him, a father can be placed on the continuum.

We choose the metaphor of multi-colored lenses/glasses because of the way that colors can be blended to create subtle variations, shades and hues. The characterization of world-view as color requires the reader to see world-view as an average of all of a father's life experiences—generally blue, purple, or rose (see Figure 14.2).

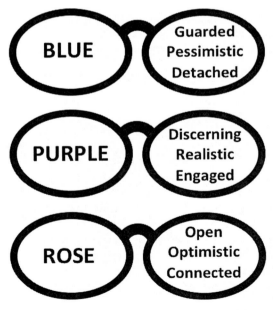

BLUE — Guarded / Pessimistic / Detached

PURPLE — Discerning / Realistic / Engaged

ROSE — Open / Optimistic / Connected

Figure 14.2—The continuum of a father's world-view.

World-view's importance as a characteristic impacting fathering stems from its potential effect on his availability to new experiences and his willingness and ability to view his "past" as only one aspect of himself, not the entirety (Gartner, 2005). Considering Jung, we can understand world-view as the filter through which a father accesses the collective unconscious and can then more clearly see its effect on archetypes usage. Certain lenses make it very challenging for a father to view and process experiences because they color and distort his vision—wearing specific glasses require him to see events through these distortions. Rose colored glasses have the effect of making experiences seem "rosy," while blue colored lenses can cast a sense "melancholy" over a father's experiences. If the colors represent a world view, then having a blue, pessimistic, world-view can lead a father to feel a sense of stoic realism when interacting with his child. Conversely, a father with a rosy, optimistic world-view can find himself always seeing the bright side. While both of these are perfectly justifiable in and of themselves, they may not always be connected to what his child needs at any given moment.

Recall Errol, the father who struggles to interact with his daughter's adolescent decision-making.

He has told his 14-year-old daughter a million times that she has a curfew and must be home for dinner by 6:00 p.m., yet she is consistently late. Errol becomes enraged, takes off his belt and threatens to hit her with it. His daughter cries and begs her father not to hit her. Errol restrains himself, but he threatens to "teach her a lesson if she is late again."

When she breaks her curfew again, he hits her on her bare legs with his belt. In the confusion of his daughter trying to escape him, and his own rage and fear, he hits her arm and her neck several times.

The next day Errol is interviewed by child protective services worker who was contacted by his daughter's school. Errol is confused and angry. He tells child protective services that he received far worse beatings by his own parents, and asks "how else was he supposed to control his daughter."

Errol maintains a world-view that is shaped by an overall sense of insecurity and vulnerability. The fixed world-view can leave a father with a typical way of relating to others included his children. The chart above indicates that a father's world-view and his connection to others can run the gamut from guardedness to openness; from pessimism to optimism (see Figure 14.2).

Errol's early relationships—his file folders—include intense levels of corporal punishment and other punitive interactions. In his experience, children follow their parents' orders. Rule breaking is strictly forbidden and not tolerated. The enforcement of rules is punctuated by threats of physical punishment, and then, if necessary, increasingly violent acting out of physical punishment. This reflects the rigidity of his parent's beliefs, their own experiences of family violence, and the oppressive legacy of their country of origin's historic, brutal slave culture. Errol's loss of control and violent outburst indicate a connection to his traumatic childhood experiences. At the same time, his agitation reflects his fear and anxiety about the real dangers that could challenge a teenager out late at night. This combination of factors drives his automatic responses to zero in on her missing curfew. It becomes the job of child protective services, mandated parenting, and anger management classes to educate Errol and provide him with alternatives, choices and options to addressing his concerns about his daughter—and hopefully begin to shift his world-view.

In applying the previously described fatherhood characteristics we can say that Errol displays

- a Strong-Willed temperament,
- an Intense attachment style,
- a Moving Against stance with a Present time orientation, and
- a Visceral emotional intelligence.

From this, we can hypothesize that Errol has a world-view on the Blue side of the continuum. He has a more pessimistic view of the world due to the number of adverse childhood experiences he has absorbed (see Figure 14.1). This inevitably shapes his understanding of his daughter's actions and defines and limits his access to collective unconscious and molds his expression of the archetypes. When we couple his personal files of familial trauma, violence, and maltreatment during childhood, with files related to a cultural violence and exploitation, Errol's fierce automatic fight response to perceptions of danger can be viewed as understandable, even appropriate, adaptations.

Unfortunately, the recipient of this fight response is his daughter and not the people he fears will hurt her. In this case, the mixture of fatherhood characteristics leads Errol to choose to express the Corporal version of the Captain as he hits his daughter. His confusion and dismay over the involvement of child protective services is based on his current inability to identify any other way to respond to his daughter's disobedience. If Errol is willing to consider alternatives, the answer to his question "How else can I control my daughter?" can be found in his other unused archetypes. His defense—that he received worse beatings as a child—indicates how his own adverse childhood experiences restricts his access and expression of his other fathering archetypes.

While Errol's expression of his Blue world-view is active, other fathers, like Miguel from Chapter 11, may communicate their version of world-view in a more passive fashion. Recall that Miguel has a 5-year-old daughter who is expressing an unwillingness to go to kindergarten. Recalling Miguel and his frustrations and inner-conflict with the school dynamics.

He becomes furious that his daughter is subject to discrimination and visits the school, meeting with the principal and the teachers. The teachers explain that the girls have formed cliques. Miguel remains angry. He tells the teachers that if the girls have formed cliques then it is their responsibility to make sure that all children are included in play. The principal agrees, Miguel worries at home, with his wife and his daughter, about how this school is ever going to handle his daughter's healthy racial identity formation. He vows to remove her from the school if he does not see a rapid response to his demands.

Miguel grew up in a home in which most, if not all, problems were "swept under the rug." He was raised by very strict, God-fearing parents and felt that he never really had a voice. They yelled a lot, criticized him and had very high standards, which he struggled to meet. Living in a small town that was racially predominately white, he was one of only three boys of color in his entire grade—a cohort that stayed together from elementary school to high school. This, coupled with his home life, left him often feeling like an outsider. Like Errol, Miguel's world-view is on the Blue side of the continuum. Unlike Errol, Miguel does not act out, he acts in. His adverse childhood experiences have left him feeling profoundly doubtful that anyone will help him. He finds it difficult to trust people who do not look like him and people who have power over some aspect of his life. He rages within his mind and often withdraws from conflict, before getting a resolution that could satisfy him.

In this situation, his daughter's actual experience of the school and the difficulties that she is trying to communicate to her father are subsumed with his pessimism and rejection. Miguel's expression of Captain archetype is as the Corporal, with his form of punishment centering on how he takes his frustration out on the school. In his effort to control the situation, he, unfortunately, under-expresses other key archetypes that could assist in mollifying his worries by empowering his daughter. Miguel as Educator is left unexpressed (Skimmer)—does he have any suggestions for her as to how to navigate a situation in which she is the only girl of color? In which she feels like an outsider? Miguel as Protector is left under-expressed with regard to empathy (Abandoner) and over-expressed in terms of safety (Secret Service agent)—how much of the intense concern that he is expressing to the school and his wife regarding his daughter's discrimination have to do with his daughter's experience and how much has to do with his own experience as a man of color? Miguel's world-view is a difficult one within which to parent. Miguel can parent holistically, but it will require trust, strength and determination and a willingness to be vulnerable and open. This is a challenging request of him for it is far more comfortable to travel the path that his old files dictated for him. These files consistently remind him to be guarded and aloof in order to preserve himself. That said, his daughter is clamoring for more.

World-View and the Archetypes

As indicated by Errol, Miguel and the fathers described in previous chapters, a father's access to archetypes and the way that he expresses them, correlates closely to his fathering characteristics. The three versions of world-view that we have created—Blue (pessimism), Purple (realism), and Rose (optimism)—represent the possible, wide-ranging perceptual identifications of his world. The attributes of each include a father's typical way of connecting to others, his overall posture toward vulnerability and safety, and his ideas (confidence or otherwise) regarding the potential for constructive change.

Blue world-view:
This father perceives that world as a hostile place. Trauma of all kinds including child maltreatment, indirectly-experienced violence, war, oppression (including individual, group, historical, institutional, and cultural), losses or abrupt life changes results in this fixed perception. This, then, can lead this father to perceive himself (and those around him) as vulnerable, requiring him to take precautions, plan for possible negative eventualities, and/or maintain distance from others. Because of this guarded nature, trust, which must be earned, is doled out cautiously and can be lost quickly if there is a disruption in a relationship. His outlook is pessimistic, in that, he expects life experiences to be complex, challenging and requiring a great deal of work. In his world-view, nothing comes easy. Unfortunately for these fathers, research on ACEs indicates that a glaring companion to their pessimism and guardedness is the fear, anxiety and anger that stems from their life events and that this multi-layered angst contributes to complications in health, work, relationship functioning, and self-esteem [Felitti & Anda, et al, 1998].

Purple world-view:
This father perceives that the world "is what it is." Like the words from the hit 1980s situation comedy *The Facts of Life* theme song, this father realistically understands that the world can be experienced in a variety of ways, from positive to negative [Thicke, Loring & Burton, 1979]. He understands that there is joy and there is sadness. This requires a certain level of caution on his part, but not so much as to be distant or detached with regard to his life experiences or choices about relationships. We describe this element of his world-view as discerning. This father perceives his life and the world around him as full of possibilities and tries to be a willing participant for he perceives Khalil Gilbran's passage in The Prophet to be accurate for him:

"When you are joyous, look deep into your heart and you shall find it is only that which has given you sorrow that is giving you joy.
When you are sorrowful look again in your heart, and you shall see that in truth you are weeping for that which has been your delight" [Gilbran, 1923, pg. 29].

This father recognizes that people will disappoint him and people will pleasantly surprise him; tragic events will occur and so will wonderful ones; he will have successes and failures; and so maintains a realistic outlook regarding his day-to-day living.

Rose world-view:

This father perceives that the world is a wholly positive place. He may:

- trust quickly and completely,
- give people a second, third, and fourth chance,
- provide people with the benefit of the doubt, even with evidence to the contrary,
- never say "no" to anyone, or
- see harmful or destructive acts of another as mistakes or inadvertent.

The rejection of all that is bad in the world (and the resulting optimism) is often accomplished by discounting, avoiding, ignoring, or forgetting those aspects of his life that are or were unpleasant, painful, distressing or even traumatic. There is extensive psychology research focusing on the idea that a person's memory of life events can be altered (through dissociation), diminished (through suppression), or become consciously inaccessible to them (through repression) [Jones, 1957; Janet, 1899]. In fact, a father with a Rose world view may have no clear memories of his/her childhood and assume this is because it was uneventful, never wondering why he does not at least have pleasant memories (instead of no memories at all). Research on ACEs indicates that altering of reality in this way is actually a form of imperfect protection [Felitti & Anda, et al., 1998]. Fathers with a Rose world-view, with their fervent and fearful need for illusory optimism and positive connections, find themselves on a world-view continuum that actually wraps around in a circle that meets up with the pessimistic unreality of the Blue-colored lenses wearing father.

When we examine how these world-views may affect a father's choices, expression and access of his fathering archetypes, we look at the three elements of that father's world-view:

1. his relationship to connectedness with his environment,
2. his level of trust in his environment, and
3. overall sense in how events in his environment will turn out

As we have discussed before, every father will place a different level of emphasis on each of these areas of world-view and so the specifics regarding archetypal expression will vary from father to father.

The open/connected/optimistic father (Rose) finds it more comfortable expressing the following archetypes because they enable him to respond to his children with closeness and connection:

- Jester (playing and having fun),
- Nurturer (providing love, affection, and intimacy) and
- Protector (expressing empathy and understanding).

What tends to be complicated is the Rose father's access to and expression of the archetypes that ask him to manage potential conflict, distress, and worry with regard to his child, including

- Captain (setting rules, limits and providing discipline),
- Educator (figuring out how to convey information), and
- Protector (awareness of safety, danger).

Devlin and his wife have 2-year-old twin girls who were born prematurely and each of whom have had gastro-intestinal complications since birth. These issues require that they be fed through feeding tubes. Devlin is a good-natured, upbeat father who loves his daughters very much. He is always willing to play with them but often physically overtaxes them. Anything that reminds Devlin of his daughters' ongoing serious medical problems makes him withdraw from them. He has not stepped into a hospital or doctor's office since the day he brought his girls home. He tells his wife he knows she can handle the visits on her own. He does not ask for any information about their condition. If his daughters do not feel well, he tends to make himself scarce and disengages from them.

We can surmise that at the very least Devlin has been traumatized by the events following his daughters' birth. His Rose view of his daughters' medical issues is marked by denial and avoidance. Devlin may expand this stance, significantly under-expressing the Captain (the Abdicator), the Educator (the Skimmer), the Protector (the Abandoner), and the Nurturer (the Rejecter) in areas of his daughters' lives that include and extend beyond their medical care. At the same time, he over-expresses the Jester (Peter Pan). Without their father's involvement in this extremely significant and overwhelming area of their lives, his daughters are left to question whether Devlin loves them unconditionally. They may compensate, over-extending themselves physically during play with their father to please him. Devlin's avoidance of the doctors maintains his Rose world-view, but at the expense of his ability to access and express other fathering archetypes his children need. His children are forced to collude with Devlin and make believe they do not have any physical limitations.

The guarded/detached/pessimistic father (Blue) finds it more comfortable expressing the following archetypes because they exercise aspects of the supervision and control over both his own inner life and his child's outer life so necessary in an unsafe world:

- Captain (setting rules, limits and providing discipline),
- Educator (figuring out how to convey information), and
- Protector (awareness of safety, danger).

The Blue father has difficulty with archetypes that require him to display and interact with a level of vulnerability, closeness and uncertainty with his child, including

- Jester (playing and having fun),
- Nurturer (providing love, affection, and intimacy), and
- Protector (expressing empathy and understanding).

Saito sees his 12-year-old son talking to a girl after school when he arrives at the school to drive him home. He rolls down the window of the car and shouts, "Come!" His son puts his head down and runs to the car. As he sits next to him, Saito stares straight ahead, saying nothing. They arrive at home and Saito asks, "Homework?" The son confirms that he has homework and Saito responds with, "Go! I will call you when dinner is ready." Saito is furious that his son is talking to girls. It is a terrible distraction. When he was young, he was told over and over again by both his father and mother to stay focused on learning. Whenever they felt he was not listening, they would beat him or yell at him. "There will be time for that, later, when you are ready," his father would say. He was introduced to his wife by his mother and her mother, after they had both finished their college education. He knows he will have to have another talk with his son about how the world will not help you if you do not help your-self.

Saito's Blue world-view drives him to shape his son's life from an emotional distance. The complex aspect of Saito's world is how important this child is to him. Even with all his pessimism, his son is the hope of a better future. Saito's expression of the Captain archetype, and its over-expressed form of the Corporal, and the Protector archetype, and its over-expressed form of the Secret Service agent, enables him to control his son's world for the stated purpose of creating a successful and focused life. We can imagine he is equally focused on the quality of his studies, as expressed through his use of the Educator archetype (Squasher). In addition, Saito under expresses the Jester and uses the Killjoy version of the archetype. Sadly, Saito's efforts to make his child a success using his grandparents understanding of that concept increases the infectious nature of his pessimism. As he shrinks his son's choices, fun, sense of connectedness, and ideas of love, the son is likely to follow in his father's footsteps, just as Saito followed his parents' pessimism about the world.

The discerning/engaged/realistic father has a comfort level with all of the archetypes and can express them in various combinations and amounts as the situation with his child requires. This world-view is not static. In fact, most Purple fathers vacillate between Blue and Rose moving back and forth depending on the many factors that make life so complex. The importance of this world-view to fathers is that it is a goal. A Purple father is a father that is able to and willing to see both sides of a situation. To have a Purple world-view is to retain a flexibility, curiosity and openness in how one sees the world.

Oppression, World-View and Fatherhood Archetypes

Oppression Theory is the subjugation of a group of people who are kept from obtaining necessary resources, social acceptance, economic/educational achievement, and social access by the power elite of a society or culture (Quintana & Segura-Herrera, 2003; Sonn & Fisher, 2003; Sidanius & Pratto, 2001; Sandoval, 2000). Oppressed populations may or may not be a minority in actual raw numbers but are disadvantaged due to a highly imbalanced power differential with others in their society or culture. Oppressed populations who are numerically smaller than the power elite or who are economically and educationally disadvantaged are often more vulnerable to genocidal attacks, enslavement, and discrimination. Oppression has a generational negative impact on the targeted population groups (Sar & Ozturk, 2013; Sar, Middleton & Dorahy, 2013; Morrock, 2010).

Oppression instills powerlessness in affected populations and in particular in the men whose sense of masculinity is often predicated on being able to provide, protect and teach their children. In having a major impact on a father's world-view, oppression also has a major impact on a father's access to and expression of the fatherhood archetypes. Oppression may lead to

- abandonment being confronted with his inability to lead and/or protect his children (Captain archetype; Protector archetype),
- punitive discipline to "toughen up" children so they may be able to "survive" oppression (Captain archetype),
- misrepresentation of typical child testing behavior as "disrespectful" and requiring correction (Captain archetype; Jester archetype),
- overprotection, hypervigilance, and anxiety when attempting to insulate children from further oppression (Nurturer archetype; Protector archetype),
- sense of overwhelm and suspicion communicated through consistent and constant messaging to children (not always adjusted to child's developmental stage) about the ubiquitous of oppression in all its forms (Educator archetype; Protector archetype), and
- diminishment and/or criticism of typical fun and playful child behavior as unnecessary and weak (Jester archetype).

Oppression is the outcome of a toxic and hostile society (Vernon–Feagens, 2011). In addition to the efforts of communities to politically combat oppression typified by "Black Lives Matter" and "We're here; We're queer; Get used to it," women's and minority liberation movements, civil rights movements, and disability advocacy movements, is the individual response to oppression called the standpoint. The standpoint is the individual's intellectual/emotional response that counters the culture's negative expectations. The engine for the individual response to oppression is resilience. Resilience is the ability to cope, manage and heal in the face of adversity (Saul, 2013; Powley, 2009; Richardson, 2002). The father who is discerning, engaged and realistic is also the father with resilience—the one who wears the Purple glasses. He has the ability to weather storms by accessing any and all necessary archetypes that can help guide his family out of a crisis.

Errol attends the mandated classes and decided to participate in individual counseling with his pastor. Errol wants to process the violence he experienced, the violence he witnessed and to ultimately forgive his parents. His goal is to free himself from the notion that he only demonstrates strength by physically overpowering others. Errol knows his physical strength is necessary in some situations but not with his daughter, his wife, or his co-workers. A resilient Errol compromises with his daughter, gives her a simple flip-phone cell phone, asks for help from his partner and advice from other parents, and addresses his daughter's safety by having her take a self-defense class.

Miguel goes with his wife to see a parenting consultant not affiliated with the school in order to get another perspective. They discuss that both partners have similar experiences of not talking through problems as children and that both want to change this as it connects with their own child. They agree that they are going to keep their daughter in the school regardless of the school's overall response and that they will discuss with their daughter using age-appropriate language why she may be struggling to go to school. Miguel decides to hold off on his judgments about discrimination until he hears from his daughter, but because it is so important to him, he ask his wife for help to devise ways of augmenting any deficits they see in their daughter's experience with regard to racial identity (even if she is not old enough to articulate it herself).

A resilient Devlin meets with his daughters' doctors and becomes an active part of their treatment. He is able to express his sadness and fear about their well-being to his partner, other parents and doctors, enjoys his daughters' strengths, takes pride in how well he cares for them. Finally, a resilient Saito realizes that he did not like the choices that his parents made for him, understands that he can make different parenting decisions, enjoys his son's interest in girls knowing that it does not mean his grades will suffer, knows that his son needs time to play, create, and expand his interests, and participates in a joyful way in his son's growth. We will explore resilience further in the following chapter yet even after this brief introduction, we are telegraphing its importance to fathers and fathering.

15

The Future of
Fatherhood Archetypes

*Progress is impossible without change, and those who cannot change,
their minds cannot change anything.—George Bernard Shaw*

You must be the change you wish to see in the world.—Mahatma Gandhi

*If you don't like something, change it. If you can't change it, change your
attitude.—Maya Angelou*

If there is no struggle, there is no progress.—Frederick Douglass

*Everyone thinks of changing the world, but no one thinks of changing
himself.—Leo Tolstoy*

As fatherhood enters the 21st century and continues to evolve and expand,
the expectations for fathering have become more complex and far-reaching.
Statistics gathered from a variety of fatherhood and census-based sources show
that the numbers associated with fathers are growing—more fathers, more children, more responsibilities. "The number of fathers in the United States
increased from 60.1 million in 2000, to 64.3 million in 2007, to 70.1 million in
2012, to 72.2 million in 2014. In 2014, 23.6 percent of all children in the United
States lived in father-absent homes. Two million single fathers were raising children in 2016, approximately 17 percent of all single parents, up from 1.96 million in 2012. Stay-at-home fathers were counted by the Census for the first
time in 2003 and totaled 98,000. By 2016, the number of stay-at-home fathers
increased by more than 113 percent to 209,000. Fathers represent 3.4 percent
of all stay-at-home parents, and approximately 32 percent of these men are
married to women working full-time. They care for almost 400,000 children
under the age of 15" (U.S. Census, 2014; U.S. Census, 2015; Livingston, 2014).

Being the primary or custodial caregiver, staying at home, or co-parenting with partners who work, all require fathers to use more of themselves, more of what Jung believed lay waiting within the collective unconscious. As we discussed earlier in this book, many of the skills and roles have been employed by fathers over the centuries, and it seems that with the increasing demands (fiscal, social and societal) of today's world being placed on families, children and communities, fathers are being asked to be prepared for everything and anything. In addition, the father's essential role in infant and child development is the subject of continued study (Yogman & Garfield, 2016; Yogman & Kindlon, 1998; Yogman, Kindlon & Earls, 1995).

As stated in our introduction, more and more fathers are taking an active role in caretaking starting in infancy. In addition to the increase in fathers as primary caregivers, one study indicates that in some larger companies, men (at a rate of 85 percent) are taking off 1 to 2 weeks of unpaid leave after the birth of their child (Gensoni & Tallandini, 2009; Gordon, Zagoory-Sharon; Leckman; & Feldman, 2010: Gray & Anderson, 2010). Between 1965 and 2011, the time that fathers spent on child care increased by almost 3 times (Gray & Crittenden 2014; Knox, 2016; LaRossa, 1997, Levant & Wimer, 2009). This added time is coming at a critically important juncture as life for children seems to be getting more complex.

Expectations and Expansions Within Core Fathering Archetypes

At the writing of this book, in-person communication is fighting a losing battle with email, texting, all forms of social media including, Twitter, YouTube, Facebook, Snapchat, FaceTime, Skype, Instagram, WhatsApp, Tumblr and the VR (virtual reality) innovations that will replace these in the near future. As forms of communication change, the basics that shape the child-father relationship becomes all the more important. Regardless of form, how people understand themselves and how they understand others never changes. As this understanding starts with parents, we believe that fathers' cognitive, physical, and emotional availability will be crucial in helping children develop the type of skills (interpersonal and others) they will need to navigate the complexities—professional, social, emotional, romantic and sexual—of this changing, often overwhelming world.

We can already observe changes that are taking place in children. We believe that the advent of instantaneous information gathering and dissemination, the constant accessibility and in-the-moment, any-time-of-day communications platforms, and the sense that events, both internationally, domestically, and locally, seem to be happening more swiftly and with more negative impact, have directly affected several important areas of child development. These areas of child development include the basic building blocks related to healthy performance in the world (within relationships, at school, at work, etc.).

- building frustration tolerance,
- developing empathy,
- engaging in problem solving,
- exhibiting perseverance,
- experiencing resilience, and
- implementing coping strategies

When we examine the list above, we can imagine the compromising impact changes to these areas of development will have over a man's lifetime and as they begin to consider and enter into fatherhood. The fathering characteristics that we have described in the previous chapters can be affected in potentially negative ways—increased anger, anxiety, worry, impulsivity, hostility, distraction, and depression, among others (see Table 15.1).

Table 15.1—Impact of Future Child Developmental Changes on Fathering Characteristics

Temperament	Relational Dynamics	Time Orientation	Emotional Intelligence	World View
Strong-Willed more energetic, more resistant, more negative, less driven	**Intense** more impulsive, more over-reactive, more controlling	**Present Focused Moving Against** more controlling, angrier, more rigid	**Visceral** more external, more over-reactive, more impulsive	**Blue** excessively pessimistic, paranoid, afraid, more rigid, more withdrawn
Reserved more sedentary, more withdrawn, more worried	**Pre-Occupied** more irritable, more distracted, more withdrawn	**Past Focused Moving Away** more withdrawn, more distracted	**Cerebral** more internal, less empathy, more withdrawn, less emotion	**Rose** Less optimistic, more detached, more depressed, more anxious
Flexible/Moveable less positive, less social, less resilient, less calm, more negative	**Accessible** less resilient, less empathic, less consistent	**Future Focused Moving Toward** more anxious, more depressed	**Mindful** less thoughtful, less balanced, less measured	**Purple** More confused, more cautious, less thoughtful, less balanced

When current technology alters the ability to achieve developmental emotional milestones, we believe that children (and subsequently these children as future fathers) could be less capable in their ability to function on a daily basis and even more so when we begin to add in external stressors. Children could grow up being more cautious, more worried, more agitated.

This is not set in stone, but it could become a reality if we are not attentive and proactive. As we will present later in the chapter, these issues may necessitate the emergence of an additional fatherhood archetype.

Recent data indicates that generally people feel more in their control with challenging issues that are "close to home," and retain a sense of greater sense of optimism over these matters. That said, with national issues and dynamics such as the nature of current political disenfranchisement and partisanship, the unclear availability of reliable, cost-conscious health care, terrorism, the challenges with job security and income disparity, the burgeoning substance-use epidemics, the uncertainties in our immigration system, and the ever-expanding occurrences of gun violence, more and more we meet parents and their children who exhibit some combination of anxiety, overwhelm, disempowerment, preoccupation, tentativeness, and, even, hopelessness.

From micro-issues within the family system to the macro ones that affect the whole population, we believe that technology has a significant impact on how fathers and mothers are being asked to parent. With the new developments in technology, comes the ubiquitous nature of information and the acceleration of knowledge acquisition, both bane and boon, at times welcome, at others, unwelcome. In some ways fathering has never been more supported. Information that we need is readily available at the touch of a few buttons on our computers.

Paradoxically, children are being confronted daily with over-stimulating data that, often, they do not know how to manage. In addition to the work of growing up, managing this complex material becomes a central task of children and the caregivers around them. The term "sharenting" has been coined in connection to the dynamics related to parental over-sharing of information. Since it takes a village to raise a child, we see it is an apt turn of phrase that can speak to the increased societal (parents, Internet, media outlets, schools) norms around excessive sharing of information with children (Bessant, 2017). We live in an age of "too much information" being accessible to children and the related need to help them understand and digest this information

At the same time their parents (regardless of affiliation, political, social, or religious) are being inundated with 24-7, media coverage of calamitous, tense, and often depressing news cycles about the world, its institutions and systems to which their children are exposed. It can often feel like too much and lead parents to want to simply tune out and turn off. News is pushed through their smart phones, television sets, and streaming feeds—it overloads one's senses and thoughts. There really is no good escape, since to father holistically is to remain connected. Since for parents, all news in some way relates back to their children, this news torrent can only exacerbate the pressures that fathers already feel creating a general sense of disquiet or unease—a dynamic that we call "pressimism."

Freddy knows his 14-year-old daughter is aware of the most recent school shooting that happened the previous afternoon—it was all over the news. He brings it up at the breakfast table, because he does not want her to get to school and hear about it from other people. He also does not want her to get the impression that he will not discuss a difficult topic. She looks at him and says, "I already know," then stares back down at her food. She does not appear to want to talk about it, but Freddy presses on about the importance talking about things that are scary and worrisome. She seems to be listening, but he cannot really tell. He asks her about lock down drills and securing in place, but she does not answer. Freddy stops "badgering" his daughter and says, "I love you, I'm sorry this is all happening." Minutes later his daughter looks up at him and asks, "Dad, do you think this is something that could happen at my school?" Freddy feels crushed and is not sure how to answer. He is silent for a long moment. With a pained look on his face, he simply says, "I wish I could say no. I really do, with all my heart and soul. I truly believe that your school is doing everything they can to keep you safe. But I want to talk to you about what you can do to prevent something from happening. If you think you may know a classmate who is having a hard time, who makes you worried or uncomfortable, please let me know. Let a teacher know. Saying something helps you protect yourself and, actually, may help you protect that kid from doing something terrible."

Freddy wants to be an effective Protector, Educator and Nurturer. He does not want to over protect his daughter or intrude on her in school, yet he also does not want her to feel that she needs to process distressing news on her own or only with her friends. It would seem tempting to become a Secret Service agent and a Smotherer—to wrap his daughter into his protected embrace, controlling her every movement (Intense Relational Dynamics) because he is increasingly feeling scared of (Blue World View) and depressed about (Future-Focused, Moving Toward Time Orientation) the country in which he is raising her. His adolescent daughter, though, needs to feel she can negotiate her world on her own with the background knowledge that her father is always there for her. This does not mean only in the physical sense, but in the emotional sense of hearing his words when a dangerous situation arises. Memories of what a father says to a child can remain with the child well into their adulthood.

With the details of child-connected tragedies making their way to our children, explaining provocative and upsetting material becomes another one of a father's duties. He must contend with the new ways that children process and talk about information as he responds, and he must find age-appropriate perspective for news that is increasingly heartbreaking such as school-based mass shootings, local law enforcement's gratuitous attacks on youths of color, the rise in adolescent use of illicit substances and addiction-related deaths, and the sundering of families confronted by shifting immigration policies.

While we imagine that no father ever really wants to have these types of conversations, we know that fathers have always needed to have difficult conversations with their children especially when children are confronted by discrimination, poverty, bullying, etc. That said, the changes to children's development and the expansion of access to information in conjunction with these myriad ongoing tragedies requires a change to our expectations of fatherhood interventions.

We believe that attempts to stop this tide of changes (both the developmental ones and the environmental ones) would be misplaced, that fathers must adapt in order to, engage, guide, protect, teach, and support the children. They must try to be in the forefront of this transformation, lest they allow their children to rush ahead alone and isolated. New events, information and research will contribute to the evolution of these archetypes and fathers will use these modified archetypes to become complete parents of the future. The changes to each archetype that we imagine could look like the following.

Movement Within the Captain Archetype

The Captain archetype will have more opportunities to account and plan as the world for children (and their parents) gets more complex. We suggest "hands-on" support, augmenting the changing norms, with important skills and knowledge from the past (see Figure 15.1). All the new rules and regulations that come from (1) technology-based communications and information transmission and (2) a variety of environmental issues will require increased understanding and knowledge acquisition by the Captain. Future Captains' abilities to change course and be creative and innovative will address changes to the global and national economy and related income/poverty challenges, to the nature of new existential dangers such as terrorism and wars, to the evolving climate of the planet including temperature shifts and natural disasters, to political discourse including oppression and power shifts around the world, and to our burgeoning awareness of how pressures within these areas affect long and short-term brain development in children. Father will need a more complete understanding how the news media and social media shapes how children see their world and their "future." All will require the Captain archetype to emphasize his hopefulness and excitement guiding the family and children into the future.

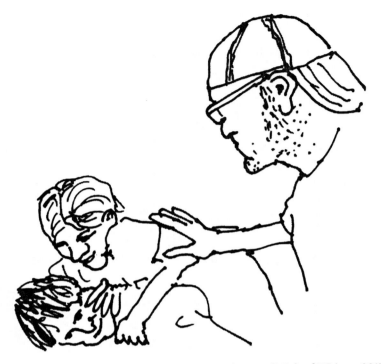

Figure 15.1—Hands-on support: the Captain archetype (Michael Weiner, 2017).

Movement Within the Protector Archetype

The Protector archetype will become increasingly important as a bulwark against new modern dangers and new version of old dangers (i.e., war around the world, local terrorism, cyber trauma, new illnesses, events associated with climate change, generational poverty, the vicissitudes of ongoing oppression, etc.). This will require seamless coordination with the Captain archetype to establish an appropriate level of safety and awareness via new rules and a level of discipline regarding these rules. Father as Protector will need to contend with new outlets for aggression, abuse, prejudice and bias that technology has afforded as individuals and movements hide behind the Internet's cloak of anonymity. In addition, the father as Protector will need to assist children in managing a society, and a world at large, that due to limited access to finite resources and seemingly intransigent religious and cultural belief systems, is populated by individuals and groups that appear increasingly without empathy, both cognitive and emotional, for one another.

During the writing of this book, it has never been more apparent to us the amount of work that will be required by the Protector in near future, as children are asked to comprehend and process the polarized and often malicious nature of the political discourse in the United States and the resulting utter lack of empathy and compromise. The economic and resource imbalances in the world from our vantage point at times seem intractable. The competition for potable water will likely continue as will access to food, education, employment, safety. While each culture has its own priorities of needs, these issues of scarcity impact on all fathers and all families. At the same time, individual, community and governmental efforts to improve the world and address the human needs of people in distress will increasingly provide ample opportunities to lend a "helping hand" as service to the common good (see Figure 15.2). These efforts provide balance to a world with many problems and give fathers as Protector tremendous opportunity to model the empowering effort of actively creating a sense of security and stability.

Movement Within the Educator Archetype

The Educator archetype will need to help his children make sense of the changes to the learning environment, access to information, and a new

Figure 15.2—Lending a helping hand: the Protector archetype (Michael Weiner, 2017).

understanding of the nature of higher education. Already well underway, the father as Educator is being asked to manage pressures being placed on children at school as less money, less training, and more blame-the-victim mentality is driving the school system in unfortunate directions. Larger class sizes, fewer teachers, mental health over-diagnosing, increasingly myopic focus on child behavior instead of child communication, decreased attention to and understanding of the need for recreation in learning, are all making learning in school more complex for children with unique requirements and disparate innate ways of learning and information acquisition. On a related matter, developmental dynamics such as differences (racial, sexual, and cultural, etc.) and identity formation, these are being unevenly addressed within our society's school systems. Even with our growing understanding of these important areas of growth, many of these problems are getting worse, not better. In response, fathers as Educator will be required to have a greater awareness and involvement in their children education and learning at an earlier stage and be willing to intervene earlier if problems are identified.

This is a form of intervention that will demand the coordination and balance of the Captain, the Protector and the Educator. In addition, as a way of containing their children's learning experience, the Educator archetype will expand its own knowledge base in order to become familiar will all the new advances in technology, including speed of information dissemination and acquisition, the varying forms information can take, and the disparate types of platforms through which information can be delivered. Fathers as Educator will need to be familiar with these burgeoning areas of technology and also have some understanding of their advantages and disadvantages. The father as Educator may even be asked to help his children reframe the age-old notion of higher education and what its meaning and purpose are, as college tuition becomes increasingly difficult for families to manage. Lastly, the move from the concrete form to ephemeral nature of information, from a brick and mortar library to the Cloud, may necessitate the Educator archetype's collaboration with the "next generation" in order to identify new methods of maintaining a sense of continuity in the histories of wisdom of each individual family and community so that it may be passed down from family to family (see Figure 15.3).

Movement Within the Nurturer Archetype

The Nurturer archetype will need to take into account all the new data being accumulated about (1) the nature of father-child relationships and (2) the understanding of the different elements of an individual (including gender, sexual orientation, neurobiology, neuro-diversity, racial identity, attach-

Figure 15.3—Collaborating with the next generation: the Educator archetype (Michael Weiner, 2017).

ment, the impact of trauma, oppression, poverty, etc.). Fathers already know that their overall involvement has a positive impact on their children development and generally lowers the rates of mental health issues in children (Erlandsson, et, al., 2006). To add to this, fathers as Nurturer will be asked to become increasingly comfortable with "tactile affection" and care (hugs, kisses, and diaper changing) and un-gendered structuring of home life (cooking, cleaning, maternal support), as mothers and other co-parents increasingly work and become primary sources of family income), and implementation of non-authoritarian forms of interaction with their children (see Figure 15.4).

Globalization may ultimately enable childrearing to be more similar and focused on the issues of quality intimacy interactions between fathers and their children. As ideas around gender expand a become less rigid, the father as Nurturer will be pressed to be less concerned about what is masculine and feminine and more comfortable with what is human and the type of intimacy and attention that children of all ages and all genders require to grow up feeling loved. Lastly, the #metoo movement, coupled with other movements such as Black Lives Matter and "We're here, we're queer, get used to it," will continue to press for change within the Nurturer archetype. There will be an enduring demand that father as Nurturer must listen, process and act on the voices, requests, and needs of those individuals who have traditionally been unheard.

Movement Within the Jester Archetype

The Jester archetype will have a key role in helping to manage how the world and children fit together in a way that does not leave the children overwhelmed and searching for hope. There are many children who suffer a sense of dislocation buy being born into poverty, into communities where gun violence is prevalent, into cultures or populations in which oppression and prejudice are ever-present. Accessibility of elicit substances, mass shootings and the pervasiveness of information due to technological advances has added to these numbers of traumatized, confused children. As more and more children have become aware of dangers that being connected to the world around them poses, their innocence has been undermined in an inverse proportion. Knowledge is power, but in this case, it is often too powerful and consequently, we see spikes in childhood anxiety, depression and trauma-related symptoms (Mojtabai, Olfson & Han, 2016; Schrobsdorff, 2016). In balance with all the other archetypes, fathers as Jester will be on the front lines

Figure 15.4—Comfort with tactile affection and care: the Nurturer archetype (Michael Weiner, 2017).

of trying to find new ways to distract, amuse, and inoculate his children, by giving them hope, and reminding them to "just be a child" (see Figure 15.5).

An example of this is the father depicted by Roberto Benigni in the 1997 movie *Life Is Beautiful*. Written by Vincenzo Cerami, and, in part, based on a true story, a father, even though he and his son are prisoners in a Nazi camp, manages to divert his child focus from the tragedy around them with his ceaseless antics. Some people were very critical of these scenes feeling the movie trivialized the horrors of the Nazi era. Yet, Mr. Benigni is demonstrating how the Jester functions under the most desperate of circumstances. Counterbalancing war, terrorism, gun violence, climate change, substance abuse, domestic violence, dysfunctional politics, poverty, oppression, discrimination, financial difficulties, high divorce rates, health coverage worries, and many other concerns, requires the ever-growing need for play, fun and joy.

Within a developmental context, the dynamics of the "terrible twos" and "teenage rebellion" will take on a more significant purpose when fathers as Jester take into consideration all the pressure that family systems and individuals therein (parents and children) are under. Coming to terms with the fact that as more strain is placed on families because of the external

Figure 15.5—Reminding your child to just be a child: the Jester archetype (Michael Weiner, 2017).

realities of the world, children will need to test limits more as a way of unloading their intense feelings and as a method of questioning all the complicated material around them. The Jester archetype must become a global thinker in the way it helps fathers to understand and intervene with their children.

New Fathering Archetypes

We believe it likely that of all aspects of fathering, the technological advances (medical, scientific, and environmental) will contribute most to the development of new archetypes just as innovations throughout history have dramatically affected in family life and individual interaction, communication, and relationships. The problem that we see is that these changes seem to be occurring faster than we can keep up. Human beings tend default to the familiar for the purpose of security and this rapid state of change is straining our society and, by extension, our children. This is not necessarily a harmful phenomenon, in and of itself, yet it does require tending, managing and containing. Unprocessed change can be destructive.

Due to the potential for dramatic and potentially overwhelming changes in our family systems, communities and societies, we can conceive of the emergence of a new archetype: father as Adapter. We use this word to convey the global augmentation that certain moments of history can require of fathering. This archetype melds with the Captain, the Educator, the Protector, the Nurturer and the Jester during times of upheaval to supplement the work of the original archetypes (see Table 15.2).

Table 15.2—Augmented Roles of the Adapter Archetype

Archetypes	Roles of the New Augmented Archetype
Captain and Adapter	Preserve processes of what was beneficial from the functions of previous and ephemeral moments from the recent past and re-interpret them with the context of change
Educator and Adapter	Create more explicit connections between "old" knowledge and new information and forms, the past and the present; remind ourselves that history tends to repeat itself
Protector and Adapter	Reinforce interpersonal relational dynamics, empathy, and mutuality that result in rewarding connections to the self, others and the world
Nurturer and Adapter	Lean on the fundamental building blocks of human nature—the need for love, sustenance, and safety—while reconceiving how changes may alter the ways these are understood and accessed

Archetypes	*Roles of the New Augmented Archetype*
Jester and Adapter	Develop a continuum of responses that acknowledges, embraces and, even, celebrates the technologically-driven changes and how these changes can be both bad and good

The father will become similar to the electricity adapter that enables electronics from one country to work in another or a software patch that allows old technology to function on more modern devices. This role as the Adapter has its precursor in the fathering required before and after wars, during other waves of rapid inventions and changes in lifestyle. It, too, remains inside all fathers as part of the collective unconscious. An old skill set that will be needed in a fast-changing world.

With rapid changes in technology, the Adapter's job centers on a process of gradualism; slowing down change, but not obstructing it. The tendency for youth to leave the old behind—to find the next cool thing—is normative, but the extreme pace is novel, and we have concerns regarding how the brisk pace of advances is affecting the integration of ideas, memories, etc. Quick changes tend to be difficult for families and children to incorporate. The lack of integration is in direct conflict with Jung's idea of collective unconscious. The Adapter's central role may be to help unify past, present, and future as a way of preserving a sense of stability within the family as a whole and within the child.

The numerous objects invented by people to enhance and simplify all manner of human endeavors can often create more time for a family to be together. The chapter on the Educator archetype offers examples of a fathers relying on his child's expertise with a new piece of technology and a father who enjoys his child sharing facts learned at school and sharing career plans while still very young. The father encourages growth in the form of acquisition of knowledge. That knowledge is increasingly comprised of material that fathers are far less familiar with than their children.

As each generation becomes more technologically advanced than the one before it, the father as Adapter, as liaison with a "more straight-forward, more connected" past, will aid fathers in coordinating archetype roles within the context of technology's impact on the family and relationships. This is critical due to the pressure technological changes will put on day to day interpersonal interactions. The scene of the family around the table sharing a meal, while each member is on their own piece of technology, demonstrates that changes in the world of communication and information sharing need to be explicitly integrated into family life without diluting the emotional intimacy families need to thrive and survive. With ever-present technology such as smart phones, here to stay, father as Adapter will find a way to characterize these changes as important yet requiring limits and containment.

Within the Adapter archetype are the skills to absorb and interpret new information quickly and efficiently, along with the ability to be comfortable with not knowing what will come next and how it will change things yet again. We are not describing a version of trying to help one's child learn to use a new method of solving a math problem. This is a more of an overarching and ongoing intervention, similar to trying to communicate with a child who uses a language other than the one we speak. The Adapter archetype will be the wellspring of fathers' abilities (balanced with the Protector, Captain, Educator, Nurturer, and Jester) of incorporating information into a logical, safe, and enjoyable structure for children. To illustrate this, we ask you to look into the future with us at a father-child interaction that has both not yet occurred and, in some ways, has occurred many times in the past.

Benjamin is sitting with his 11-year-old daughter as she stares straight ahead through her iFrames. He has not gotten used to the look that she has when she is logged in to the Cloud server; that distant, calm look, that however peaceful, makes him feel alone even when he is with her. He recalls the concerns his father had about all the time he spent on the computer. She sends him a message that he reads on the lenses of his own iFrames. She writes: "Dad, I know you don't like it when I do this with you in the room, but there is no other way to get the information that I am searching for." Benjamin sighs preferring to hear his daughter's voice. He always feels frustrated at these moments, like he is being ignored. He thinks to himself, "Whatever happened to talking?"

He unwraps one of the many pieces of candy he always seems to have handy. His daughter smells the candy and says, "Mmmm, I smell that." As if on cue, Benjamin unwraps a piece of candy and pops it into his daughter's mouth, so she does not have to stop what she is doing. This little intimacy, repeated many times by father and daughter (who "inherited" his love of candy), makes Benjamin smile to himself. Naturally Cerebral in his use of emotional intelligence, he has learned to grab the opportunities that present themselves to him to show his daughter how much he loves her; he thinks of it like a game.

He knows that she needs his help and that eventually she will tell him what she needs him to do. Gone are the days he would just show her what to do, realizing that she did not like it when he would just take over. She will project something onto the home uplink screen or upload something onto his iTab. This technology makes him feel anxious at times because he always likes to feel in control. Benjamin realizes that it is not possible for anyone to feel that way in light of all the new tech that seems to come out every six months. It's something his father always talked to him about ... and stills tries. He is tremendously proud of his daughter, how smart she is and how capable.

She is so independent when it comes to learning and so he is happy to be a part of it. It makes him smile that she still struggles with math just like he did when he was a child. He thinks of how he and his father sat around the dining room table and did math with a pencil and paper at 6:00 a.m. Things were so different just 30 years ago. Now that paper has been banned due to deforestation, everything is virtual. He got the digital stuff, but this virtual learning makes him cringe. He pushes aside his feelings of discomfort and tries to relax by listening to some soothing music emanating from his iFrames.

Benjamin knows how to adapt, accepting some innovations and hanging on to old-school ways as a source of comfort. He kisses his daughter's shoulder and she shrugs him away. He grabs her head with both hands and kisses the top of her head making loud smacking noises that make her laugh. He loves to tease her, and she loves to be teased by him. The Jester may not be his most comfortable archetype due to Benjamin's serious earnestness, but he can still make his daughter laugh.

Final Thoughts

The fatherhood archetypes are part of our shared human history both positive and negative—a trove of jewels and sharps that are the inheritance of all fathers. In this way the past, present and future are connected. The cave drawings of the past are the texting of today and the virtual messages of the future. The world indeed is connected. It has become smaller as information and knowledge is shared more rapidly and with fewer and fewer boundaries. There is more conveying and sharing of ideas, culture, and history, than ever before and, sadly, there is also an increase in uncertainty, fear misunderstanding, prejudice, conflict, and malady. Children will always rely on fathers and the roles of fathering to navigate whatever challenges and boons their moment in history offers. The archetypes—the Captain, the Protector, the Nurturer, the Educator and the Jester, and one day, the Adapter, each in its own way and together, provide a continuity for this process. One that transcends time, and we hope, offers solace to fathers—that fatherhood is a wonderful and wild journey that has a purpose and a plan. And finally, that this journey is one in which fathers never travel alone. They are accompanied by each and every father that came before him through time immemorial.

Bibliography

Ainsworth, M.D.S., M.C. Blehar, E. Waters, & S. Wall (2014). *Patterns of attachment (Classic Edition): A psychological study of the strange situation.* Florence, KY: Guilford Press Taylor & Frances Group.

Alexander, R. (2009). *Wise mind, open mind: Finding purpose and meaning in times of crisis, loss, and change.* Oakland: New Harbinger.

Allport, G. (1937). *Personality: a psychological interpretation.* New York: Holt, Rinehart, & Winston.

Allport, G. (1954). *The nature of prejudice.* Cambridge, MA: Addison-Wesley.

Allport, G. (1955). *Becoming: Basic considerations for a psychology of personality.* New Haven: Yale University Press.

Allport, G. (1961). *Pattern and growth in personality.* New York: Holt, Rinehart & Winston.

Aubrey, A. (2017, August 31). Fatherhood After 40? It's Becoming A Lot More Common. Retrieved from https://www.npr.org/sections/health-shots/2017/08/31/547320586/fatherhood-after-forty-its-now-a-lot-more-common-study-finds. Accessed on 11/14/2017.

Axline, V.M. (1981). *Play therapy: The groundbreaking book that has become a vital tool in the growth and development of children.* New York: Ballantine Books.

Bailey, K.D. (1984). Equilibrium, entropy and homeostasis: A multidisciplinary legacy. *Systems Research, 1*(1), 25–43.

Bailey, K.D. (1994). *Sociology and the new systems theory: Toward a theoretical synthesis.* Albany: State University of New York SUNY Press.

Bandura, A. (1969). *Principles of behavior modification.* New York: Holt, Rinehart & Winston.

Barel, E., M.H. Van IJzendoorn, A. Sagi-Schwartz, & M.J. Bakermans-Kranenburg (2010). Surviving the Holocaust: a meta-analysis of the long-term sequelae of a genocide. *Psychological bulletin, 136*(5), 677.

Barker, G., & E. Weingarten (2016, July 15). Why America's fathers aren't living up to expectations. Retrieved from http://time.com/4355643/fathers-day-expectations/. Accessed on 2/1/2018.

Barnes, S., K.W. Brown, E. Krusemark, W.K. Campbell, & R.D. Rogge (2007). The role of mindfulness in romantic relationship satisfaction and response to relationship stress. *Journal of Marital and Family Therapy, 33*(4), 482–500.

Bateson, P., & P. Gluckman (2011). *Robustness, plasticity, development and evolution.* New York: Cambridge University Press.

Beddoe, A., & S. Murphy (2004). Does mindfulness decrease stress and foster empathy among nursing students? *Journal of Nursing Education, 43*(7), 305–312.

Beldoch, M. (1964). Sensitivity to emotional expression in three modes of communication. In Davitz, J.R. (Ed.), *The communication of emotional meaning.* New York: McGraw-Hill, 31–42.

Bell, D. (Ed.). (2006). *Memory, trauma and world politics: Reflections on the relationship between past and present.* New York: Springer.

Bellack, L. (1973). *Ego functions in schizophrenics, neurotics and normals* (Wiley Series on Personality Processes) Hoboken: Wiley.

Belsky, J. (1981). Early human experience: A family perspective. *Developmental Psychology, 17*(1), 3.

Benzimen, G., R. Kannai, & A. Ahmad (2012). The wounded healer as cultural archetype. *CLCWeb: Comparative Literature and Culture, 14*(1) Gale Academic Onefile. Accessed on 12/2/16.

Benzinger, T.H. (1969). Heat regulation: Homeostasis of central temperature in man. *Physiological Reviews, 49*(4), 671–759.

Bergland, C. (2016, April 9) Violent video games can trigger emotional desensitization. Retrieved from https://www.psychologytoday.com/blog/the-athletes-way/201604/violent-video-games-can-trigger-emotional-desensitization. Accessed on 10/10/17.

Bernard, J (1981) The good-provider role: Its rise and fall. *American Psychologist, 36*(1): 1–12. http://dx.doi.org/10.1037/0003–066X.36.1.1.

Bessant, C. (2017, September 20) Too much information? More than 80% of children have an online presence by the age of two. Retrieved from https://theconversation.com/too-much-information-more-than-80-of-children-have-an-online-presence-by-the-age-of-two-83251. Accessed on 2/2/18.

Blumberg, M.S. (2005). *Basic instinct: The genesis of behavior.* New York: Basic Books.

Boeree, C.G. (2006). *Personality theories.* Psychology Department: Shippensburg University, Original E-Text-Site, http://www.ship.edu/%7Ecgboeree/perscontents.html. Accessed on 12/2/16.

Bowlby, J. (1969). *Attachment and loss: Volume 1 attachment.* New York: Basic Books.

Bowlby, J. (1982). *The mind in conflict.* New York: International Universities Press.

Bracha, H.S. (2004). *Freeze, fight, flight, faint, fright: Adapatationist perspectives on the acute stress response spectrum. CNS Spectrums, 9*(9): 679–685.

Brofenbrenner, U. (1981). *The ecology of human development: Experiments by nature and design.* Cambridge: Harvard University Press

Brofenbrenner, U. (2004). *Making human beings human: Bioecological perspectives on human development.* Sage Program on Applied Developmental Science, New York: Sage.

Cabrera, N.J., C.S. Tamis-LeMonda, R.H. Bradley, S. Hofferth, & M.E. Lamb (Jan./Feb. 2000). Fatherhood in the twenty-first century. *Child Development, 71*(1), 127–136.

Cannon, W. (1915). *Bodily changes in pain, hunger, fear, and rage.* New York: D. Appleton. See also Bracha.

Carrano, J. (2006). The father-child relationship, parenting styles, and adolescent risk behaviors in intact families. *Journal of Family Issues, 27*(6), 850–881.

Carson, J.W., K.M. Carson, K.M. Gil, & D.H. Baucom (2004). Mindfulness-based relationship enhancement. *Behavior Therapy, 35*, 471–494.

Cattell, H.E.P., & A.D. Mead (2008). The sixteen personality factor questionnaire (16PF). In Boyle, G.J., & G. Matthews (eds.), *Sage Handbook of personality theory and assessment.* New York: Sage.

Cattell, R.B. (1946). *The description and measurement of personality.* Oxford: World Book.

Cattell, R.B. (1957). *Personality and motivation structure and measurement.* Oxford: World Book.

Cattell, R.B., & P. Kline (Eds.). (1977). *The scientific analysis of personality and motivation.* Oxford: Academic Press.

Cerami, V., & R. Benigni (1997). *"Life is beautiful"* screenplay based on the book: *In the end, I beat Hitler* by Rubino Romeo Salmoni.

Chess, S., & A. Thomas (1990). 11 continuities and discontinuities in temperament. In Robins, L.N. (Ed.), *Straight and devious pathways from childhood to adulthood.* New York: Cambridge University Press.

Chess, S., & A. Thomas (1996). *Temperament: Theory and practice.* New York: Brunner/Mazel.

Coates, T. (2015, October). The black family in the age of mass incarceration. Retrieved from https://www.theatlantic.com/magazine/archive/2015/10/the-black-family-in-the-age-of-mass-incarceration/403246/. Accessed on 11/20/16.

Conn, S.R., & M.L. Rieke (1994). *The 16 (PF) fifth edition technical manual.* Champaign, IL: The Institute of Personality and Ability Testing.

Connery, C.M., V. John-Steiner, & A. Marjanovic-Shane (Eds.). (2010). *Vygotsky and creativity: A cultural-historical approach meaning making and the arts.* New York: Peter Lang.

Cordell, J.E. (2014, April 9). The myth of the "deadbeat dad" Label. Retrieved from https://www.huffingtonpost.com/joseph-e-cordell/the-myth-of-the-deadbeat-_b_4745118.html. Accessed on 1/27/18.

Crenshaw, D.A. (1993). Responding to sexual acting out. In Schaefer, C.E., & Swanson, A.J. (eds.), *Children in residential care: Critical issues in treatment.* 2nd ed. New York: Van Nostrand Rheinhold.

Cutty, E., & R.V. Reeves (2014, November 6). Hitting kids: American parenting and physical punishment. Special Report, Brookings Institute, brookings.edu/research-hitting-kids. Accessed 12/16/16.

Davidson, R.J., J. Kabat-Zinn, J. Schumacher, M. Rosenkranz, D. Muller, S.F. Santorelli, F. Urbanowski, A. Harrington, K. Bonus, & J.F. Sheridan (2003). Alterations in brain and immune function produced by mindfulness meditation. *Psychosomatic Medicine, 65,* 564–570.

Davies, C.T.M., M.J. White, & K. Young (1983). Muscle function in children. *European Journal of Applied Physiology and Occupational Physiology, 52*(1), 111–114.

Davis, R.L.F. (1982) *Good and Faithful Labor: From Slavery to Sharecropping in the Natchez District, 1860–1890.* Westport, CT: Greenwood Press.

DeMolen, R.L. (1991). *Richard Mulcaster (c. 1531–1611) and educational reform in the Renaissance.* New Milford, CT: Hes De Graaf /Brill.

Denham, T., J. Iriarte, & L. Vrydaghs (Eds.). (2015). *Rethinking agriculture: Archeological and ethnoarchaeological perspectives.* New York: Routledge.

Dewey, J. (1986). Experience and education. *The Educational Forum, 50*(3), 241–252.

Diamond, J. (8 August 2002). Evolution, consequences and future of plant and animal domestication. *Nature, 418,* 700–707. doi: 10.1038/nature01019.

Donaldson, C., & R. Flood (2014). *Mascupathy: Understanding and healing the malaise of American manhood.* Grand Rapids: The Institute for the Prevention and Treatment of Mascupathy.

Edinger, E.F., & G.R. Elder (2002). *Archetype of the apocalypse: Divine vengeance, terrorism and the end of the world.* Chicago: Open Court.

Ellenberger, H. (1970). *The discovery of the unconscious.* New York: Basic Books.

Ellis, A. (1994). *Reason and emotion in psychotherapy revised.* Secaucus: Carol Publishing.

Ellis, A. (2001). *Overcoming destructive beliefs, feelings and behaviors.* Amherst, NY: Prometheus Books.

Ellis, B.J., G.L. Schlomer, E.H. Tilley, & E.A. Butler (2012.) Impact of fathers on risky sexual behavior in daughters: A genetically and environmentally controlled sibling study. *Journal of Developmental Psychopathology, 24*(1), 317–32. doi: 10.1017/S095457941100085X.

Erikson, E. (1950). *Childhood and society.* New York: W. W. Norton.

Erikson, E. (1968). *Identity, youth and crisis.* New York: W. W. Norton.

Erlandsson, K., A. Dsilna, I. Fagerberg, & K. Christensson (2006). Early father involvement moderates biobehavioral susceptibility to mental health problems in middle childhood. *Journal of the American Academy of Child and Adolescent Psychiatry, 45*(12), 1510–20.

Eyerman, R. (2001). *Slavery and the formation of African-American identity.* Cambridge: Cambridge University Press.

Fairbairn, W.R.D. (1954). *An object relations theory of personality.* New York: Basic Books.

Fairbairn, W.R.D., & D.E Scharf (eds.). (1994). *Vol. II From instinct to self: Selected papers of W.R.D. Fairbairn. Applications and early contributions* (Library of Object Relations, Vol. II) Lanham, MD: Jason Aronson.

Fairbairn, W.R.D., D.E. Scharf, & E. Fairbairn-Birtles (Eds.) (1995). *Vol. I From instinct to self: Selected papers of W.R.D. Fairbairn, Clinical and theoretical papers* (Library of Object Relations) Lanham, MD: Jason Aronson.

Felitti, V.J., R.F. Anda, D. Nordenberg, D.F. Williamson, A.M. Spitz, V. Edwards, M.P. Koss, & J.S. Marks (1998). Relationship of childhood abuse and household dysfunction to many of the leading causes of death in adults: The Adverse Childhood Experiences Study. *American Journal of Preventive Medicine*, 14(4): 254–258.

Frank, J.D. (1973). *Persuasion and healing (2nd Edition)*. Baltimore: Johns Hopkins University.

Frankel, V.E. (1963). *Man's search for meaning*. New York: Washington Square Press.

Freud, A., & D. Burlingham (1967). *The writings of Anna Freud: The ego and the mechanisms of defense, vol. 2*. New York: International Universities Press.

Freud, S., & J. Strachey (Ed.). (1990). *The Ego and the Id: Standard edition of the complete works of Sigmund Freud*. New York: W. W. Norton.

Gallo-Silver, L. (2016). Palliative care communication and sexuality. In Wittenberg, E., Farrell, B.R., Goldsmith, J., Smith, T., Ragan, S.L., Glajchen, M., & Handzo, G. (Eds.). *Textbook of palliative care communication*. New York: Oxford University Press.

Gallo-Silver, L., & D. Bimbi (2012). Human sexual health. In Gehlert, S., & Browne, T. (Eds.), *Handbook of health social work, second edition*, 343–370.

Galton, F. (1883). *Inquiries in human faculty and its development*. London: JM Dent.

Gander, E.M. (2003). *On our minds: How evolutionary psychology is reshaping the nature versus nurture debate*. Baltimore: Johns Hopkins University Press.

Genesoni, L., & M.A. Tallandini (2009, December). Men's psychological transition to fatherhood: An analysis of the literature, 1989–2008. *Birth Issues in Prenatal Care, 36*(4), 305–318.

Gilbran, K. (1923). *The prophet*. New York: Alfred A. Knopf.

Goleman, D. (1995). *Emotional intelligence: Why it can matter more than I.Q.* New York: Bantam.

Goloboy, J.L. (Ed.). (2008). *Industrial revolution: People and perspectives*. Santa Barbara: ABC-CLIO.

Gordon, I., O. Zagoory-Sharon, J.F. Leckman, & R. Feldman (2010). Prolactin, Oxytocin, and the development of paternal behavior across the first six months of fatherhood. *Hormones and Behavior, 58*(3): 513–518. doi: 10.1016/j.yhbeh.2010.04.007.

Gottlieb, G. (2007). Probabilistic epigenesist. *Developmental Science, 10*(1): 1–10.

Gottman, J., & J. Declaire (1998). *Raising an emotionally intelligent child: The heart of parenting*. New York: Simon & Schuster.

Graff, G. (2014). The intergenerational trauma of slavery and its aftermath. *Journal of Psychohistory, 41*(3),181–197.

Gray, P.B., & K.G. Anderson (2010). *Fatherhood: Evolution and human paternal behavior*. Cambridge: Harvard University Press.

Gray, P.B., & A. Crittenden, (2014, Spring). Father Darwin: Effects of children on men, viewed from an evolutionary perspective. *Fathering, 12*(2), 121–142.

Gurven, M., & H. Kaplan (2007, June). Longevity among hunter-gatherers: A cross-cultural examination. *Population and Development Review, 33*(2), 321–365.

Hall, C.S., & V.J. Nordby (1999). *A primer of Jungian psychology*. New York: First Meridian.

Hankivsky, O. (2014). *Intersectionality101*. Vancouver: The Institute of Intersectionality Research and Policy, Simon Fraser University.

Harlow, H.F. (1959). Love in infant monkeys. *Scientific American, 200*(6), 68–74. http://dx.doi.org/10.1038/scientificamerican.

Hewlett, B.S. (2004). Fathers in forager, farmer, and pastoral cultures. In Lamb, M. (Ed.), *The role of the father in child development, fourth edition*. New York: J. Wiley and Sons.

Hewlett, B.S., & M.E. Lamb (2005). *Hunter-gatherer childhoods: Evolutionary, developmental, and cultural perspectives*. Piscataway, NJ: Transaction.

Hinton, E.K. (2016). *From the war on poverty to the war on crime: The making of mass incarceration in America, first edition*. Cambridge: Harvard University Press.

Horney, K. (1945). *Our inner conflicts: A constructive theory of neurosis*. New York: W. W. Norton.

Horney, K. (1950). *Neurosis and human growth: The struggle toward self-realization*. New York: W.W. Norton.

Hutcherson, C.A., E. Seppala, & J.J. Gross (2008). Loving-kindness meditation increases social connectedness. *Emotion, 8*(5), 720–724.

Iacoboni, M. (2008). *Mirroring people*. New York: Farrar, Straus & Giroux.

Inhorn, M.C., W. Chavkin, & J.A. Navarro (2014). Globalized fatherhood. In Inhorn, M.C., Chavkin, W., & Navarro, J.A. (Eds.). *Fertility, Reproduction and Sexuality: Social and Cultural Perspectives, 27*.

Jablonka, E., & M. Lamb, (2005). *Evolution in four dimensions: Genetic, epigenetic, behavioral and symbolic variation in the history of life* (Life and Mind: Philosophical Issues in Biology and Psychology). Cambridge: A Bradford Book, MIT Press.

Janet, P. (2014). *Subconscious phenomena*. Primary Source Edition. Charleston, SC: Nabu Press, BiblioBazar/BiblioLife.

Jones, E. (1957). *The life and work of Sigmund Freud. Vol. I The young Freud 1856–1900; Vol. II Years of maturity 1901–1919; Vol. III The last phase 1919–1939*; New York: Basic Books.

Jung, C.G. (1951). *Aion: Researches into the phenomenology of the self (Collected Works Vol. 9, Part 2)*. Princeton: Bollingen.

Jung, C.G. (1956). *Mysterium conjunctiones: An inquiry into the separation and synthesis of psychic opposites in alchemy (2nd edition, 1970 Collected Works, Vol 14)*. London: Routledge.

Jung, C.G. (1957). *The Undiscovered Self (Present and Future), 1959 ed.* New York: American Library. *1990 ed.* Princeton: Bollinger.

Jung, C.G. (1959). *Flying saucers: A modern myth of things seen in the skies*. London: Routledge & Paul.

Jung, C.G. (1968). *The psychology of the child archetype in collected works of C J Jung (Vol 9, Part 1) Bollinger Series XX (2nd Edition)*. Princeton: Princeton University.

Jung, C.G. (1970a). *Four archetypes: Mother, rebirth, spirit trickster (Collected Works 9, Part 1)*. Princeton: Princeton University Press.

Jung, C.G. (1970b). *The collected works of C. G. Jung, volume 8: Structure and dynamics of the psyche*. Princeton: Princeton University Press.

Jung, C.G. (1981). *The archetypes and the collective unconscious. (1981 2nd ed.) Collective Works Vol. 9, Part 1*. Princeton: Bollingen.

Jung, C.G., & V.S. De Laszlo (1958). *Psyche and symbol: A selection from the writings of C. G. Jung*. Garden City, NY: Doubleday.

Jung, C.G., & V.S. De Laszlo. (1959). *Basic writings*. New York: Modern Library.

Jung, C.G., & R.A. Segal (1998). *Jung on mythology*. Princeton: Princeton University Press.

Jung, C.G., R.I. Evans, & E. Jones (1964). *Conversations with Carl Jung and reflections from Ernest Jones*. New York: Van Nostrand Rheinhold.

Kenklies, K. (2012). Educational theory topological rhetoric: The concepts of pedagogy of Johann Friedrich Herbart and Friedrich Schleiemacher. *Studies in Philosophy and Education, 31*(3), 265–273. Doi:10.1007/s11217-012-9287-6.

Kilmartin, C., & A.P. Smiler (2015). *The masculine self.* Cornwall-on-Hudson: Sloan Educational.

Kimmel, M.S. (2012). *Manhood in America: A cultural history*. New York: Oxford University Press.

Kimmel, P.R., & C.E. Stout (2006). *Collateral damage: The psychological consequences of America's war on terrorism*. Westport, CT: Greenwood, Houghton Mifflin Harcourt.

Klein, M. (1932). *The psycho-analysis of children*. New York: W.W. Norton.

Klein, M., P. Heimann, & R.E. Money-Kyrle (Eds.). (1955). *New directions in psychoanalysis: The significance of infant conflict in the pattern of adult behavior*. New York: Basic Books.

Knox, R. (2016, June 17). Wired to be a dad: Recent science fuels a new view of fatherhood.

Retrieved from http://www.wbur.org/commonhealth/2016/06/17/fatherhood-science. Accessed on 12/10/16.

Kohut, H. (1971). *The analysis of self: A systemic approach to the psychoanalytic treatment of narcissistic personality disorder.* New York: International Universities Press.

Kraemer, S. (1991). The origins of fatherhood: An ancient family process. *Family process, 30*(4), 377–392.

Kris, E. (1975). *The selected papers of Ernest Kris.* New Haven, CT: Yale University Press

Krumwiede, A. (2014). *Attachment theory according to John Bowlby and Mary Ainsworth: A seminar paper.* English language version. Munich: GRIN Verlag Gmbh.

Landreth, G.L. (2012). *Play therapy: The Art of relationships (3rd Edition).* New York: Routledge.

Langer, E. (2014). Mindfulness: 25th anniversary edition. Cambridge, MA: Da Capo Lifelong Books.

Lanza, R., with B. Berman (2016). *Beyond biocentrism: Rethinking time, space, consciousness, and the illusion of death.* Dallas: BenBella.

Larisey, K.C. (2012). The wounded healer: A Jungian perspective. C. G. Jung Society of Atlanta, Jung Society Newsletter Articles, jungatlanta.com/articles.html Accessed on 12/11/16.

LaRossa, R. (1997). *The modernization of fatherhood: A social and political history.* Chicago: University of Chicago Press.

Laslett, P. (2000). *The world we have lost: Further explored.* New York: Routledge.

Lazar, S. W., C.E. Kerr, R.H. Wasserman, J.R. Gray, D.N. Greve, M.T. Treadway, M. McGarvey, B.T. Quinn, J.A. Dusek, H. Benson, S.L. Rauch, C.I. Moore, & B. Fischel (2005). Meditation experience is associated with increased cortical thickness. *NeuroReport, 16*(17), 1893–1897.

Lee, R.B., & I. DeVore (Eds.). (1968). *Man the hunter.* Piscataway, NJ: Transaction.

Leeming, D. (2005). *The Oxford companion of world mythology.* New York: Oxford University Press.

Lerner, R.M. (1982). Children and adolescents as producers of their own development. *Developmental Review, 2*(4): 342–370.

Levant, R.F., & D.J. Wimer (2009). The new fathering movement. In Oren, C.Z., & Oren, D.C. (Eds.), *Counseling Fathers* (pp. 3–21). New York: Routledge.

Lewontin, R.C. (2000). *The triple helix: Gene, organism and environment.* Cambridge: Harvard University.

Lickliter, R. (2008). Developmental dynamics: The new view from the life sciences. In Fogel, A., King, B. & Shanker, S. (Eds.), *Human development in the 21st century: Visionary policy ideas from systems scientists.* Cambridge: Cambridge University Press.

Livingston, G. (2014). Growing number of dad's home with the kids. Washington, D.C.: Pew Research Center Social and Demographic Trends Project Blog. Available at: www.pewsocialtrends.org/2014/06/05. Accessed 3/24/15.

Lutz, A., J. Brefczynski-Lewis, T. Johnstone, & R.J. Davidson (2008). Regulation of the neural circuitry of emotion by compassion meditation: Effects of meditative expertise. *PLOS ONE* (Public Library of Science One), *3*(3): open access online journal, plos.org. Accessed 12/11/16.

Mahler, M., F. Pine, & A. Bergman (1975). *The psychological birth of the human infant.* New York: Basic Books.

Mahoney, M.J. (1974). *Cognition and behavior modification.* Cambridge, MA: Ballinger.

Mallet, C.A. (2016 April). The school-to-prison pipeline: Disproportionate impact on vulnerable children and adolescents. *Education and Urban Society, 49*(6), doi: 10.1177/0013124516644053,

Maltz, W. (2012). *The sexual healing journey: A guide for survivors of sexual abuse,* 3rd ed. New York: HarperCollins.

Marsh, M. (1990). *Suburban lives.* New Brunswick: Rutgers University Press.

Martone, R. (2012, December 4). Scientists discover children's cells living in mother's brains.

Retrieved from https://www.scientificamerican.com/article/scientists-discover-childrens-cells-living-in-mothers-brain. Accessed on 12/9/16.

Maslow, A. (1968). *Toward a psychology of being (2nd Edition)*. Princeton: Van Nostrand Rheinhold.

Maslow, A. (1971). *The further reaches of human nature.* New York: Viking.

Maslow, A. (2013). *A theory of human motivation.* Eastford, CT: Martino Fine Books.

May, R. (1953). *Man's search for himself.* New York: Norton.

May, R. (1967). *Psychology and human dilemma.* New York: Norton.

May, R. (1969). *Love and will.* New York: Norton.

May, R. (1975). *The courage to create.* New York: Norton.

Megarry, T. (1995). *Society in prehistory: The origins of human culture* New York: New York University Press.

Meichenbaum, D. (1977). *Cognitive-behavior modification: An Integrative approach.* New York: Plenum.

Meierhenrich, J. (2007). The trauma of genocide. *Journal of Genocide Research, 9*(4), 549–573.

Merchant, J. (2009). A reappraisal of Jungian archetype theory and its implications for theory and practice. *Journal of Analytical Psychology, 54*, 339–358.

Merriam and Webster Dictionary New Edition. (2018). Springfield, MA: Merriam and Webster.

Mojtabai, R., M. Olfson, & B. Han (2016). National trends in the prevalence and treatment of depression in adolescents and young adults. *Pediatrics 30*(6). doi: 10.1542/peds2016–1878.

Morgan, D.H.J. (2014). *Social theory and the family.* New York: Routledge.

Morrock, R. (2010). *The psychology of genocide and violent oppression: A study of mass cruelty from Nazi Germany to Rwanda.* Jefferson, NC: McFarland.

Murdoch, H.A. (2009). A legacy of trauma: Caribbean slavery, race, class and contemporary identity. *Research in African Literatures, 40*(4), 65–88.

Murphey, D., & P.M. Cooper (2015, October). Parent behind bars. Retrieved from http://www.childtrends.org/wp-content/uploads/2015/10/2015–42ParentsBehindBars.pdf. Accessed on 2/15/17.

Nuekrug, E.S. (2015). *The world of the counselor: An introduction to the counseling profession,* 5th Edition. Independence, KY: Brooks Cole, Cengage Learning.

Oxford Dictionary (2018). New York: Oxford University Press,

Oyama, S. (2000). *The ontogeny of information: Developmental systems and evolution.* Durham: Duke University Press.

Pancsofar, N., L. Vernon-Feagans, & Family Life Project Investigators (2010). Fathers' early contributions to children's language development in families from low-income rural communities. *Early Childhood Research Quarterly, 25*(4), 450–463.

Pavlov, I.P., & G.P. Anrep (Eds.). (2003). *Conditioned reflexes.* New York: Dover.

Peetz, J., & A.E. Wilson (2008) The temporally extended self: The relation of past and future selves to current identity, motivation and goal pursuit. *Social and Personality Psychology Compass, 2*(6), 1090–2106. DOI: 10.1111/j.1751.9004.2008.00150.

The Pew Charitable Trusts, 2010. Collateral Costs: Incarceration's Effect on Economic Mobility. Washington, D.C.: The Pew Charitable Trusts.

Piaget, J. (2001). *The psychology of intelligence.* New York: Routledge.

Piaget, J., & B. Inhelder (1969). *The psychology of the child.* New York: Basic Books.

Powley, E.H. (2009). Reclaiming resilience and safety: Resilience activation in the critical period of crisis. *Human Relations, 62*(9), 1289–1326.

President's Council on Fitness and Nutrition. (2011). https://www.fitness.gov. Accessed 12/16/16.

Quintana, S.M., & T.A. Segura-Herrera (2003). Developmental transformations of self and identity in the context of oppression. *Self and Identity, 2*(4), 269–285.

Raeburn, P. (2014). *Do fathers matter? What science is telling us about the parent we've overlooked.* New York: Scientific American, Farrar, Straus & Giroux.

Railey, J.A. (2010). Reduced mobility or the bow and arrow? Another look at "expedient" technologies and sedentism. *American Antiquity, 75*(2): 259–286.

Regoli, R., & J. Hewitt (2001) Differential oppression theory. In *Encyclopedia of Criminology and Deviant Behavior, Volume 1*. C Bryant Edition. Philadelphia: Taylor & Francis.

Richardson, G.E. (2002). The metatheory of resilience and resiliency. *Journal of clinical psychology, 58*(3), 307–321.

Ridley, M. (2003). *Nature versus nurture: Genes, experience, and what makes us human.* New York: HarperCollins.

Robertson, R. (1995). *Jungian archetypes: Jung, Godel and the history of archetypes.* York Beach, ME: Nicolas-Hays.

Rodolfo, K. (2000, January 3). What is homeostasis? Retrieved from https://www.scientific american.com/article/what-is-homeostasis. Accessed on 12/8/16.

Rogers, C. (1939). *The clinical treatment of the problem child.* Boston: Houghton Mifflin.

Rogers, C. (1995). *On becoming a person.* New York: Houghton Mifflin (reprint 1961).

Rogers, C.R. (1951). *Client-centered therapy.* Boston: Houghton Mifflin.

Rosen, D. (2002). *Transforming depression: Healing the soul through creativity.* York Beach, ME: Nicholas-Hays.

Rotter, J.B. (1975). Some problems and misconceptions related to the construct of internal versus external control of reinforcement. *Journal of Consulting and Clinical Psychology, 43*, 56–67.

Salavoy, P., & J.D. Mayer (1990). Emotional intelligence. *Imagination, Cognition and Personality, 9*(3), 185–211.

Sandoval, C. (2000). *Methodology of the Oppressed (Vol. 18).* Minneapolis: University of Minnesota Press.

Sar, V., & E. Ozturk (2013). Stimulus deprivation and overstimulation as dissociogenic agents in postmodern oppressive societies. *Journal of Trauma & Dissociation, 14*(2), 198–212.

Sar, V., W. Middleton, & M. Dorahy (2013). Individual and societal oppression: Global perspectives on dissociative disorders. *Journal of Trauma & Dissociation, 14*(2), 121–126.

Saracho, O.N., & B. Spodek (1995, January 1). Children's play and early childhood education: Insights from history and theory. *Journal of Education, 177*(3): 129–148.

Saul, J. (2013). *Collective trauma, collective healing: Promoting community resilience in the aftermath of disaster* (Vol. 48). New York: Routledge, Taylor & Francis Group.

Schrobsdorff, S. (2016, October 27) Teen depression and anxiety: Why the kids are not alright. http://time.com/4547322/american-teens-anxious-depressed-overwhelmed/. Accessed on 1/15/18.

Schrobsdorff, S. (2016, November 16) There's a startling increase in major depression among teens in the U.S. Retrieved from http://time.com/4572593/increase-depression-teens-teenage-mental-health/. Accessed on 1/15/18.

Schulte, B. (2014, June 5). Don't call them Mr. Mom: More dads at home with kids because they want to be. Retrieved from https://www.washingtonpost.com/news/parenting/wp/2014/06/05/dads-who-stay-home-because-they-want-to-has-increased-four-fold. Accessed on 12/7/16.

Searles, H. (1955). The informational value of the supervisor's emotional experience. *Journal for the Study of Interpersonal Processes, 18*, 135–146.

Shapiro, J. (2014, August 30). The truth about parenting and smartphones. Retrieved from https://www.forbes.com/sites/jordanshapiro/2014/08/30/the-truth-about-parenting-and-smartphones/#720338e9794a. Accessed on 10/4/17.

Shapiro, S., J.A. Astin, S.R. Bishop, & M. Cordova (2005). Mindfulness-based stress reduction for health care professionals: Results from a Randomized Trial. *International Journal of Stress Management, 12*(2), 164–176.

Shephard, M.T. (1996). *Maria Montessori: Teacher of teachers.* Stamford, CT: Lerner Publishing Group.

Sidanius, J., & F. Pratto (2001). *Social dominance: An intergroup theory of social hierarchy and oppression.* Cambridge: Cambridge University Press.

Silberman, S., & O. Sachs (2016) *Neurotribes: The legacy of autism and the future of neurodiversity.* Wayne, NY: Avery Publishing Group.

Singh, N.N., A.N. Singh, G.E. Lancioni, J. Singh, A.S.W. Winton, W.J. Curtis, R.G. Wahler, & K.M. Mcleavey (2007). Mindful parenting decreases aggression and increases social behavior in children with developmental disabilities. *Behavior Modification, 31*(6), 749–771.

Skinner, B.F. (1966). Conditioning responses by reward and punishment. *Proceedings of the Royal Institution of Great Britain, 41,* 48–51.

Skinner, B.F. (1974). *About behaviorism.* New York: Knopf.

Smith, E.J., & S.R. Harper (2015). Disproportionate impact of K-12 school suspension and expulsion on Black students in southern states. Philadelphia: University of Pennsylvania, Center for the Study of Race and Equity in Education.

Sonn, C.C., & A.T. Fisher (2003). Identity and oppression: Differential responses to an in-between status. *American Journal of Community Psychology, 31*(1–2), 117–128.

Sotero, M. (2006). A conceptual model of historical trauma: Implications for public health practice and research. *Journal of Health Disparities Research and Practice, 1*(1), 93–10.

Sroufe, L.A., B. Egland, E.A. Carlson, & W.A. Collins (2005). *The development of the person: The Minnesota Study of risk and adaptation from birth to adulthood,* New York: The Guilford Press

Stein, M. (1998). *Jung's map of the soul: An introduction.* Chicago: Open Court.

Stein, R. (1999). *The betrayal of the soul in psychotherapy* (originally published under the title *Incest and human love*). New Orleans: Spring Publications.

Stern, D.N. (2004). *The present moment in psychotherapy and everyday life.* Norton Series on Interpersonal Neurobiology. New York: W. W. Norton.

Stevenson, B.E. (1996) *Life in black and white: Family and community in the slave south.* New York: Oxford University Press.

Stewart, A.J., & N. Newton (March 2010). The middle ages: Change in women's personalities and social roles. *Psychology of Women Quarterly, 34*(1), 75–84.

Strachey, J. (1966). *The complete introductory lectures in psychoanalysis: Sigmund Freud. Dreams (1916)* VII the Manifest Content of Dreams and the Latent Dream Thoughts: 113–125. New York: W.W. Norton.

Strachey, J. (1966). *The complete introductory lectures in psychoanalysis: Sigmund Freud. General Theory of the Neuroses (1917)* XVII the Sense of Symptoms: 257–273. New York: WW Norton & Company Inc.

Strachey, J. (1966). *The complete introductory lectures in psychoanalysis: Sigmund Freud. General Theory of the Neuroses (1917)* XXII Some Thoughts of Development and Regression: 339–357. New York: W.W. Norton.

Strachey, J. (1966). *The complete introductory lectures in psychoanalysis: Sigmund Freud's general theory of the neuroses (1917)* XXIII the Paths to the Formation of Symptoms: 358–377. New York: W.W. Norton.

Strachey, J. (1966). *The complete introductory lectures in psychoanalysis: Sigmund Freud's general theory of the neuroses (1917)* XXVII Transference: 431–447. New York: W.W. Norton.

Sullivan, H.S. (1953). *Sullivan conceptions of modern psychiatry.* New York: W.W. Norton.

Sullivan, H.S. (1974). *The psychiatric interview.* New York: W.W. Norton.

Tabery, J. (2014). *Beyond versus: The struggle to understand the interaction of nature and nurture.* Cambridge: MIT Press.

Tang, Y.Y., Y. Ma, J. Wang, Y. Fan, S. Feng, Q. Lu, Q. Yu, D. Sui, M.K. Rothbart, M. Fan, & M.I. Posner (2007). Short-term meditation training improves attention and self-regulation. *Proceedings of the National Academy of Sciences, 104*(43), 17152–17156.

Taylor, M.L. (2004). *Remembering Esperanza.* Minneapolis: Fortress Press.

Taylor, S.E., L.C. Klein, B.P. Lewis, T.L. Gruenewald, R.A. Gurung, & J.A. Updegraff (2000). Biobehavioral responses to stress in females: Tend-and-befriend, not fight-or-flight. *Psychological Review, 107*(3), 411.

Thomas, A., & S. Chess (1956). An approach to the study of sources of individual differences in child behavior. *Journal of Clinical and Experimental Psychopathology, 18*(4): 347–357.

Thomas, A., & S. Chess (1977). *Temperament and development.* New York: Brunner/Mazel.

Thorndike, E.J. (2010). Educational psychology: The original nature of man. Charleston, SC: Nabu Press.

Ulanov, A.B. (1999). *Religion and the spiritual in Carl Jung.* Mahwah, NJ: Paulist Press.

United States Census Bureau. (2013). Facts for features: Father's Day, June 16, 2013. Available at www.census.gov/newsroom/facts-for-features/2013/cb13-ff13.html. Accessed 3/24/15.

United States Department of Justice. (2017). Citizen's Guide to the U.S. Federal Law on Child Support Enforcement, July 7, 2017. Available at www.justice.gov/criminal-ceos/citizens-guide-us-federal-law-child-support-enforcement. Accessed 2/27/18.

Van Den Berghe, P.L. (1979). *Human family systems: An evolutionary view.* Westport, CT: Greenwood Publishing Group.

Van Der Kolk, B. (2014). *The body keeps the score: Brain, mind, and body in the healing of trauma.* New York: Viking.

Vernon-Feagans, L., & The Family Life Project Investigators. (2011 February). Assessing the impact of paternal involvement on racial/ethnic disparities in infant mortality rates. *Journal of Community Health, 36*(1), 63–8. doi: 10.1007/s10900–010-9280–3.

Wakefield, S., & C. Uggen (2010). Incarceration and stratification. *Annual Review of Sociology, 36*, 387–406.

Webb, N. B., & L.C. Terr (2016) *Play therapy with adolescents and children in crisis, fourth edition.* New York: Guilford Press.

Weiner, M., & L.P. Gallo-Silver (2015). *You and your child's psychotherapy: An essential guide for parents and caregivers.* New York: Oxford University Press.

West, M.J., & A.P. King (1987). Settling nature and nurture into an ontogenetic niche. *Developmental Psychobiology, 20*(5), 549–562.

Whitman, W. (2007). "O captain! My captain!" *Leaves of grass, original 1855 edition.* Dover Thrift Edition. New York: Dover.

Wilkinson, M. (2006). *Coming into mind: The mind-brain relationship: A Jungian clinical perspective.* New York: Routledge.

Wilson, A.E., G.R. Gunn, & M. Ross (2009). The role of subjective time in identity regulation. *Applied Cognitive Psychology, 23*(8), 1164–1178.

Winnicott, D.W. (1953). Transitional objects and transitional phenomena: A Study of the first not me possession. *International Journal of Psychoanalysis, 34,* 89–97.

Winnicott, D.W. (1963). *Maturational process and facilitating environment.* Madison, CT: International Universities Press.

Winnicott, D.W. (1990). *Home is where we start from: Essays by a psychoanalyst.* New York: W. W. Norton.

Winterhalder, B. (2001). *Hunter-gatherers: An interdisciplinary perspective.* Cambridge: Cambridge University Press.

Yogman, M., & C.F. Garfield (2016 July). Fathers' roles in the care and development of Ttheir children: The role of pediatricians. *Pediatrics, 138*(1). PMID: 27296867.

Yogman, M.W., & D. Kindlon (1998 January). Pediatric opportunities with fathers and children. *Pediatric. Annals, 27*(1),16–22. PMID: 9494972.

Yogman, M.W., D. Kindlon, & F. Earls (1995 Jan). Father involvement and cognitive/behavioral outcomes of preterm infants. *Journal of American Academic Child Adolescent Psychiatry, 34*(1):58–66. PMID: 7860458.

Young, I. (2004). *Five faces of oppression.* In Heldke, L., & O'Connor, P. (Eds.) *Oppression, Priviledge, and Resistance.* Boston: McGraw-Hill.

Zamon, R. (2017, September 1). The age of first-time fathers is creeping up, and that might be great. Retrieved from http://www.huffingtonpost.ca/2017/09/01/age-of-first-time-fathers_a_23193788/. Accessed on 12/15/17.

Zickl, D. (2017, August 31). First-time dads are getting older—but are there risks? Retrieved from https://www.menshealth.com/health/new-fathers-are-getting-older. Accessed on 1/27/18.

Zimring, F.M. (2000). Empathic understanding grows the person. *Person-Centered Journal,* 7(2): 101–113.

Zoldbrod, A. (1998). *Sex Smart: How your childhood shaped your sexual life and what to do about it.* Oakland: New Harbinger.

Zoldbrod, A. (2003) Assessing intrapsychic blocks to pleasure using the Milestones of Sexual Development Model. *Contemporary Sexuality, 37,* 7–14.

Index

Numbers in *bold italics* indicate pages with illustrations

249